AF895643

For my mother, whose courage never failed,
for every child longing for protection,
and in loving memory of JD Roberts.

CONTENTS

FOREWORD

Growing up, Lauren was my best friend. Our families were incredibly close, and she was the first true friend I ever made. I was only four years old when she was kidnapped.

My parents were private investigators, so when Lauren's mother, Cathy, called to say that Lauren had been taken by her father, they immediately jumped into action. Because I was so young, my parents tried to shield me from the reality of what had happened. But I could see in my mom's tears and my dad's set jaw that something was terribly wrong. All I knew for certain was that I missed my friend.

Then, one day, my parents shared the news I had been desperately waiting for: Lauren was coming home, and we were going to meet her at the airport. As she walked down the ramp from the plane, I was so overwhelmed with excitement that I broke free from my parents and ran straight toward her. I hugged and kissed her, completely oblivious to airport security and my parents calling after me. I was just so happy that my best friend was back.

Years later, when we were in high school, Lauren moved in with my family. I became her little sidekick, and she let me tag along everywhere she went. As we grew older, she began to trust me with the deeper parts of her story, and I started to understand the reality of what she had endured.

She shared how her dad hadn't taken care of her—how there was no bathroom where she lived, how she couldn't speak the language, and how frightening it was to be so far away from her mom. Little by little, I came to understand the strength it took for her to survive that chapter of her life—and what it meant to carry the scars long after it was over.

It was heartbreaking to hear, but those conversations also taught me about forgiveness, courage, and what it means to lean on faith when life asks you to be braver than you ever expected you'd need to be.

In *Stolen*, Lauren brings everything I knew about her story—and so much more—to life. She thoughtfully walks readers through her journey with honesty, heart, and grace.

Every one of us has faced something that once felt impossible. Some of you may even be in the middle of that kind of journey right now. As you turn these pages, you'll find strength in the story of a mother and daughter, in the love of family and friends, and even in the unexpected kindness of strangers who show up when it matters most. That strength is in this story—and it lives in you, too.

Lauren, you were then, you are now, and you will forever be one of the bravest people I know. To say I'm proud of you barely scratches the surface of what I feel.

To my friend, my sister: Walk in the freedom that sharing your story makes possible.

You did it.

—Foreword by Miranda Lambert, Grammy Award-winning country singer, songwriter

PROLOGUE

It was a bright spring day, the kind that tempts you to tackle projects before summer's heat sets in. My husband and I were in the garage, sifting through stacks of boxes, clearing space, and creating order. Growing up, my mom and I moved often, and she taught me to "pitch it" if we hadn't used or worn something in a while.

Then I saw it. The box. *The* box. On one side, my mother had written in black permanent marker one word—*Jordan*. My eyes widened, and my heart stopped.

Why was it in my hot garage?

My stomach twisted as if the air had suddenly thickened. I froze, staring at it, dread washing over me. I'd completely forgotten it was there, buried beneath years of life and clutter, and part of me wished I hadn't seen it at all. Memories I'd worked hard to suppress stirred, sharp and painful. My instinct was to ignore it, to shove it back onto the shelf and pretend it didn't exist. I wanted to be like my mom and put that box on a shelf and move on.

In my college years, opening that box meant opening years of hurt and disappointment. In my young twenties, I was focused on my career and new marriage, looking toward my future and not my past.

But I couldn't ignore it. Not this time. Even as hurt and hesitation clawed at my chest, the Divine's unmistakable tug called. This wasn't just a box of forgotten things—it was a piece of my story that I needed to confront, to redeem, to share. Tears pricked my eyes as

I stood there, overwhelmed by a mix of fear and awe. My journey wouldn't be easy to revisit.

It was as if the box itself became God's way of tapping me on the shoulder, His gentle yet firm reminder cutting through my hesitation: *Lauren, trust me*. The thought stopped me in my tracks, piercing through my doubt. What I'd seen as an inconvenient discovery now felt like divine timing. This wasn't about my strength or my comfort—it was about surrendering, trusting that even the most broken parts of my story could serve a greater purpose.

Three months before cleaning out the garage, I felt called to finally write my story. To not only tell what I have gone through but *how* I walked through it all. The highs and lows, the grief and anger, the ache and the mercy, the long road to forgiveness. All of it.

It is funny the ways God chooses to speak to us, such as the day I sat in my living room reading *Y'all Eat Yet?*, my childhood friend Miranda Lambert's cookbook. It's filled with stories of her parents, grandparents, and friends. When I saw the photos in her book and read about Beverly and Rick—her parents—who are like second parents to me…my eyes filled with tears, and I heard a whisper, *Lauren, write your story*.

See, the Lamberts are a big part of my story, and to this day they are a big part of my life, so, in my brown leather recliner, with my heart full of energy and emotion, I began to pray over the decision to write a book. And over the next few months, that seed of an idea grew and grew.

But I kept resisting. I have dyslexia and struggled my whole life in school. I have a full-time job. I have two active boys.

But when you are supposed to do something, and when your story is meant to be told to help other trauma survivors heal and forgive and grow—when it is your destiny—the ways to make it happen open up.

I never imagined that while working full time, shuttling to soccer, and digging through records on my own abduction, I'd also be building a public platform. When the desire to tell my story wouldn't let go, I did the work—months of prayer and reflection, researching how to launch a podcast, studying the true-crime space, and seeking advice from producers, authors, and podcasters. With a clear plan, I launched the *Redeemed* podcast. Within six months, it gained real traction: guests with national followings, steady audience growth, and listeners writing from around the world. That momentum opened doors I hadn't anticipated, like media interviews and a full speaking calendar, which provided me with a credible, ongoing channel to share a survivor's perspective and practical hope.

It was as if a light broke through the shadows, and the fear melted away. A deep, unexplainable peace washed over me, calming my racing heart. Yet, as peace settled over me, so did the question: Was I truly ready to take a hard look at my past? The box held many photographs of my father and details of what he did.

After so many years of healing, I can finally say that it is okay to forgive someone who has caused you immense hurt and heartache. I feel this is why the box reappeared when it did, dusty and almost forgotten. Almost. Because now, I can't deny it was my nudge to remind you that you are not alone in your suffering.

If you are ready, let us open that box together and see what we find.

CHAPTER ONE

OPENING THE BOX: UNPACKING A PAST I TRIED TO FORGET

The stifling heat of the garage pressed down on me as I stood there, a worn cardboard box in my hands, its edges frayed from years of storage. Inside, memories I wasn't sure I was ready to confront called to me like whispers from the past. Anticipation, fear, and sadness tangled in my chest—a cocktail of emotions I couldn't quite sort out. My thoughts swirled while I tried to predict what I might find inside, but a sharp argument broke the spell.

"It's your turn!" one of my boys shouted, a broom clattering against the cement floor.

"No! You didn't carry as many boxes!" the other cried. Their voices snapped me back to the present, pulling me away from the silent lure of the box. Sighing, I set it aside and returned to the task at hand: sweeping out cobwebs and sorting through dusty clutter.

Later that evening, when the house was finally quiet, I carried the box into my closet, the only place where I could steal a moment of solitude. I sat cross-legged on the floor, my heart racing as I pulled open the flaps, exposing its contents for the first time in years. A wave of anxiety washed over me as I stared at the chaotic mess inside.

A tangled collection of folders, papers, and mementos spilled out of the box. My mind raced as I pulled out a thick, yellow folder. It was stuffed with typed and handwritten notes, each page meticulously documenting details about my father's family: names, descriptions of their immediate families, jobs, appearances, and even snippets about their character. I was struck by the precision of it all. I traded the yellow folder for a bright blue one, its edges well-worn. It was a step-by-step guide from the State Department about what to do if your child has been abducted. The words on those pages, though distant now, were echoes of my mother's desperate search for answers.

Beneath the folders lay stacks of old magazines, newspapers, and faded photographs. I began sorting them—press on one side, legal documents on the other—trying to impose order on the chaos. On top of a glossy pile, a cover screamed in blocks: "RAMBO RAIDERS SAVE TOT." Inside, a two-page spread staged me at seven—hair brushed smooth, posing in a field of flowers—set beside a stark map of Jordan with arrows tracing routes and timelines.

Another page showed my rescuers, dressed in typical Jordanian clothing. A small box held a grainy picture of my father and me when I was barely three. Near the back, another photo captured my mother in a doorway, arms wrapped around me, my face turned away from the camera as if I already knew how to hide.

The newspapers' black-and-white headlines read, "International Kidnapping" and "Mom Rescues Daughter," sidebars promising "exclusive details" and quotes from people who only knew pieces of the story. Each clipping felt like a verdict handed down by strangers. This wasn't just a box of paper; it was a record of how the world told the story of my life before I was old enough to tell it myself, and the weight of it settled on my chest as I realized how much of me had been translated into headlines.

EWYORK POST

SPORTS FINAL

TONIGHT:

TOMORROW:

1988

Founded by Alexander Hamilton in 1801

35 CENTS in New York City

50 CENTS

RAMBO RAIDERS SAVE TOT

Mom hires Delta Force veterans

PAGE 7

ER: In the running.

ERT'S

CAR

Headlines that told my story before I could.

Underneath the magazines and files lay a stack of old photos, their edges slightly curled with time. My breath caught as I uncovered them, a surge of emotion I hadn't expected gripping me. For years, a single image of my father could send me spiraling, a torrent of fear, anger, and sadness crashing over me. But this time was different. As I held the top photo, its faded colors still vivid in my memory, my heart ached for the father I'd known back then.

It was a picture of me as a toddler, no older than two or three, cradled in my father's arms. Alongside the ache was a swell of anger for what came later and sadness for all that was lost. The photo stack revealed more: snapshots of Jerash, Jordan, where my father grew up and photos of my parents during their marriage.

My mom, Cathy, was just nineteen when she took a leap of faith and left her small-town roots in Florida behind. She grew up with one sister, three brothers, and two hardworking parents, but her dreams pushed her beyond the familiar. Determined and fiercely independent, she landed in Dallas, juggling waitressing shifts while attending classes at El Centro Junior College in the heart of downtown. It was there, in that season of new beginnings, that her path crossed with my father's, setting the stage for a story neither of them could have predicted.

My father, Ali, had traveled a much greater distance to arrive in Texas. Born and raised in Jerash, Jordan, as one of twelve siblings, he had grown up in a bustling household steeped in tradition. Seeking opportunities beyond his hometown, he moved to the United States at twenty years old. He first attended Navarro Junior College in Corsicana, Texas, before transferring to El Centro Junior College where his path eventually crossed with my mother's. Like her, he worked long hours at Denny's, but in the kitchen as a cook.

My mother's first visit to Jordan, stepping into a world that would later shape my story.

Their connection grew amid shared shifts and conversations in the rhythm of their busy lives. My dad's strong work ethic and worldly charm must have caught my mom's attention, while her determination and beauty drew him in. Despite their cultural and religious differences (my father, a Muslim from Jordan, and my mother, a Christian from the United States), they were both willing to take a chance on their relationship.

As I continued to sift through the box, I grabbed another stack of worn photographs of my parents from their visit to Jordan. My mom had often shared stories about this trip. It was the first time my father took her to meet his family and marked the beginning of her immersion into his world. The faded images transported me to a time long before I was born, offering a glimpse into a pivotal chapter of their lives. In one photo, my mom stood with her hair modestly covered, framed by the timeless beauty of ancient Greek ruins and the silver-green leaves of olive trees. In another, she wandered the narrow, sunlit streets of Jerash, her expression a mix of curiosity and wonder.

The images of Jerash stirred memories of a town I had long forgotten. That's the thing about trauma and being so young: It blurs the edges of your past until a photograph awakens something deep inside you. The photos told a story of connection and contrast—a bridge between my father's heritage and my mother's new reality. I stared at them longer than I intended, wondering how much of that world my mother had truly understood when she stepped into it.

That was the first time she had ever visited Jordan, but it would not be the last. She'd recounted to me how they had traveled to Jerash to share the news of their engagement with his family. The festivities included a feast where a goat was sacrificed, a gesture of hospitality that stunned her. She described standing in the courtyard, frozen for a moment, before stepping gingerly over the goat lying in the entryway to reach the home. It was one of many moments where she began to grasp the depth of the cultural differences between her world and my dad's.

During their stay, Mom met my father's large, close-knit family for the first time. She spoke fondly of his brothers and several of his sisters, who greeted her warmly despite the unspoken tension in the room. In my father's culture, arranged marriages were the norm, and it was expected that he would marry a Muslim woman. By choosing an American Christian, my dad had defied deeply held family traditions. Even so, my mom said she felt a genuine sense of acceptance during that visit, unaware of how her presence marked the beginning of a quiet conflict that would linger beneath the surface.

The stack of photos revealed scenes from around Jerash. As I sifted through them, I found myself transported not only to my parents' past but also to fragments of my own memories of Jordan. My emotions fluctuated as I struggled to remember details of the town, my father's family, and all that had happened.

What if my mother had realized during that visit just how vast the differences between their worlds truly were? The weight of their religious beliefs, cultural traditions, and opposing values could have easily convinced her that their lives were too different to merge. What if she had decided it was all too much to overcome? Perhaps they would never have married. Perhaps I would never have been born. And this story—my story—would never have been told.

Yet, here I am, a living testament to how God can take the most unlikely circumstances, even the messiest moments, and weave them into a beautiful message. It's a powerful reminder that His plans often defy human understanding, turning what seems impossible into something extraordinary.

I picked up another stack of photos, this time of my parents' wedding. The images captured a small, intimate ceremony held in their modest apartment. Only a handful of guests were present, including my grandparents and one of my uncles on my dad's side, who lived in the Dallas area. Among the attendees were my parents' closest friends, Rick and Beverly Lambert, neither knowing how deeply they would impact my life one day.

I spied a white envelope tucked beneath a pile of disheveled folders. The corners were slightly bent, and the paper felt thin and worn. I carefully picked it up, noticing my mother's handwriting across the front, faded but unmistakable. My heart quickened as I opened it and pulled out an old Pan Am Airlines ticket.

The ticket was delicate, its ink slightly smudged from years of being tucked away. As I read the details, a lump rose in my throat: The flight was from Cyprus to Amman, Jordan. This wasn't just any ticket—it was *the* ticket, the one that had brought my mother back to me. The realization hit me hard, and I clutched the paper in my hands as if holding it could somehow bring me closer to the moment it represented.

I could almost picture her boarding that plane, her heart heavy with fear but unwavering in her determination. It was the flight that carried her into the unknown, trusting that God would guide her to me. The thought of what she must have endured—her courage, her faith—made my chest ache. Tears welled in my eyes as I held that fragile piece of paper, overwhelmed by the significance it carried. It wasn't just a plane ticket; it was the bridge between my mother's prayers and the moment she held me in her arms again.

This really did happen. It is funny how one ticket, one box can change everything. I have shared my story more times than I can ever count, but at that moment, with the ticket in my hand, it was visceral.

There I was, the scared little seven-year-old who had been kidnapped by her father and taken to Jordan; the nine-year-old little girl, scared that she would never have a normal life again; the ten-year-old longing to have the love of a father; and the fourteen-year-old angry at God and the world, trying to figure out who she was.

Overwhelmed, I closed the box and rested my head on my knees, the weight of emotions and memories pressing down like a heavy blanket. The silence of the closet, once my refuge, now felt stifling and too small, as if the walls themselves carried the echoes of my past. I squeezed my eyes shut and whispered a prayer, barely audible in the stillness. "God, give me strength," I pleaded, my voice trembling. This task felt insurmountable.

After a few steadying breaths, I opened my eyes, still uncertain but resolved to take it one step at a time. The flood of memories and emotions would have to be faced slowly, piece by piece. It was only 7:00 p.m., so I had a little more time before I had to put the kids to bed. With a deep inhale, I reopened the box, determined to uncover whatever lay inside.

As I sifted through the contents, my fingers brushed against something I hadn't noticed before—a spiral notebook. Flipping through the pages, I recognized my mom's cursive handwriting. I read as fast as I could, trying to figure out what treasure I had just found. It was my mom's journal—one she had written in every day after I was taken. *Every single day*, and this was the first time I had ever seen it.

After reading a few lines, I quickly dialed her number with shaking hands. The phone barely rang before she picked up, and before she could even say hello, the words spilled out of me: "Mom, I found the Jordan box in the garage. You won't believe what I've discovered inside." My voice wavered with a mix of urgency and awe as I tried to convey the weight of what I'd unearthed.

Her voice softened on the other end, steady and familiar, as if she'd been waiting for this moment. Prior to finding the box, I had shared with her that I was determined to write a book about my kidnapping and rescue—a prospect that both moved and terrified me. She responded without hesitation.

"Lauren," she said, her voice thick with emotion, "I always knew it was your job to write this book. That's why I kept all the details of the rescue in a box for you."

Her words hung in the air, heavy with meaning. She had been quietly preparing for this day, preserving pieces of our story so I could tell it fully. Now, as I held her journal and heard her words, it all began to make sense. My calling to write this story started long before I imagined writing a single word.

At the top of each page, my mom had written the date and time. Some journal entries were emotional: how difficult the days were without me and without hearing from me day after day. Others were factual: what she had done that day, who she spoke with, and the information she had learned. The entirety of the journal focused on finding a way to get me back. I began to read portions of it to my mother as I sat in the closet. The line was quiet for a moment, and then her voice, trembling, came through. "Lauren," she said softly, "that journal was my lifeline. I wrote every word for you—for this moment."

I began to read one of the earliest entries aloud to her over the phone. The words were raw, heavy with heartbreak and guilt: "Ali has taken Lauren. How could I be so stupid to trust him? Why didn't I see this coming? No one can help me, but I will continue to try. Rick and Beverly are calling everyone they know. I have to trust that Lauren is safe. I have to believe that I will see her again."

My voice faltered as I read her words, feeling the weight of her pain as if it were my own. Tears stung my eyes. I paused for a moment, struggling to continue, then snapped a picture of the page and sent it to her, thinking it might be easier for her to see it than to hear me read it.

There was a long silence on the other end of the line after she received the image. Finally, she spoke, her voice trembling. "Lauren, this is…this is too much for me right now. But I am so happy you found the journal."

Her words carried a mixture of relief and pain—relief that the memories she had poured onto those pages were now in my hands, but pain from revisiting the agony of those days. I wanted to say something to comfort her, but the truth was, I didn't have the words. In that moment, I realized just how much she had endured, how deeply she had fought for me, and how these pages weren't just her story—they were ours.

Reading the journal as a mother myself, the weight of my mom's words hit hard. I found myself not just reading of her heartbreak; I felt it through the lens of what I would do for my own children. The fear, the fight, the faith, it all became more vivid. In that moment, I realized just how much she had endured and how deeply she had fought for me.

After we hung up, a surge of energy and curiosity coursed through me. I set the journal aside and reached for a gallon-sized Ziploc bag crammed with old cassette tapes, relics from decades past. My hands wavered as I held the bag. I hadn't seen a cassette tape in over twenty years, and I had no idea if they would even still work. But what if they did? What secrets might these tapes hold? Would they bring memories to life or answers to questions I didn't even know I had?

One of those questions hit me like a jolt—was I ready to hear my father's voice again? Just the thought made my heart race. I opened my Amazon app, found a pink cassette player, and purchased it for $31.00. As I clicked "Buy Now," my mind raced with possibilities. I couldn't wait to find out what stories, messages, or emotions were trapped within those little spools of magnetic tape, waiting for their moment to be heard.

A few days later, an Amazon package arrived on our doorstep, igniting an immediate squabble between my boys over whose it might be. Their voices rose in anticipation as they examined the box like detectives. When I caught sight of the small blue-and-white box, I chuckled and said, "Boys, that one's mine."

Caleb, my youngest, grabbed it eagerly and brought it over. "What did you buy, Mom?" he asked, his eyes alight with curiosity. I tore open the package and revealed a small pink cassette player. Caleb frowned, tilting his head. "What's that?" he asked, skepticism dripping from his voice.

Stifling a laugh, I said, "This is what we used to play music back in the day." The explanation was enough to extinguish their interest. They wandered off, leaving me alone with my nostalgic discovery. I couldn't wait to retreat back to my quiet closet, open the Ziploc bag of cassettes, and uncover the voices waiting for me after all these years.

I hurried into my husband's office, clutching the cassette player like it was a long-lost treasure. "Do we have any double A batteries?" My voice shook with emotion and nervous energy.

He glanced up from his desk, mildly amused, and reached into a drawer. As he handed me the batteries, his curiosity got the better of him. "What's this for?" he asked, studying my face. I took a deep breath, my fingers tightening around the cassette player. "I'm hiding in the closet to listen to the tapes," I said, my words rushing out. "I need to do this without distractions."

He smiled, catching the mix of eagerness and apprehension in my tone. "Got it." He nodded, his easy acceptance reassuring me. He'd keep the boys and dog at bay, but as I turned to leave, my heart thudded in my chest. What if the tapes didn't work? Or worse, what if they did? The anticipation buzzed through me as I headed to my quiet refuge, batteries in hand.

My boys already knew my story. They grew up understanding that the abduction in 1987 was why their biological grandfather wasn't in our lives—and why marriage, faith, family, and resilience are non-negotiables for me. I'd always planned that, when they were old enough, I would not only tell them everything but I'd also let them watch the film about my case. But writing this book was different. It meant opening boxes of documents and tapes and hearing voices I'd never heard before. This wasn't just a retelling of the past; I would be learning things I did not already know about myself and my life.

I knelt on the floor of my closet, surrounded by the familiar scent of my clothes and the faint smell of leather from my husband's shoes. The quiet hum of the house felt distant, muffled by the door I had shut firmly behind me. Clearing a small space on the carpet, I reached into the Ziploc bag and pulled out a tape buried at the bottom. Its label, written in faded ink, read *Calls to Family.* My breath hitched. My fingers hovered over the words as memories surged—fragmented and hazy, yet powerful enough to make my chest tighten. Could this cassette hold my father's voice?

Over the years, my father and I had spoken only in jagged intervals—brief calls, long silences, each conversation reopening wounds that had never fully healed. And at this point, it had been seven years since I'd heard his voice at all. I had *never* heard a recording from those days—from *that* season—the months in Jordan when I was separated from my mother.

I slid the tape into the player and braced myself, wondering what would surface when the past finally had a voice.

I hesitated, overwhelmed. Was I truly ready for this? I steadied myself. With deliberate care, I placed the cassette into the pink player and pressed the play button. My heart raced as the machine whirred softly to life.

Wow, it actually worked. Every word was as clear as if the conversation had just happened yesterday. With a mix of relief and disappointment, I realized it wasn't my father's voice coming through the speaker; it was my uncle's. As I sat cross-legged in the closet, the world around me faded, and I was transported back to 1987.

My uncle spoke with my mother. Her voice gripped me, the raw emotion and urgency there as she asked my uncle, "Why did Ali take her? Why did he do this?" Her words were heavy with confusion and heartbreak. As the conversation on the tape shifted, memories of my own surfaced, brought to life by my uncle's mention of The Country Skillet—the restaurant my father and uncle owned in Dallas.

Instantly, I was a little girl again, standing in the bustling kitchen of that restaurant. I could hear the clang of pots and pans, smell the sizzle of food on the grill, and feel the warmth of the kitchen as I stood on tiptoes to peer over the counter and watch my father cook. Those moments were among the few untarnished memories of my father that I had left—a time when life felt simple and safe, untouched by the pain he would later cause. For a moment, time stood still, and I was wrapped in the warmth of love and security that came from our father-daughter bond.

But the tape kept playing, jolting me back to the present and the mission at hand. I needed to uncover the buried past, to piece together the fragments of my story, no matter how painful or complex they might be.

As I continued to listen, I learned the business hadn't been doing well, and the brothers were discussing its uncertain future. My uncle's voice was firm, almost exasperated, as he told my mom repeatedly, "Cathy, Ali has lost his mind. I don't know what he's doing."

I heard my husband calling my name from somewhere deeper in the house. "The boys are heading to bed!"

I froze, the spell momentarily broken. With a sigh, I hit the stop button on the cassette player, the mechanical click echoing in the confined space. Carefully, I placed the tape back in the box, tucking it away as if safeguarding a secret too fragile to leave exposed. But even as I closed the lid, my thoughts remained tethered to the voices on the tapes. They had become a lifeline, pulling me deeper into the story of my own life, piece by piece.

I found myself returning to the box at every opportunity, consumed by an insatiable need to hear more. Late into the night, I would sit on the floor, pressing play again and again, scribbling frantic notes in a journal. Come morning, I'd be up early, drawn back to the tapes as if they held answers I'd been chasing my entire life.

The obsession spilled into my days. On my commutes to work, the cassette player rode shotgun, my car transforming into a time capsule as voices from the past filled the space. After each tape, I called my mom, eager to share what I'd uncovered. "Do you remember this?" I'd describe snippets of conversations that I could only partially piece together. Sometimes, her voice would falter, the memories too painful to confront all at once. She'd ask for time to process, and days later, she'd call back with stories, her words deepening the picture I was slowly assembling, each one adding more and more to my journey.

CHAPTER TWO

PREGNANT AND ALONE

The early morning sky remained cloaked in darkness as I backed the car out of the garage. I slipped on my earphones, slid a cassette into the player, and pressed play. The rhythmic hum of the tires on the pavement filled the background as I drove. I had about twenty minutes to immerse myself in the past before reaching my office.

I instantly recognized the first voice as the raspy, smoker's drawl of my Aunt Joyce. Joyce had been gone for twelve years at this point, but through the speakers, she felt alive again. My chest tightened, and tears welled up, spilling down my cheeks as her familiar cadence wrapped around me. Hearing her voice again was an unexpected treasure, like stumbling upon an old photograph you thought had been lost forever. She wasn't really my aunt, but she'd loved me fiercely, as though I were her own daughter.

Another voice emerged—my mother's, warm and unmistakably Texan, her thick accent so much stronger on the cassette tape. I couldn't help but smile through my tears, marveling at how the tapes captured not just words but the essence of who they were.

Joyce's tone was urgent and indignant. "Cathy, how could he do this? How could Ali take Lauren like this? I know he abandoned you when you were pregnant, but did you ever think he'd do something like this?" Her words hit me like a jolt. *Abandoned?* The word reignited a trauma response in me, though the circumstance of the traumatic event was from a long-lost, barely there memory, yet it had been within me all along, whether I acknowledged it or not. I hadn't even been born when this traumatic event occurred; I was just a baby growing deep in my mother's womb. All the same, pain, confusion, and anger resurfaced as I hung on every word, driving in the dark of the morning with my past playing out through the tiny headphones.

As I pulled into the parking lot at work, I pressed the stop button with the voices still echoing in my mind. I grabbed my journal and jotted down a quick note: *Call Mom. Ask about the conversation with Aunt Joyce.* I tucked the journal and cassette player carefully into my bag, wiped away the lingering tears, and took a steadying breath before stepping out of the car.

The cool morning air brushed against my face as I walked toward the office, trying to push the emotional weight of the recording aside. Inside, the familiar routine of the workday awaited. I greeted our secretary with a smile, her cheerful response grounding me in the present.

Later that afternoon, before driving out to pick up the boys from the bus stop, I dialed my mom's number as I was getting into my car, my fingers shaking as I placed the phone down. When she answered, I wasted no time. "Mom, do you have a minute?" I asked, my voice already quivering with emotion. "I listened to a conversation between you and Aunt Joyce today." My words faltered, cracking under the heaviness of what I was about to ask.

Excitement and curiosity rose in her voice. "Really? What did she say? What did I say?"

I hesitated and gripped the phone tighter. "That's why I'm calling," I said softly. "Aunt Joyce mentioned something about Dad abandoning you when you were pregnant with me." The words hung in the air, heavy and raw. "I know you've told me bits and pieces about my birth before, but…can you tell me more?" My voice trailed off, a quiet plea for the truth I wasn't sure I was ready to hear.

My mom responded almost immediately, her voice steady yet tinged with a hint of uncertainty. "Of course, Lauren. I'll tell you everything I can remember, but my memory isn't what it used to be. You might need to call Bev and ask her to fill in the missing pieces."

I smiled at the mention of Beverly. She'd always been the keeper of details, the one with a memory sharp enough to recall even the smallest moments. Bev's recollections were like pieces of a puzzle Mom and I couldn't complete on our own. If anyone could provide clarity, it would be her.

I pulled into the church parking lot, waiting for the kids' school bus as my mom began recounting the early years of her marriage. She shared vivid memories of how she'd met Rick and Beverly and the details of her pregnancy with me. I grabbed my journal to take notes as my mother's voice carried me into our past.

She told me about the time she took a job at the apartment complex where she and my dad lived. It was there that she struck up a fast friendship with her manager, Wanda, who eventually introduced her to her daughter, Beverly Lambert. My mom and Beverly instantly hit it off. They were two peas in a pod—outspoken, energetic, and fiercely strong-willed women who thrived on tackling life's challenges head-on.

Beverly's husband, Rick, a homicide detective with the Dallas Police Department, soon became part of their close-knit circle. Mom and Dad, Beverly, and Rick bonded deeply. They weren't just friends; they were like family. They spent countless evenings together, sharing meals, laughter, and stories that made their little group feel like something extraordinary.

As my mom spoke about Rick and Beverly, I began to truly understand why I loved them so deeply and why they've always felt like home to me. They weren't just friends of the family; they were part of my life from the very beginning. They carried pieces of my story that no one else ever knew. They knew my dad—not just as a husband or a father, but as the person he was in those early, formative years. Their connection was woven into my history, making their presence feel both inevitable and irreplaceable.

Mom's voice became heavy with what she was about to share. "There are things about our marriage I never wanted you to know, but maybe it's time." She paused, as if gathering her thoughts. "Even with the friends we had around us, your dad and I started falling apart. The arguments became more frequent, and he was working longer hours—too long, if you ask me. He wasn't home much, and I could feel in my gut that something wasn't right."

She sighed, the kind of sigh that carries years of unresolved hurt. "I'd confront him, but he always denied it. Still, the signs were there. Like the time he came home without his wedding ring. I'll never forget that. Or the whispers I heard from one of the residents in our complex, hinting at things I didn't want to believe. But no matter what, I loved him. I loved him so much, and I fought to save our marriage. I fought harder than I think he ever realized."

I sat in my car, hanging on every word. Even after all these years, I had never known this. The idea that my father might have been unfaithful was a revelation I wasn't prepared for. Yet, even in the midst of her pain, my mom's voice carried a quiet strength that kept me glued to the conversation. I found myself hoping the kids' bus would be late, desperate to hear more.

My mom continued, her tone softening as she recounted when she became pregnant with me. "Four years into our marriage," she said, "I thought maybe this was it—the miracle that would bring us back together. When I told your dad, he was thrilled. Family was everything to him. Becoming a father gave him a sense of pride and purpose I hadn't seen in a long time."

But even as joy bloomed, shadows lingered. "Things felt better for a while," she admitted, "but then he changed again. He started spending more time at the mosque, praying on his rug at home, and reconnecting with his family back in Jordan. It felt like he was slipping away."

Then came the day that changed everything. My mom's voice grew quieter as she described it. My father sat her down and told her he needed to return to Jordan urgently—his father was gravely ill. "I didn't know what to think," she said. "He didn't know how long he'd be gone, and I was left with so many questions."

After he left, the silence became deafening. His calls were infrequent and vague, offering little reassurance, and my mom's unease only deepened. She confided in Beverly, who quickly became her lifeline. Though Beverly and Rick didn't have children yet, Beverly's empathy and strength gave my mom some comfort. I tried to imagine how overwhelming it must have been for her, pregnant, alone, and facing the uncertainty of whether her husband would return at all.

"Mom," I interrupted, unable to hold back any longer, "how did you handle all of that, the fear, the uncertainty, not knowing what was happening?"

She paused. "I don't know if I *did* handle it," she said finally, her voice thick with emotion. "I think I just survived it. When you're in the middle of something like that, you don't have time to break down. You just keep going because you have to."

Sitting in my car, I glanced at the road, knowing the bus would arrive any minute. But I couldn't hold back the pressing question. "When did Dad come back?"

She let out a long sigh before answering. "Three months later," she said quietly. "By then, I was thirty weeks pregnant. I was exhausted physically and emotionally, and when he finally walked through the door, I didn't know whether to cry or scream. But I couldn't hold it in any longer. I confronted him right there, demanding to know how he could leave me like that when I needed him the most."

Her voice wavered with a rawness, even after all these years. "And then he said something that stopped me in my tracks. He told me he hadn't just gone to Jordan to visit his father. He'd been preparing a home for us. He said he wanted to move there, to raise you in Jordan, and to embrace his faith more fully. I couldn't believe it. Despite everything I'd endured while he was gone, I had been waiting for him to come home so we could pick up the pieces and move forward. But instead, he was telling me he wanted to uproot everything and take us somewhere I didn't even want to go."

With the frustration and sadness in her voice while telling me this, I could only imagine how she must have felt back then, the overwhelming mix of emotions—relief at his return, anger over his absence, and confusion about the future he envisioned for our family. "How did you react? What did you do?"

"It hit me like a freight train," she admitted. "He had never talked about wanting to leave the US, let alone raising you in another country or as a Muslim. It felt like he'd been planning a life I didn't agree to, a life I couldn't see myself living. I told him straight—I wasn't going anywhere and neither was my baby."

Her words were resolute, but it couldn't have been an easy decision. "We argued," she continued, her voice thick. "It was the worst fight we'd ever had. All the love, all the hope I'd held onto felt like it was unraveling right there in front of me. The differences between us, our cultures, our beliefs, and even how we saw the future, felt like walls we couldn't climb. Finally, I'd had enough. I packed up his things, put them by the door, and told him to leave. I couldn't do it anymore."

I sat in silence, grappling with all I'd just heard. Her strength was undeniable, and the enormity of her decision left me awestruck. This wasn't just about ending an argument; it was about drawing a line, standing her ground, and protecting both herself and me. Her choice didn't just alter the course of her life; it also shaped mine.

But as I sat there absorbing the gravity of what she had been through, a chilling thought crossed my mind: Neither of us could have foreseen what was coming next. Her decision, as brave and final as it seemed, was only the beginning of a new chapter. It would be filled with twists, challenges, and consequences that would test her resolve in ways neither of us could imagine.

I glanced out my window as the bus pulled up, parents already forming a line on the sidewalk. Still, I sat in the car, reluctant to break the connection with my mom.

My phone buzzed with a text from Cooper: *Mom, I can see you. Why aren't you getting out of the car to come get us?* His message made me chuckle, snapping me out of my thoughts.

"I have to go," I told my mom reluctantly. "But can we talk more later if you're up for it?"

"Of course," she softly replied.

After getting the boys settled in the car and hearing all about their day, my mind drifted back to Mom's words. I couldn't stop picturing her—young, pregnant, and caught in a whirlwind of stress and turmoil, unsure of what the future held.

Later that evening, after dinner was cleaned up, the kids' homework was done, and I'd managed to squeeze in a quick bike workout, I called my mom. I couldn't wait another day to hear more of her story. She often got tired in the evenings, but hearing more of what she'd shared earlier wouldn't let me wait.

When she picked up, I hesitated for only a second. "Mom, is it too late? Are you too tired?"

"No, I'm good," she replied, her voice warm but steady. "Where did we leave off? What do you want to know?"

I took a deep breath and asked her to tell me about the day I was born.

She started with a memory that felt almost cinematic in its intensity. "I was at work, trying to push through the day, but you know…the worry and uncertainty was overwhelming. Then, out of nowhere, I felt a sudden rush. I turned to Wanda and blurted out, 'I just peed myself!' Wanda gave me the most incredulous look and said, 'Cathy, that's not pee—your water just broke. You're going into labor!'"

At just thirty-four weeks pregnant, she was panicked with fear, unsure of what would happen next. Wanda immediately sprang into action. "She didn't waste a second," my mom said. "Wanda and her son, Stan, got me to the hospital as fast as they could. Stan was a firefighter, so he knew exactly what to do. I was terrified. For you, for me, for everything."

Her voice came quieter, as if the memory still carried a sting. "The doctors told me stress had pushed me into labor. Six weeks early. You were so small."

As she spoke, I could picture her, twenty-five years old, living by herself with a premature baby arriving any minute. "Even in the hospital, your father and I were arguing," she continued. "He wanted to give you an Arabic name, but I wasn't having it. I told him you were going to be named after my mother, Barbara Lauren. And that was that. But I always called you Lauren. It just felt right."

When she brought me home from the hospital, my father wasn't with her. "I didn't let him stay," she said, her voice laced with emotion. "The apartment felt so quiet, so heavy, but I needed it that way. I needed time to figure out how to move forward—how to be your mom and how to rebuild after everything that had happened."

Her words painted a vivid picture of resilience and love, and I sat there in awe of the young mother she had been, fighting to create stability in a world that had felt anything but stable.

Her apartment, once filled with shared dreams and the routine of married life, now symbolized a fresh start. My mother turned her energy toward creating a peaceful environment for me, despite the emotional turmoil she faced. Her days were a mix of joy and sadness. She remained grateful for the blessing of her child but was burdened with an unraveling marriage.

Friends like Beverly and Wanda rallied around her, offering encouragement and practical support. They brought meals, ran errands, and simply sat with her during those lonely and exhausting early days. My mother leaned heavily on her faith, finding comfort in whispered prayers during the quiet moments when I finally slept. She was determined to build a life for us, even if it meant navigating the unknown as a single mother.

At six weeks old, my life took a drastic and defining turn. My mom, overwhelmed but resolute, filed for divorce, a decision that set the course for the rest of our lives. The decree was issued on December 30, 1980, granting custody to my mom while allowing my dad "reasonable" visitation rights. As a newly single mother, she faced the daunting task of raising me alone, navigating the uncertainty of a new chapter while trying to make ends meet.

I can only imagine the emotions she must have felt—grief over the end of her marriage, fear of the unknown, and the immense pressure to provide for me as both mother and father. It was a pivotal moment, not just for her, but for me as well, as we stepped into a life that would test her strength and shape my earliest memories.

It was getting late, and I could hear the weariness in my mom's voice. I told her how much I loved her and thanked her for revisiting the past to share our story with me. After we hung up, I sat in the quiet stillness of my living room, letting her words wash over me.

After the divorce, Mom and I moved in with Joyce, who overflowed with kindness and generosity. Joyce didn't just open her home to us, she took me in as if I were her own daughter. She showed her care in the little things, like teaching my mom how to warm my milk properly or making sure my diapers were always changed on time. Wanda, ever the loyal friend, had been the one to introduce my mom to Joyce, knowing she would be the steady anchor we needed during such a turbulent time.

Joyce and Beverly weren't just a lifeline for my mom during those uncertain days, they became the foundation of something far greater. Their love wasn't fleeting or conditional; it was enduring, unwavering, and the kind of love that can weather any storm. Together, they built a network of resilience and faith, a shelter of grace that would prove to be essential in the trials ahead.

The role these women played in my story wasn't over by a long shot. This was just the beginning of their impact on my life, and it was a beginning that would prepare us for the unexpected battles yet to come. Their courage, faith, and willingness to fight for me would be tested in ways none of us could have imagined.

CHAPTER THREE

SILENCE BEFORE THE STORM

After hanging up with Mom, my mind buzzed with an overload of information. The temptation to dive back into the box and continue unraveling the mysteries of my past was overwhelming, but a glance at the clock reminded me that 5:00 a.m. would come far too soon. With early shifts at the clinic and a packed schedule awaiting me, I reluctantly pushed the urge aside and forced myself to get some sleep. The following days blurred together in a whirlwind of work, the kids' activities, and the relentless rhythm of daily life.

By Thursday evening I'd finally carved out a moment to indulge my curiosity. While the boys gathered their soccer cleats, shin guards, and water bottles, I snuck back into my closet and retrieved the cassette labeled "Wife." My journal, tape player, and laptop in hand, I joined the flurry of activity, rushing to get everyone fed and out the door on time. Once at the soccer field, I parked and told the boys I'd be in the car if they needed me.

I sat alone in the dim glow of the dashboard lights, holding the cassette in my hands. My pulse quickened as I slid it into the player and pressed play. What truths—what secrets—were waiting for me on this tape?

"Hello, this is Cathy. Have you heard anything?"

"No, Cathy. Nothing. He won't tell me anything."

The woman speaking to my mother was my stepmother. Her voice was unmistakable, marked by an accent I knew well, and there was strain and worry in her tone. I could hear the tremble in her words so crisply through the threads of the tape that I felt the depth of her unease.

My father married her a few years after my parents divorced, and they had two children together, a daughter and a son. I was so young at the time that I have no memory of attending their wedding, though when I think of my father, I think of my stepmother, because she was always there, seamlessly present in our lives. She wasn't just "Dad's wife" to me. She was the one who took care of me every time I went to visit.

She had a way of making you feel at home, no matter the chaos swirling around. Though her family hailed from the Middle East, she was born and raised in the United States, weaving together two cultures in a way that made her endlessly intriguing yet entirely relatable.

Hearing her voice brought it all back—the stability she somehow glued together for a fractured family and the love she gave me without hesitation, always making me feel like I was one of her own daughters.

Listening to my stepmother's voice, I couldn't help but think about the stark contrast between her and my stepfather. My mom had also remarried, though I can't quite pinpoint when it happened, and the two could not have been more different. While my stepmother embodied nurturing warmth and a natural knack for parenting, my mother's new husband was not the fatherly type. He had no children of his own and seemed more at ease loving my mom than stepping into a parental role.

What he did bring into our lives, however, was a sense of stability and luxury we hadn't experienced before. Coming from a wealthy family, he owned a beautiful house on Caddo Lake near Marshall, Texas. That house became the backdrop to some of my most cherished memories with my mother. It was the only time I remember her not having to work tirelessly to make ends meet. For the first time, we had the freedom to simply be together—to laugh, relax, and enjoy each other's company without financial strain hanging over us. Those moments felt rare and precious, a fleeting glimpse of the life I wished we could have always had.

As the cassette tape continued, my mother's shrill voice pierced my car, filled with desperation and urgency. "Where is Lauren? Why did Ali do this? What is his plan? Are you going to Jordan with him? Please, don't go. You can't go! If you go, he might never bring Lauren back." Her questions came like rapid fire.

My stepmother's voice cracked. She began to cry, her vulnerability raw and palpable, revealing the turmoil she was facing. At the time, she was pregnant with their third child, and my father's insistence on moving to Jordan also had thrown her into an impossible situation. "Cathy, Ali has been pressuring me to uproot our family and move to Jordan, but I never imagined he would take Lauren there. He wants to raise the kids close to his family, in his culture. He says it's important for them to know their roots. But I don't want to go. I can't! My life is here, Cathy. My support, everything I've built! I can't just leave it all behind."

"Does he understand what he's asking of you? What about the baby? You're pregnant, for God's sake!"

"I've tried to make him see," my stepmother whispered. "But you know Ali. When he decides something…."

Unspoken words hung heavy between them.

"Cathy," my stepmother began hesitantly, her voice barely above a whisper, "Ali told me when he moves, he is *never* coming back."

"*What?* He'd leave you and the kids behind? Would he really do that?"

My stepmother's voice trembled as she recounted the conversation with my father. "He told me he wanted to move back to Jordan, to return to his homeland, but he said he planned to leave Lauren here in Texas with you."

My mother's silence on the other end of the line spoke volumes, but my stepmother continued. "He said it like it was nothing, that we could come back to Texas to visit Lauren often. He never mentioned taking her to Jordan, not once."

"That's insane," my mother said, her voice rising. "He has been planning this all along."

"And that's not all. He threatened me, Cathy. He said if I told you about his plans, it would cause trouble, that you'd demand more child support, and he can't deal with that."

My mother let out a bitter laugh. "Child support? What child support? Ali has never paid a dime! He's supposed to, but I've never seen a single penny from him."

The line went quiet for a moment before my stepmother replied softly, "I didn't know, Cathy. He's been lying about that too...."

"Of course he has," my mother said, her voice heavy with frustration and exhaustion. "It's always the same with him—promises, excuses, and nothing to show for it. And now this? Dragging you into his mess?"

"I don't know what to do," my stepmother whispered, her despair palpable. "I feel like I'm trapped, Cathy. Completely trapped."

"Well," my mother said firmly, "you're not alone. We'll figure this out. Don't let him bully you into something you'll regret."

I hit pause on the cassette player, my heart racing as I sat back in the car, absorbing it all. The words swirled, and as I sat there in silence, memories from my childhood started to resurface—some sharp and clear, others faded with time. But there was one thing I had never known: that my father hadn't paid child support. It was a truth my mother had carried for years, a burden she never shared with me.

What I *did* know was that my mom had always worked tirelessly to support us. I remembered the late nights she'd spend at her desk, her determination unwavering. One memory stood out in particular: the story of how she started her own personnel agency after the divorce. It began when, several months after working at the apartment complex, a resident had come into her office and offered her a position at their agency. She took the leap, and in just two years, my mom had risen to become one of the top twenty agents in the entire Dallas/Fort Worth area. It was a remarkable accomplishment, and I could see how proud she was of her success.

Prior to remarrying, my mom had built and run her own business, and her hard work paid off in ways I couldn't fully appreciate at the time. She bought her first home, a townhouse in Richardson, Texas, a suburb of Dallas. It felt like the physical manifestation of all the late nights, the sacrifices, and the relentless drive she'd put into building something for us. Riding that wave of success, she didn't stop there. She went on to open her own agency—Career Contacts—bringing Beverly on board to work with her. The business flourished for years, standing as a testament to her dedication, resilience, and unshakeable belief that she could build a life beyond the hardships.

My mom and Beverly Lambert at Career Contacts, the business she built during a season of rebuilding—long before we knew how deeply this friendship would shape our future.

But the late eighties economic downturn hit even the most successful businesses hard. Mom was no stranger to overcoming obstacles, but this challenge tested her in ways she hadn't anticipated. Yet through it all, she persevered with that same unwavering faith which kept her moving forward, adapting to whatever came her way.

I felt my mother's pain while I sat in the car clutching the cassette player, not just in her words, but in the way she spoke. Every syllable was laced with years of struggle, sacrifice, and unrelenting hope. Hearing the desperation in her voice was almost unbearable. The memory of those years felt so vivid that I couldn't help but wonder: *What would I have done if this had happened to my children? How would I have faced such unthinkable betrayal and despair?*

The thoughts made my chest tighten, and for the first time, I realized I could never fully grasp the depth of strength my mother had summoned during those years of hardship. She had been more than a mother. She was a warrior.

I replayed the end of their conversation in my head, each line echoing louder with every passing second. "Have you heard from Ali?" my mother pleaded, a sense of urgency in her tone. "Do you have any phone numbers for his family? Anyone who can help?"

But both women were caught in a whirlwind of shock and uncertainty. Neither was able to provide the answers they so desperately needed. They were both fighting a battle they could not see a way out of.

My stepmother reassured my mom, her voice steady despite the turmoil: "Cathy, I will help you in any way I can, and I won't go to Jordan. I'm not Lauren's mother. You are." Her words, raw and honest, lingered in the air, a shared understanding that transcended their differences.

With thirty minutes left until practice was over, my mind was still spinning with everything I'd just heard. I wiped away the tears that had unexpectedly surfaced. The emotions were raw: grief, confusion, and a deep yearning for clarity.

Despite the pain, I could still remember the good times. Moments from my childhood that now felt like precious treasures. Fleeting moments with my father, warm despite their brief nature, and surprisingly, even moments with my stepfather. But the memories that truly brought me comfort were those from the lake house—the place where some of my most cherished memories with my mom were made.

That house wasn't just a building. It was a sanctuary. My mom transformed the attic into a beautiful bedroom just for me. She painted the dark, wood-paneled walls a crisp white, and the slanted ceiling felt like it was pushing the room higher into the sky. The space felt open, almost light enough to breathe in, and from my bed, I could touch the ceiling. My collection of Care Bears covered the walls, turning the small attic into a haven that was truly mine

We spent our days outside, working in the yard, splashing in the pool, and attempting (and often failing) to keep up with the Jane Fonda workout sessions we followed on the VCR. My mom's love for the outdoors was contagious, and I can still remember the joy on her face, and the way the sun made her laugh feel even brighter. Evenings were filled with more laughter as we played Mrs. Pac-Man on the life-sized arcade machine or battled it out in long, competitive games of Monopoly. Those were the moments that seemed to stretch out indefinitely, frozen in time, creating memories I would forever hold close. Even now, when I play Monopoly with my own boys, I feel the echoes of those days. My mom's laughter makes me feel like she's right there with us.

But as much as those moments felt timeless, they were not immune to the inevitable changes that come with life. As a child of divorce, the back-and-forth between two homes became my norm. Every other weekend spent at my dad's house, though never ideal, was simply all I had ever known. But by the summer of 1987, something shifted. The cracks in the routine and the subtle changes in my dad's behavior were starting to show. These weren't just the usual annoyances of divorced parents—they reminded my mom of the man he had been when he left her during the most vulnerable time of her pregnancy.

When she called his house to arrange our weekend visits, it was often my stepmother who answered. Her voice, warm yet hesitant, would explain that my dad couldn't come to the phone because it was his prayer time, or he was away at the mosque. At first, these responses seemed innocent enough, but they planted seeds of concern in my mom's mind. Something was changing, and she could feel it.

The move to Caddo Lake had made our visits less predictable, turning the once-steady every-other-weekend routine into something far more sporadic. The three-hour drive made coordination more difficult, and instead of seeing my dad regularly, our visits dwindled to just once or twice a month. Tyler, Texas, became our halfway point for pickup and drop-offs between my parents.

I remember my mom telling me about our meetings on the side of Interstate 20. It was during one of those meetings that my mom saw something that shocked her. My dad stepped out of his car wearing traditional Middle Eastern clothing—a long robe and a headscarf. While he had dressed this way when I was a baby, he had stopped after their divorce. Now, he seemed to be reclaiming parts of his religion and culture in a way that was both familiar and foreign to her. My mom realized that my father was returning to his faith in a way she hadn't anticipated. It was a transition that would ripple through all our lives.

The sound of my stepmother's voice unlocked moments I had long buried. One particular visit with my dad stood out vividly. Afterward, my mom asked, "Did your dad take you to the mosque in Richardson?" I nodded, unsure why she seemed so concerned.

I explained how things were different there compared to our church. We had to remove our shoes, wash our feet, and cover our hair before praying. I told her I couldn't join the men in prayer because they prayed separately from the women, so I stayed with my stepmother in another room. My mom listened quietly, but I could sense her unease. She didn't want to upset me or my dad, so she simply asked me to let her know if he ever took me again.

At the same time, my mom was dealing with her own storm of challenges. Her marriage was unraveling, and she was seriously considering separation. But just when things seemed like they couldn't get worse, the stock market crashed on October 19, 1987. Black Monday. My mom had invested a significant amount of money, and the crash sent her financial plans into a tailspin.

This, combined with the strain of her faltering marriage and the growing emotional distance from my dad, pushed her to make a decision.

It was time to leave Caddo Lake and return to Richardson.

She called the leasing office to see if our old townhome was available. To our surprise, the tenants agreed to move out on short notice, and within weeks, we packed up and said goodbye to Caddo Lake.

Back in Richardson, my mom threw herself into rebuilding our lives. She searched for a job and enrolled me in a school just a few blocks from our townhome. It was a fresh start—and for the first time in a long while, I was closer to my dad again, no longer having to endure the three-hour drives for weekend exchanges.

What we didn't know, though, was that this was only the beginning. The change that had been quietly brewing in the background was about to arrive, sweeping through our lives like a tidal wave. And when it did, nothing would ever be the same.

My father was becoming increasingly devoted to his religion. He began going to the mosque more frequently to pray, dressing more traditionally, and slowly introducing new expectations into our daily lives. He told my mom that I should no longer wear shorts and instead needed longer skirts and pants. At the time, these changes seemed small and gradual, but they marked the beginning of a deeper shift—one that would soon reshape our family in ways none of us fully understood.

CHAPTER FOUR

KIDNAPPED

Returning to Richardson felt like slipping into a well-worn pair of shoes—comfortable and familiar. Our old townhouse welcomed us back with the warmth of memories, and the transition was seamless. It was 1987, the year I turned seven, and I couldn't wait to start school again. My birthday in September always made me one of the oldest kids in class, a small detail I secretly took pride in. My mom was busy searching for a new job, her determination a steady hum in the background of our days, while I was thrilled about one thing above all else: being closer to my dad. The long, exhausting road trips every other weekend for our visits were finally behind us. Life felt like it was settling into something steady, but even at seven, I was beginning to learn that "steady" doesn't always last.

October in Texas is always a welcome change—a much-needed break from the relentless summer heat. The air turns crisp, inviting everyone to step outside and savor the cooler weather. For Mom and me, weekends often meant a trip to the bustling farmers' market in downtown Dallas. Nestled beneath the overpasses, the market offered a cozy shelter from the occasional fall rain, its atmosphere alive with the hum of vendors and the scent of fresh produce. Farmers rolled in with trucks overflowing with colorful vegetables, fragrant flowers, and homemade goods. My mom and I would wander down each lane, hand in hand, picking out our favorite vegetables and daring to try something new.

Fall also brought the State Fair of Texas, an event that still glows brightly in my memories. I can still see myself perched on my dad's shoulders, my tiny hands clutching a light-up toy he had bought from one of the street vendors. The fair was pure magic—bright lights, carnival rides, and the kind of joy only a child can fully experience. Those moments with my dad were rare and precious, the kind you hold onto tightly.

This October felt different. Not just because of our move back to Richardson but because of the energy building at school. As we returned from our fun fair day off, the hallways were alive with fall decorations—die-cut paper pumpkins, watercolor cutout leaves, and scarecrows made with real straw smiled down from every corner. The festive atmosphere made everything feel new and exhilarating.

I sat at my desk, absentmindedly tapping my pencil against the edge, when my teacher's voice pulled me back to the moment. "Class, I have some news! In two weeks, we're hosting a Harvest Festival, and all of your families are invited!" The room erupted in whispers and smiles as she continued, explaining how each class would contribute to the event.

With contagious enthusiasm, she handed out bright, colorful flyers (this was the eighties, so there were no emails or social media memes to spread the word, only our cherished flyers to show our parents). "You'll each need to bring something to share—food, decorations, or supplies." Her eyes sparkled as if she'd just revealed the best secret. When the flyer landed on my desk, I eagerly scanned the list of options, my imagination kicking into high gear. *Cupcakes!* The idea struck me like lightning. Not just any cupcakes—ones with orange icing, maybe even topped with little candy pumpkins.

When the bell rang, I stuffed the flyer into my backpack, barely able to contain my fervor. All I could think about was convincing Mom to help make my cupcake vision a reality.

As soon as the final bell rang, I bolted out of the classroom, my backpack bouncing against my shoulders. I spotted Mom's car in the pick-up line and raced toward it, barely waiting for it to come to a full stop before yanking open the door. "Mom, guess what?" I practically threw myself into the seat.

She glanced over with a smile. "What is it?"

I unzipped my backpack in a rush, pulling out the slightly crumpled flyer and thrusting it into her hands. "We're having a Harvest Festival in two weeks, and we have to bring something to share. Can we make cupcakes? With orange icing? Maybe even with little candy pumpkins on top?"

My words tumbled out so quickly, I barely paused to take a breath. My mom looked at the flyer, nodding as she read through it. "A Harvest Festival, huh? That sounds fun. Sure, we can do cupcakes. Just let me know how many your teacher needs."

Relief and delight flooded through me as I grinned up at her. "Thanks, Mom, it's going to be so much fun!" I couldn't wait to tell my friends the next day that we were making the best cupcakes in the class.

The weeks leading up to the Harvest Festival were filled with work and planning. Every day after school, Mom and I brainstormed costume ideas, each one more elaborate than the last. First, it was a pumpkin, then a princess, and even a cat. But none felt quite right. Finally, one evening while I was sitting at the kitchen table drawing on a scrap of paper, the idea struck.

"What about a cheerleader?" I asked, my eyes lighting up. "I've always wanted to be a cheerleader."

My mom smiled and leaned against the counter, considering it. "That's a great idea. What colors should we use?"

"Blue and yellow," I said instantly. "Those are my school colors!"

She nodded with approval. "Perfect. We'll get you a little skirt and top, and we can put your hair in pigtails with blue and yellow ribbons."

"Can I wear a little makeup?" I hoped she wouldn't say no.

She tilted her head, pretending to think it over. "I think that would be okay. Just a little—maybe some blush and lip gloss. Cheerleaders always look polished, right?"

I couldn't contain my grin as I imagined the costume coming together. Every trip to the store became an adventure as we hunted for the perfect pieces: the ribbons, the pom-poms, and even a sparkly pair of sneakers. The excitement at the school was equally contagious, and as the festival drew closer, I could barely wait to see everything come to life.

The weekend before the Harvest Festival, I spent time with my dad, stepmom, and my little sister and brother. As we sat in the living room, I told my dad all about the upcoming event at school and the cheerleader costume my mom had helped me pick out.

"Dad, it's blue and yellow—my school colors. And I even have pom-poms," I gushed.

My dad leaned back in his chair, his expression shifting from curious to slightly concerned. "Lauren," he said, his tone thoughtful, "why do you want to be a cheerleader? I hope that skirt isn't too short."

I paused, caught off guard by his reaction. For a moment, I thought about mentioning the makeup Mom had agreed to, but I quickly decided against it. Instead, I smiled and reassured him. "Don't worry, Dad. It's not too short. It's just for fun."

He gave me a small nod, but his protective nature was clear. As much as I loved his concern, I also couldn't help but feel a little self-conscious.

When the day of the Harvest Festival finally arrived, the school gym had been transformed into a festive wonderland. Hay bales, pumpkins, and scarecrows were scattered across the space, and colorful streamers hung from the ceiling, creating an atmosphere brimming with autumn charm. The air buzzed as students and their families filled the gym, moving from booth to booth.

While Mom and I walked through the lively scene, we stopped to explore the activities. There was bobbing for apples, pumpkin painting, and my personal favorite—the ping pong toss. Its booth had a row of glass bowls filled with water, each one shimmering under the gym lights.

A teacher standing behind the table handed me a ping pong ball and smiled. "If your ball lands in one of the bowls, you win a goldfish!"

My heart raced as I held the ball in my hand, carefully aiming for a bowl. With a deep breath, I tossed it, watching intently as it sailed through the air. The moment it landed with a satisfying plop into one of the bowls, I gasped. I had won!

The teacher congratulated me and handed my mom a plastic bag containing my very first pet—a tiny goldfish, swimming in tight circles in the sloshing water. I couldn't stop grinning as I stared at the little fish.

My mom carried the bag carefully as we wandered through the rest of the festival, and on the way home, we talked about setting up a place for our new family member. That goldfish may have been small, but to my seven-year-old heart, it was the most thrilling prize I could've ever imagined.

The following weekend was Halloween, and my dad asked if I could spend it with him. He said he would take me trick-or-treating with my stepmother, little sister, and brother and promised to get me to school on time Monday. He sounded eager—maybe too eager—but I was thrilled. The thought of another chance to wear my cheerleading costume and go door-to-door with my siblings filled me with exhilaration. I didn't notice the way my mom's smile didn't quite reach her eyes or how my dad kept saying, "*Trust me.*" I only felt the thrill of Halloween. I had no idea it would be the last time I'd see my neighborhood for a very long while.

Halloween 1987—my cheerleading costume for a night I thought would be ordinary. I didn't know my dad was about to take me to Jordan.

I could already picture the fun we'd have, our candy bags growing heavier with each stop. Plus, I couldn't wait to share the news about my goldfish. I imagined the look on their faces when I told them about winning it at the Harvest Festival.

I eagerly packed my little pink suitcase with my costume, my favorite stuffed animal, and a drawing I'd made of my goldfish. The crisp autumn air was filled with the promise of spooky fun.

I overheard my parents talking in the next room; my mom was going over the details for the weekend. "Ali, *please* make sure Lauren gets to school on time Monday, and don't forget her homework in her backpack."

"Don't worry, Cathy, I've got it covered. I'll get her to school. I'll just go to work early on Monday. She'll be fine."

My mom gave me a tight hug, kissed me on the cheek, and reminded me not to eat too much candy. "And make sure you give the kids and your stepmother a big hug from me."

With my suitcase in hand, I eagerly jumped into my dad's car, already filled with anticipation for the weekend ahead. As we pulled away from Mom's house, I asked, "Dad, are we going trick-or-treating in your neighborhood or at Uncle's?"

My dad, glancing down at me with a mysterious smile, responded, "Well, I have a big surprise for you."

My heart skipped a beat. "What is it? Are we going to a Halloween party? Did you get my favorite candy?" I practically bounced in my seat.

My dad's smile widened. "Well, we're not going to my house," he said. "And we're not going trick-or-treating. We're going to the airport. I'm taking you on a big trip to Jordan so you can see my home and meet all of your relatives."

The words didn't immediately register. I was full of questions and surprise. "Wait—what? Does Mom know about this?" I blurted. "She didn't tell me anything. She said we were going trick-or-treating, and I packed my cheerleading costume!" Panic built up inside.

My dad quickly consoled me. "Yes, of course she knows. Don't worry; everything's fine. It's going to be an adventure." But even though he said everything would be okay, a knot of unease still tightened in my stomach. I couldn't get past the feeling that something wasn't quite right.

As we drove down the highway toward the airport, a nervousness settled. It was as if the world outside the car had grown quieter, and I was incapable of getting past the unease troubling me. The joy I'd felt earlier dissolved, replaced by a mix of hesitation and bewilderment. My mind was spinning, and I finally asked, "Dad, where's Nora? And why aren't Layla and Hasan coming with us?"

My dad glanced over at me briefly before answering, his voice steady but tinged with something I couldn't quite place. "Your stepmom couldn't come on such a long trip because she's pregnant with the new baby," he said. "And actually, she's out of town visiting her family right now. She took the kids with her."

I processed his words, but something still didn't sit right. "Wait, they're all gone? But…why now? Right before Halloween? I was supposed to go trick-or-treating with them," I said, my voice rising.

"Don't worry. We'll have fun in Jordan, just the two of us." His words did little to calm the questions in my mind. The whole thing felt too sudden, too strange. Why was I the only one going? And what about Halloween?

But the more I asked, the more he smiled and told me not to worry, as if that would somehow make everything okay.

As the miles stretched on, the air in the car grew thicker. I couldn't help myself—questions kept coming up, each more urgent than the last. "Why didn't Mom say anything about this? Why didn't anyone tell me?" My voice trembled.

My dad's body tightened, and his eyes flickered to me, his smile now strained. "Lauren, stop asking questions. Everything's fine. Just trust me, okay?" The words came out almost like a command, and for a moment, the air between us seemed to freeze. I didn't want to push my father any further, didn't want to make him angry. So, I bit my lip and fell into silence, even though the questions kept turning in my head.

The tension in the car was palpable. My dad's hands were clenched on the wheel, his jaw tight. Walls were closing in around me, and I knew—deep down—that something wasn't right, but I couldn't bring myself to say so. Instead, I stared out the window, trying to steady my breath, and tried to convince myself that everything would be fine, just like he said. But that knot of dread in my stomach kept tightening.

I had never had a reason not to trust my dad. Sure, I'd seen him get upset a few times—maybe when work got stressful or when things didn't go as planned—but nothing that ever made me question his intentions. He had never lied to me, at least not in a way that felt intentional. But this was different. The way he was acting and avoiding my questions—it didn't sit right with me.

I kept replaying the conversation with my mom in my head. She had been so concerned about my homework and making sure I got to school on Monday. But if she'd known I wasn't going to school, why would she even bring it up? Why would she send my backpack with me if I wasn't going to need it? It didn't make sense. As we drove on, the questions kept mounting. And with every new question, the more unsettled I became.

Looking back at my childhood, I'm flooded with questions and emotions I never fully understood until now. As I sat at my computer, writing down the details of my life, I began to grasp the full weight of that day. Now, with kids of my own, I can't help but put myself in my mom's shoes and realize just how quickly everything can change.

I often wondered what the day was like for my mom when she realized I was gone. Did she start her morning like any other, pouring herself a cup of coffee, turning on the news, and carrying on with her routine? Or did she sense something was wrong right away? I could picture her, quietly sipping her morning brew, maybe even feeling a little tug of confusion at the unusual silence in the house.

It wasn't until later that evening, when the house had settled into an almost eerie stillness that I found myself drawn back to my closet, pulling out the "Jordan" box and carefully sifting through Mom's old, worn journals—her handwriting looping gracefully in cursive. The pages were filled with memories of our life together, but one entry caught my eye. The first sentence leaped off the page: "God, why? You knew this was going to happen, but why? You even pulled me away from work to have lunch with Lauren in the middle of the day, but why didn't you stop this from happening?"

A chill ran through me as I sat on my couch with a blanket draped over my lap. My fingers trembled slightly while taking notes. Witnessing her pain and fear all these years later kept me in a state of frailty.

As I read, I realized the timeline felt jumbled in my mind. So much had happened, and the details were hard to piece together. I needed clarity, so I picked up the phone and called my mom, asking her to take me back to the day she knew my father had taken me. She paused, taking a breath before replying, "Yes, of course. I can't forget it."

While my dad and I were boarding a flight to Jordan, my mom's world was about to be turned upside down. She told me everything she remembered.

"Remember, we had just moved back to Richardson a few weeks before all this happened," she began. "I was working non-stop, trying to get back on my feet financially. You had just started that new school, and my days were packed. But on that Monday, something shifted. I had this strong urge to go have lunch with you at your school—something that was very unusual for me, given how full my days were with work. Now, looking back, I know it was the Lord telling me I needed to be there...."

After moving back to Richardson, my mom had never had the chance to surprise me with lunch at school. But after Halloween weekend, she decided to break from her routine and show up at Greenwood Hills Elementary with my favorite sandwich and a note.

When she arrived, my teacher greeted her with an unexpected question. "Where's Lauren?"

Confused, my mom responded, "She should be in class. My ex-husband was supposed to drop her off this morning."

My teacher's expression shifted. "Lauren never came to school today."

Those words hit my mom like a gut punch. Anger and sheer terror surged through her as she rushed to the nearest payphone. This was 1987, so she had no immediate way to reach anyone. Frantic, she called my dad's house—no answer. Then, she dialed his restaurant, hoping to find some clue. My Uncle Amir picked up the phone, and when she asked where my dad was, his response was blunt, "I don't know. I haven't heard from him in days."

I could only imagine the cold grip of panic constricting my mom's chest, the awareness dawning that something wasn't just *wrong*—it was far *worse* than she could have imagined.

Feeling a surge of desperation, my mom knew she had to do something—*anything*—to find me. She felt a voice deep inside urging her to reach out to the one place she feared the most but needed to consider: the airlines. Years ago, when she'd traveled to Jordan, the major airport there had been the Queen Alia International Airport, and a glimmer of hope flickered as she recalled that detail. Trusting her instincts, she dialed the airline's headquarters in New York, every fiber inside her vibrating.

The woman who answered was cold, professional, and immediately reluctant to share any information. "I'm sorry, ma'am, I can't help you," she said, her tone flat. But my mom, frenzied, wouldn't back down. She explained—pleaded, even—that she believed my dad had taken me without her consent. She begged for any information that could confirm where I was.

After a long, agonizing silence, the woman finally spoke, her voice now more cautious. "I'm sorry, ma'am," she repeated. "I can confirm that a flight from Dallas to Jordan is scheduled to arrive tonight. The tickets are under the names Ali and Lauren."

The reality slammed into her so hard it took her breath away. My dad had taken me—*kidnapped* me—and was already halfway across the world. From Dallas, Texas, to Jerash, Jordan, he had stolen me away without a word and without warning.

It was too surreal to comprehend, but there was no denying it. My dad had abducted me. Comprehension swept over my mother in waves. This wasn't just an unexpected trip; this was an escape—a calculated move to completely uproot me from everything and everyone I knew. All of it was part of his plan to start a new life with me in Jordan—one I never agreed to.

The feeling of betrayal was suffocating. My mom knew my father wanted to live in Jordan again, but she never thought my father would *kidnap* me and take me with him. Her world, which had always been grounded in the routines of her busy life, was spiraling into chaos. And I was nearly 7,000 miles away, unknowingly at the center of it all.

Sitting on the couch with my mother's journal spread out in front of me, every emotion I had fought to suppress came rushing to the surface. Tears blurred my vision as I read the words she had written, each sentence soul-crushing. It's strange how memories blur over time, fading into something more like a dream than reality. But as I read her journal, I was no longer the clueless seven-year-old girl. I could feel it all again—the shock, the fear, the helplessness.

The moment my dad took me, my life as I knew it was over. I was no longer Lauren, a typical little girl running around in the suburbs of Richardson, Texas. I became *Lauren,* the seven-year-old American girl kidnapped by her Jordanian father, taken from everything familiar and tossed into a world I couldn't even begin to understand. Instead of walking into the second grade classroom of a school I loved, I was suddenly starting kindergarten in a small desert town in Jordan, unable to speak or understand those around me, struggling to learn how to read and write in Arabic. Everything—every part of my life—slipped away, long before that plane even touched down.

After hanging up with the airline, my mom immediately dialed Rick Lambert's pager (remember, this was the eighties) with a 911 message. Her worst nightmare had just become her reality—the horrifying possibility that she might never see her daughter again.

Over the years, Rick and Bev had shared pieces of my story with me. They were deeply involved, having run a private investigation company at the time, but there were still so many unanswered questions. So, I decided to reach out to Bev. I sent her a quick text asking if she had time to talk about my kidnapping, and she immediately replied that it was as good a time as any. "Rick's here with me," she added.

Rick and Bev live busy lives, running the Pink Pistol—Miranda's store in Lindale—and frequently traveling for Miranda's concerts and events. But on this particular day, they were home and available to talk. When I called, Bev answered the phone, her eagerness to help evident in her voice. "What do you need? If I don't know the answer, Rick will; he's sitting right next to me with a dog in his lap."

"Hi, baby, I love you," Rick said.

I took a deep breath before asking, "Can you tell me about the day my mom paged Rick with 911?"

Bev let out a sigh. "Ugh, yes…we can. But I need to grab a box of tissues first. This is a hard one to talk about." I could hear the weight of those words in her voice. She paused for a moment, then began. "Rick and I normally didn't work together on cases. We usually split up to get more done in less time. But on that day, we were at the Dallas County courthouse working a case together when your mom's page came through."

Beverly and Rick filled in all the pieces I didn't know from that day. They were going about their day when Rick's pager went off. He glanced at it, then looked up at Beverly with a furrowed brow. "Something's wrong. Cathy's paging me 911," he said, his voice low but laced with concern.

Rick walked to the clerk's desk and asked to use her phone. His hands were steady, but his mind raced as he dialed my mom's number. When she answered, the raw, broken sound of her voice stopped him cold. "Rick," she gasped between sobs, "Ali took Lauren. He took her to Jordan. They're arriving at 5:00 p.m. today. He took my baby."

Rick froze, his face pale, his thoughts scrambled. Beverly, standing next to him, saw the look in his eyes and felt the air around them shift. Without needing to hear what my mother said, she knew exactly what had happened. "Ali took Lauren," she whispered, already bracing for an avalanche of action.

Rick's voice was steady but urgent as he spoke to my mom, telling her to head to her townhouse. "We'll meet you there. We're coming." Without waiting for a response, he grabbed his coat, but Beverly was already two steps ahead. She knew what needed to be done.

They rushed out of the courthouse, the reality of the situation setting in. Rick slammed the car into gear, his foot pressing hard on the pedal. The car roared to life as they sped down the highway, driving a hundred miles an hour. Every contact they had, every person they could call, raced through their minds. They *had* to get me back. Time was slipping through their fingers, and they had no idea what they would find when they reached my mom. But one thing was certain: The fight to bring me home had already begun.

Beverly glanced over at Rick, eyes wide, her voice tight with urgency. "We have to get Lauren back. No matter what it takes." Rick's jaw clenched, his grip tightening on the wheel as he sped through traffic. They both knew how complicated getting me back was going to be.

With each passing mile, the Lamberts couldn't help but feel the crushing load of the unknown. They had worked on domestic kidnapping cases before, but nothing like this. They had never faced the prospect of international law, of fighting for a child across borders, much less ones with extreme cultural and religious barriers. How could they possibly break this to my mom? How could they tell her that getting me back would be nearly impossible?

When they finally arrived at the townhouse, my mom was pacing the kitchen floor, smoking two cigarettes at a time, each step a mix of rage, fear, and confusion. She stopped, her eyes wild, her voice trembling. "Ali said he was just taking her trick-or-treating, that he'd bring her to school today. Why didn't I see it? Why didn't I *know*?" Her voice cracked, and she wiped tears from her eyes.

"I should have known when he left to go to Jordan during my pregnancy. I should have known!" Her words were a mixture of guilt and heartbreak. "I should have stopped him. I should have never let her go. How could he do this? How could he take my baby?"

Her eyes were frantic, desperate. "I have to get her back." The words came out like a vow. But in her voice, Rick and Beverly could hear the raw fear—the fear that she might never be able to keep that promise.

Beverly stood beside my mom, her face etched with concern. She spoke gently but firmly. "Cathy, you need to call the police." My mom nodded, her shoulders sinking as the reality set in. After she made the call, Rick stepped forward, pushing aside his personal connection to my mom, and adopted the cold, professional demeanor that had served him in countless investigations before.

"Cathy, listen," he said, his voice firm and commanding, "you need to go to Radio Shack and get a recording device. We need to put it on your phone." His words were blunt, practical, and they cut through the fog that had overtaken my mom. "I'll set it up for you. You need to record every phone call. We can't afford to miss a single detail."

He paused, locking eyes with her. "Your mind will be all over the place, Cathy. I know this is hard, but if Ali calls—*when* he calls—we need to know exactly what he's planning. We need to figure out where Lauren is, and we need to be ready."

Even all these years later, I could almost feel the tension in the air, the determination in Rick's voice as he guided my mom to set up that recording device. Just for a brief moment, as I held the tapes in my hands, I felt this unspoken connection to the Lamberts and to my mother. I closed my eyes and imagined what it must have been like for them—facing the unknown, doing everything in their power to get me back. I could almost hear their voices, echoing across the years. I breathed in, feeling the moment take its full shape, before turning the page to continue reading, not wanting to miss a single detail.

The cassette tapes Rick insisted my mom record—real-time evidence of the calls, leads, and heartbreak that followed my kidnapping.

Back in the townhouse, Rick wasn't wasting any time. The moment my mom had set up the recording device, he laid out a plan. His thoughts were sharp, focused; he knew every second counted. There was no room for error, no time to guess. Rick's voice broke through the air in the dimly lit kitchen, steady with purpose. "We need to stay ahead of this. The first call we get from Ali…we're not just listening. We're learning everything we can from him. We'll figure out where Lauren is and what his next move is."

His voice remained calm, but there was an urgency behind it now. Rick didn't have time for emotions. He had to think like a professional, like someone with the knowledge and resources to pull off a miracle. But even as he spoke, a gnawing sense of helplessness clawed at him. He picked up the phone, calling anyone and everyone he knew: fellow investigators, law enforcement contacts, anyone who might have a solution, a clue, an answer.

But each call only brought more frustration. One by one, the people he reached out to told him the same thing—this wasn't something they could handle. This was beyond their expertise. They didn't know how to rescue someone from a situation like this—not when it involved crossing international borders, not when it meant dealing with the complexities of kidnapping laws in a foreign country.

Rick's heart sank with each phone call, but he refused to give up. Time was slipping away, and *time* was the very thing that could be the difference between finding me and losing me forever.

Beverly turned to my mom, her voice calm but resolute. "You need to make a list. Every person you know who has any connection with Ali. We need names, numbers, anything that might give us a lead."

Beverly's focus was razor sharp, her instincts honed from years of working side by side with Rick. They had been in the business long enough for her to trust her gut. Her mind was already calculating who could help, who might have information, who was connected in ways they hadn't thought of yet. But beneath that professional exterior, Beverly was human. This was her best friend's daughter, the girl she had watched grow up, her own daughter's best friend. But there was no room for emotion, not now. Beverly had to put her feelings aside and approach this like the job it was.

As she moved through the townhouse, her eyes took in the traces of my life scattered everywhere—baby dolls, Barbies, Care Bears—all silent reminders of a little girl who was now lost in a world that wasn't her own. The presence of these childhood memories only deepened the ache in Beverly's chest. She could feel the loss as if it was her own child who had been taken. But she couldn't let herself get lost in it. Not now. They had a job to do.

My mom scribbled furiously on a piece of paper, the list of names growing longer second by second. At the top of the list was my Uncle Amir's name.

After getting off the phone with the Lamberts, a sudden urge pulled me toward the Jordan box. My mind kept circling back to the idea of finding something—anything—that had my uncle's name on it. Maybe there was another piece of history hidden inside, something that could help me make sense of it all. Determined, I started sifting through the contents, my fingers brushing over old papers and trinkets until I pulled out the Ziplock bag full of cassette tapes. Sitting on the couch, I started reading through the labels on the tapes. A sense of awe washed over me as I saw my mother's familiar handwriting on each one. It felt surreal, knowing how pivotal this moment was in telling my story. What I hadn't known as a scared seven-year-old, was that I was never truly alone; every day, my mom was fighting to get me back while a circle of people refused to give up. I could hardly believe these recordings—the ones Rick had insisted on—were not just key to my rescue but also to preserving everything that happened afterward. These tapes held fragments of my past—the fear, the determination, and the relentless drive that had pushed my mom, Beverly, and Rick to their limits and beyond. They were the evidence of all that was going on while I was on the other side of the world, afraid, homesick, and not knowing if I'd ever see my mother again.

When I spotted Uncle Amir's name on one of the tapes, a wave of recognition hit me. I'd listened to a clip of him a few weeks earlier, his voice crackling through the tape player's speakers, thick with tension. I paused, the conversation rushing back. I reached for the tape, put it in the pink player, and pressed play, ready to hear his voice again.

It came through the speakers almost immediately, raw and unfiltered. "Cathy, I had no clue he was going to take Lauren…I can't believe he did this to you. He's lost his mind." He continued, his voice growing more urgent. "The restaurant's not doing well, Cathy. Ali sold his share of the business a few weeks ago. He's been having problems with his wife, and to top it off, he sent her out of state to her family with the kids, saying they needed a vacation."

My mom's breath caught in her throat. As Amir spoke, I could almost feel the thudding of her heart growing louder and faster with each revelation. Everything was beginning to fall into place. My dad had planned this—all of it—and she hadn't seen it coming.

"Wait," my mom's voice cracked as she interrupted Amir. "Ali sent Nora and the kids to Springfield *two weeks ago*? Why didn't you tell me?" Her voice rose with anger. Dad had been lying, keeping her in the dark while executing his plan. "How did you not know what he was planning, Amir?" My mom's voice was trembling, her words sharp with the sting of betrayal. "How am I supposed to trust you now?"

There was a raw edge in her voice as it all settled in—the understanding that everyone around her had been blind to what Dad was planning, and now it was too late. As my mom listened to Amir on the phone, her emotions were all over the place. Rick had told me that Beverly, ever the calm and collected one, stood by her side, taking meticulous notes, her pen scratching against paper as she tried to make sense of every detail. She knew this was critical—the more information they could gather, the better. But as Amir spoke, it was clear my mom was unraveling. Beverly placed a hand on her shoulder, offering silent support as Mom's eyes welled up with tears.

The reality of it crashed back into me as I thought about the phone conversation with the Lamberts. It was as if I had been transported back thirty-seven years; it felt like I was standing in that townhouse beside my mom, witnessing everything unfold through her eyes. I could feel the tension, the fear, and the heartbreak all over again. I continued listening to the recording of my uncle, my emotions pulling me in different directions.

Amir's voice spat through the receiver. "Cathy, I swear to you, I had no idea what Ali was planning. I knew he was acting strange lately, but I never thought he would go this far. I never thought he would take Lauren from you."

After a long silence, my mom finally hung up the phone. She wiped her tears and turned to Rick and Beverly, her voice shaking as she pulled out another cigarette. "Ali sent his wife and the kids out of state two weeks ago. I didn't know, Rick. I didn't know any of this. Why didn't anyone tell me?"

Rick and Beverly exchanged a look, knowing this was just the beginning of a nightmare they couldn't yet fully grasp. But as Beverly continued to jot down the details, her eyes never left my mom, who was now trembling, the heaviness, betrayal, and helplessness pressing down on her shoulders. The road ahead was uncertain, but one thing was clear—there was no turning back.

I hit the pause button on the cassette tape, the voice of my uncle still echoing in the quiet room. I wanted to keep listening, to push forward, but I needed a moment. The rawness of hearing my uncle's voice—someone I had trusted, someone who should have known—was too much to take in all at once. I set the tape aside, took a deep breath, and jotted down a few notes and questions I wanted to ask my mother when the time was right.

With a quiet sigh, I picked up the cassette again, hit play, and settled back into the couch, determined to continue.

A faint static on the line crackled, heightening the anticipation of whose voice would come through next. It was Aunt Joyce. Her raspy, smoker's voice sliced through the air with a certain bluntness. "Hello, um, yes, this is Joyce Alston. I need to cancel my nail appointment for today." I couldn't help but smile, a small moment of levity in the midst of everything. It was a little dose of reality—every conversation, even the mundane ones, were being recorded, no matter how far removed from the gravity of my kidnapping they were. But in that moment, I realized something else: Life was still happening around my mother, even in the midst of the chaos. And for just a second, I needed that reminder. I needed a little laughter.

The cassette tape continued to play, and this time it was my mother's voice. I could almost picture her—taking a slow drag from her cigarette, then exhaling deeply as she dialed my stepmother's number. Her heart raced with every ring, each one a painful reminder of the uncertainty she was suffocating under. When my stepmother finally picked up, her voice was just as shaken, full of disbelief. Ali's choices stunned her, and her voice trembled as she tried to make sense of it.

But my mom wasn't going to waste time with pleasantries. Her voice was tight. I could hear her take another puff of her cigarette as she asked with emotion and exhaustion, "Did Ali discuss his plans with you? What was his motive? Were you planning to go to Jordan with him?"

My stepmother hesitated before answering, her words coming out slowly. "Ali and I had been fighting for months about him wanting to move to Jordan. The last month, though, he stopped talking about it. Things seemed to be getting better. He bought me gifts, suggested I take the kids on vacation to visit my family. I had no idea he was planning something like this."

My mother's heart sank with every word, the threads of Ali's deception weaving tighter and tighter. My stepmother continued, "I would never have gone to Jordan with him, certainly not if I knew he was going to take Lauren. You have to believe me, Cathy. I never knew."

The silence on the other end of the line stretched out, and in that space, both women's grief collided. They didn't have the answers, but for that brief moment, they shared something deeper than just their pain—they shared the gravity of the unknown. Both of them, mothers in different ways, bound by the loss of a daughter, each struggling to make sense of the chaos that had suddenly overtaken their lives from one man's actions.

Through her tears, my mom begged my stepmother, her voice raw and desperate, "Please, help me; talk to Ali. Do something. I'll do whatever it takes. Please help me get Lauren back."

My stepmother promised that she would do whatever she could. Neither of them knew how or where to begin, but in that moment, they clung to the hope that together, somehow, they might find a way.

A few hours later, my stepmother called with news that shattered what little hope my mom had left. Her voice was barely a whisper, thick with devastation, as she relayed Ali's cold, unyielding response to her desperate pleas. Ali had firmly declared that he would *never* bring Lauren back, no matter what. He wouldn't listen to reason, not even to her threats of keeping his other children in the US unless he returned Lauren. His answer was simple: "No." He insisted that Lauren was happy in Jordan, that it was now his home, and that nothing—*nothing*—would change his mind. In his eyes, the matter was settled, and he assumed my stepmother would eventually give in and join him, taking the kids to Jordan.

Ali's words—the cold, callous refusal to even consider bringing me home—crushed my mom in a way nothing else could. She was overcome with grief, and for a long moment, there was nothing but another silence on the line. In a voice barely above a whisper, Mom told my stepmother that it was too much to bear, that she couldn't take it anymore, and then she hung up. I sat there on my couch, my chest tight as tears streamed down my face, taking in the magnitude of everything that had just transpired.

The pain between my mother and my stepmother was palpable—raw, like a wound that couldn't be healed. It dawned on me how young my stepmother had been at the time. She was pregnant with her third child, younger than my mom, and had been abandoned by a man she trusted. My father had taken his *other* daughter to Jordan, leaving her and their children behind. I could only imagine the swirl of emotions she must have been feeling—horror, confusion, rage, and desperation. She must have been wondering how it could have all gone so wrong, how the man she loved could betray her like this, just as he had done before.

This time, though, was different. This time, he had taken me. And in this moment of reflection, sitting with my mother's journal in one hand and the cassette tapes in the other, everything began to click. It was as if the pieces of a puzzle I had never fully put together were finally falling into place. My father had abandoned yet another wife, left her in the midst of pregnancy. Only this time, he had gone even further. This time, he kidnapped his own child. Like an abuser who escalates, his actions had escalated.

I could only imagine the devastation my stepmother must have felt, watching her family unravel, her life turned upside down. But even as I thought about her, I could see my mother, collapsed on the floor, her body shaking with uncontrollable sobs. Her world, once full of the promise of raising me and creating a life for us together, was slipping through her fingers. Everything she thought she knew was being torn apart, and she was powerless to stop it. The life she had planned for us, the future she had imagined, seemed to dissolve in an instant.

This is more than just *my* story. It's my mother's story, my stepmother's, my father's. And through the pages of those journals and the voices on those tapes, I began to see the ripple effects of one man's choices, the destruction left in his wake, and the endless, heart-wrenching love of two women trying to hold everything together in the face of unimaginable loss.

In the depths of her despair, my mom did what she had always done when life became too much—she turned to her faith. There, on that cold floor, she cried out to God, desperate for His help, for His strength, for a glimpse of hope in the darkness that consumed her.

When her sobs finally subsided, she managed to crawl into bed, but sleep wouldn't come. Through my mother's journal entries and the hiss of those cassette tapes, I finally realized—I wasn't the only one taken. Fear had kidnapped her too. On tape, you can hear the timeline: calls logged, leads chased, doors slammed shut, prayers turning into strategy. The exhaustion is right there in her voice; so are the pleas for help, the dead ends, and the decision to keep moving anyway.

Those notebooks and tapes don't just preserve a memory; they document a siege—my mother's relentless campaign to get her child back. Faith and adrenaline lived side by side. Desperation never stopped her courage. This had been larger than a single victim and a single crime; it became a story of two lives held hostage and one woman who refused to surrender.

CHAPTER FIVE

OUT OF OPTIONS, NOT OUT OF HOPE

I needed to call my mom to share everything I'd uncovered, but the pain was still raw, and I couldn't bring myself to overwhelm her with all the details. Too many years, too much hurt. Instead, I decided to ease into it, testing the waters to see what she could handle. Reopening these old wounds wasn't something I could do alone. It was something we both had to face together, at our own pace, on our own terms.

That evening, I dialed her number, my heart heavy. "Mom, I spent some time reading through one of your journals, and I listened to another cassette tape...."

Her voice softened with curiosity, "What was this one about?"

I recounted the story of my stepmother and uncle, piecing together the gaps with her help. But as I asked more questions—questions about the early days after I was gone—she faltered, struggling to remember. "Lauren," she said, "I don't really remember...I think there was someone named Teddy Bear, but you'll have to ask Rick."

We chatted a bit longer, but I could tell she was weary. Our conversation, while still filled with the familiar warmth of shared history, was beginning to feel like a delicate balance. Both of us were tired, and it was time to wrap things up. The next day, I picked up the phone to call Beverly, eager to update her on my progress and to ask for help remembering the details of our past. I held the receiver and paused, my heart heavy with emotion. I closed my eyes, reflecting on everything that had led me to this moment.

Rick, Beverly, Miranda, and her little brother Luke had always been part of my life in one way or another. There was a time when our paths diverged—when I was caught up in the whirlwind of college and trying to figure out what it meant to be an adult. Meanwhile, Rick and Beverly had poured their energy into Miranda's music career. I'll never forget the moment I saw Miranda on *Nashville Star.* I was away for a weekend trip with friends and turned on the television. There she was—my beautiful friend, standing on a stage in front of millions of people, singing with the kind of confidence and grace that had always seemed to radiate from her. I sat on the edge of the bed, in awe of her talent, bravery, and strength.

For a beat, my thoughts shifted to something unexpected: *What if the Lamberts were no longer in my life? How could I tell this story, walk through this journey, without the people who had played such an essential role in my rescue and healing?*

It was then that I felt a sense of clarity, like a voice speaking directly to my soul. *Lauren, I have been with you every step of the way. I surrounded you with the people you needed then, and I have surrounded you with the same people now. I have orchestrated every detail because you have trusted me in the process.*

A wave of peace and love settled over me as I dialed Beverly's number. I shared my progress with her, the pieces I had uncovered in the tapes and journals, feeling a sense of purpose in the work ahead. It was as though the journey, despite its pain and complexity, was unfolding exactly as it was meant to.

Beverly's voice came through, thick with tears. "Lauren, you are a daughter to me and Rick. We want to help you in any way we can. I'm so proud of the work you're doing, and I know Miranda will be excited too. This story must be told." Beverly couldn't believe all that I had uncovered, especially the fact that the cassette tapes still worked after all these years. The idea that they could hold the key to the truth was almost too much to grasp. I told her that once I figured out how to digitize the tapes and store them on my computer, I'd send her a copy.

"Well, I have an idea," Beverly said, her voice steady now. "Rick and I will be in Austin next weekend. Do you and your mom want to meet up? We can figure it out together."

The invitation felt like a lifeline, a tangible reminder that I wasn't walking this journey alone. The thought of sitting with them again, of sharing memories and ideas, filled me with warmth and excitement.

"Yes!" I replied without hesitation. "Anytime I get a chance to see my favorite people, I'll take it."

The next weekend, we gathered in Austin for brunch. As we sat around the table, the conversation ebbed and flowed—sometimes heavy, other times light. We laughed, we cried, and then laughed some more. Listening to Rick, Beverly, and my mom reminisce about the powerful memories they shared was nothing short of amazing. The pieces of the puzzle I'd been slowly putting together from the journals and cassette tapes started to fall into place in real-time. In those moments, it was as though I was living day to day with them, absorbing the story from multiple angles and finding healing in the shared laughter and tears.

During brunch, Rick shared his determination to keep fighting back then, no matter how complicated the path might become. As I listened, I was struck by how focused he had been, even in the face of something so overwhelming. He wasn't going to let the tangled web of international law or the uncertainty of the situation stop him. Rick was a man of action, and he'd made it his mission to find the right people who could help us.

He told me about Ramsey Clark—an unexpected but crucial name. Clark had negotiated the release of American hostages during the Iranian crisis in 1979, a moment that had solidified Clark's reputation as someone capable of navigating high-stakes international issues. Rick's choice to contact him was bold, but it made sense. If anyone could understand the legal complexities of recovering an abducted child in another country, it was Ramsey Clark.

Mr. Clark agreed to speak with him. When they connected, Rick outlined the gravity of the situation, explaining that he needed help getting an American child out of Jordan. But what happened next threw Rick for a loop: Mr. Clark suggested he contact King Hussein of Jordan directly for help. The thought of involving the Jordanian monarchy was both tempting and daunting. At first, it felt like it might be the solution—after all, who could deny the authority of a king?

But Rick's instincts kicked in, sharp and clear. He immediately declined the suggestion. His mind raced with the potential fallout. If Ali or his family caught wind of any royal involvement, it could make everything worse. Rick was playing a delicate game of strategy, and revealing too much too soon could backfire, jeopardizing any chance of getting me back. Like a seasoned chess player, he understood the stakes. Every move had to be calculated, every decision weighed carefully, because even the smallest slip-up could tip the balance and undo everything they were working for.

Before Rick could finish his sentence, my mother interjected, "What about Ross Perot? Was I the one who called him, or was it you?"

Rick had been poring over every lead, searching for someone—anyone—who could help. One name in particular stood out in his mind: Ross Perot. He recalled reading *On Wings of Eagles*, the gripping account of how Perot, the American business tycoon, had orchestrated the daring rescue of two American prisoners in Tehran in 1979. The mission, led by the formidable Army Colonel Arthur "Bull" Simons, had been a triumph of ingenuity and determination. Inspired by this story, Rick reached out to Perot's office at E-Systems in Richardson, Texas.

When the executive assistant answered, the response was a cold splash of reality. The US government, the assistant explained, wouldn't intervene. If Rick wanted help, he would have to find a way to handle it himself. Those words hit hard, another door slamming shut.

Then I spoke up, trying to piece together the last remaining details. "Rick, my mom mentioned someone named Teddy Bear, but she couldn't remember anything else."

Beverly chuckled, shaking her head. "Cathy, how could you forget this part?"

Rick leaned in, a slow smile creeping across his face as the memory surfaced. "Ah yes, I remember now." He paused, glancing around the table, the wheels turning in his mind as he recollected the strange, unsettling encounter. Rick sighed, his tone more serious than it had been all morning. "Teddy Bear was a contact that came through the back channels from a news report I saw on television. Lauren, we were desperate and racking our brains on how to find help to get you back."

Rick paused, his fork hovering over his plate. The light in his eyes dimmed slightly, and I could tell the memory was as fresh for him as if it had happened just yesterday. His fingers tapped gently on the table, a subtle sign of his deep thinking. "Teddy Bear came into the picture when I reached out for help. After running into dead ends with the usual channels, I remembered a news story about kidnapped Coca-Cola workers in Brazil. I managed to get in touch with a reporter, and through a series of mysterious calls, I was eventually directed to him."

He leaned forward, his voice dropping low. "At first, it felt like a long shot. But the moment I made the call, things started to feel a bit too...calculated. The woman who gave me the number was precise, almost eerie in how exact she was about the timing: 'dial in *exactly* fifteen minutes,'" he mimicked, his expression growing darker. "And then, when I finally reached Teddy Bear, the demand came immediately. No explanation, no pleasantries—just a flat, deadpan request: a million dollars for help in getting you back. That was it. No details, no plan, just a price tag."

A chill crept down my spine as I absorbed Rick's words. His voice softened as he continued, "But it wasn't the money that rattled me. It was the finality in his tone. The cold certainty that this was the only way. No room for negotiation, no chance of a different outcome. And when I couldn't meet that demand, he just...hung up. No warning, no second thought—just dead silence."

I sat back in my chair, but Rick wasn't done. "I dialed the number again and the same thing happened. A million dollars, no more, no less. Before I could even respond, the phone went dead. I tried a third time. Nothing. No answer. That was it. I had lost my chance."

The fact that there was someone out there—someone powerful enough to make such demands and disappear into the shadows—made everything feel much more real. And much more frightening.

And it all painted a clearer picture for me of the complex and frightening web they had found themselves tangled in.

Rick's gaze flicked to Beverly. "Do you remember the Randall brothers?"

Beverly's eyes met his with a knowing, somewhat skeptical look. She let out a quiet, almost amused sigh. "Oh, yes. How could I forget? This one always gets Rick worked up."

Rick's expression turned serious. "Bill and Dave Randall, two brothers who worked for me back when I was in the oil and gas business in East Texas. Both had solid law enforcement backgrounds. Bill, especially, had some serious credentials. He was a CIA contractor during the Vietnam War. After they left the business, they started their own investigation firm, Randall Brothers Investigations, over in West Monroe, Louisiana."

Beverly raised an eyebrow, clearly uncomfortable with the direction the conversation was heading.

Rick turned to my Mom, his expression regretful. "I never would've suggested them if I'd known, Cathy. I was friends with those guys for years. We did a lot of work together—hell, we trusted each other. But what they did to you...that ruined our friendship." His voice tightened, it was a betrayal that had hit him just as hard as it hit my mom.

My mom sat there, silent. It was clear how much it hurt to hear Rick speak of it.

I quickly pulled out my phone, typing the name "Randall Brothers" into the notes app. I needed to remember every detail, every name, every lead. The journal and tapes had already uncovered so much, but I couldn't afford to miss any of it. I'd have to go through my mother's journals again and cross-reference everything. What other pieces were hidden there? What else had my mom endured in this exhausting fight to get me back?

A heavy silence hung in the air as Rick's words settled in. The web of people involved was growing wider, and with it, the stakes were rising. Each move felt more like a game of chance than a rescue mission, and the price of failure was far too high.

That day, over the clinking of coffee cups and half-eaten brunch plates, we weren't just reminiscing. We were piecing together fragments of a story that had shaped all our lives in ways we still couldn't yet fully understand.

Later that night, after we returned home, I sat down and began to process everything we had discussed—the pieces from our conversation, the entries in my mom's journal, and the voices captured on the tapes. Slowly, the story that had once felt scattered and confusing began to come into focus, revealing a clearer picture of what had truly happened.

I made my way into the closet, pulled out the Ziplock bag from the Jordan box, and sifted through its contents until my gaze landed on it—the cassette tape labeled "Randall Brothers." A chill ran down my spine as I popped the tape into the player and pressed play.

The familiar sound of a dial tone filled the room, followed by Rick's unmistakable voice, his East Texas accent more pronounced than I remembered. "Hey, Dave, this is Rick Lambert." There was a noticeable edge to his tone, a tension that made my heart race. "Why'd you take that money from Cathy? She needs every bit of it to get her daughter back."

On the other end, Dave's voice was defensive, almost dismissive. "I used it to pay my informant. You know this stuff costs money. I didn't know they were going to bail on me."

Rick's voice grew firmer, colder. "You did Cathy wrong, Dave. We'll deal with this after she gets her daughter back. You ruined a lifelong friendship over this."

The finality in Rick's words echoed as the tape clicked off. The betrayal was crystal clear now, and it left a bitter taste in my mouth. I had always known there were obstacles, but hearing this conversation made everything feel more personal. My mother had been betrayed by my father and his family, and Rick had been betrayed by people he trusted to help—people who should have been allies in a time of crisis.

It was a painful revelation, yet one that underscored the immense courage it took for my mother to keep moving forward despite the countless times she had been let down. The more I uncovered about my story, the heavier my heart became. The desperation of those early days spent in the townhouse searching for any trace of me was suffocating. Rick and Beverly had put their lives on hold—abandoning everything they had worked for, their jobs, their responsibilities—all to find me. Even Miranda, so young and innocent, had been swept up in the whirlwind of uncertainty. Her laughter, bright and pure, was the only joy that filled the home amidst the turmoil.

As I listened to the old cassette tapes, their background held the hum of everyday life. Beverly's voice, calm but tinged with stress, would occasionally cut through the static, asking Miranda to put away the toys or reassuring her that she'd be off the phone in a few moments. Miranda would play with my toys—my Barbie dolls, my Care Bears—her small hands holding them with a quiet reverence, as if she hoped they might offer the answers to the questions she asked in her childlike innocence: "Where is Lauren? Why isn't she here?" Beverly would calmly explain that I was with my dad and they were working on bringing me home. I remember Bev telling me that even at five years old, Miranda could sense something was terribly wrong. She could feel the tension in the air, even if she didn't fully understand it.

As the days wore on, Beverly took it upon herself to research Jordanian law, hoping to find a loophole or any way to bring me back. Countless hours slipped by as she sifted through documents, her brow furrowed with concentration. And then, one day, she stumbled upon something that shook her to the core: According to Jordanian law in 1987, all parental rights went to the father once the child turned seven. I had turned seven just months before—in September—and my dad had taken me in November, just six weeks after my birthday.

This had been a carefully orchestrated plan by my father right from the start. He'd known about this law. Beverly shared her findings with my mom. Both understood the gravity of this. It wasn't just a kidnapping—it was a legal battle they were ill-prepared for.

As I continued to listen to the cassette tape, there was a long pause, a dial tone, and then my mother's voice. "Hello, my name is Cathy, and my daughter has been abducted by my ex-husband. He took her out of the country to Jordan." My mother's voice cracked, heavy with emotion. She was placed on hold before a woman's voice came on the line.

"Hi, this is Ruth Lincoln with Citizen Counsel Services in Washington, DC. How can I help you?"

"I'm a US citizen, and my ex-husband was born and raised in Jerash, Jordan. We were married in the United States, but after our divorce, I retained full custody of our daughter, Lauren. Over Halloween weekend, he took her to Jordan and refuses to bring her home."

Ruth's tone turned professional as she asked a few more questions, wanting to understand how my mom knew for sure that I was in Jordan. She detailed her conversations with the airlines, her communication with my stepmother, and the information she had gotten from Uncle Amir. Ruth listened carefully and then dropped a bombshell.

"I'm sorry, Cathy, but the United States cannot get involved. It's out of our jurisdiction. We don't have a treaty with Jordan,"

Ruth explained, the words like cold water to my mother's burning hope.

Mom's heart sank. All of her efforts, all the phone calls and research, were a dead end. Ruth took my mother's information down and promised to send her details about international kidnapping, along with contacts for support groups she could reach out to. But it was clear now: If Mom wanted to get me back, she would have to take matters into her own hands.

Ruth, though compassionate, was blunt about the idea. "You'll need to get a passport for Lauren. But I must warn you, going to Jordan alone is risky. The US government won't be able to intervene."

These words hit hard. Not only had the system failed her, the reality of what lay ahead—venturing into foreign territory with little more than her determination—was now more apparent than ever. The road to getting me back would be long, dangerous, and filled with uncertainty. Yet, she had no choice. She *would* push forward.

As I listened, other things began to fall into place. I remembered finding a large blue envelope filled with pamphlets and support group information—titles like "Children Held Hostage" and "Paternal Kidnapping" jumped out at me. I dug through the box again, pulling the paperwork out. As I glanced over the contents, a wave of emotion hit me. Everything was starting to feel more real, more tangible. Sitting there, listening to the recording with the yellow packet in my hands, it felt like I was walking through the experience all over again, but this time through my mom's eyes.

I couldn't hold back the tears. I picked up the phone and called her, my voice trembling as I spoke. "Mom, do you remember the name Ruth?"

After some more prompting, my mom remembered the yellow envelope. "Lauren, you know how much I hate paperwork and tedious tasks. When that yellow envelope showed up at my house, I wanted to scream. But I went through every single piece of paper. I called every number if there was even the slightest chance it would help me bring you back. The information inside only made the situation feel more impossible."

I could hear the exhaustion in her voice as she continued. "I sifted through the pages, feeling hopeless. Each word felt like another door slamming shut, another obstacle keeping me from bringing you home. Lauren, this is hard to relive, but I'm so glad you are doing it," my mom said. "I could never listen to those tapes now. It's painful to even hear you talk about it."

Despite her pain, she wanted to know what was on the recording, so I told her. "I just heard a conversation between you and a grandmother who was also trying to get her grandchild back."

Looking for any form of help, she had called one of the support numbers Ruth had provided. My mom was connected to a woman who shared her own heartbreaking story. The woman explained that she had been searching for her grandson for three years following his abduction. There was a heaviness in her voice when she recounted how, twice a year, she was allowed to travel to Iran to see him. But those visits were anything but simple—she was forced to sit in a room with her grandson, always watched and always knowing someone would make sure she didn't take him away.

The grandmother's pain was palpable, and it was clear this wasn't just her personal nightmare; she had turned her suffering into a mission. She'd started a support group to help others like her—people fighting to bring their loved ones home. My mother's heart likely broke for this woman, but I kept thinking she may have also found a strange kind of solace in knowing she wasn't alone.

The grandmother asked my mother where she lived, and when she said Texas, the woman's voice softened. "I know someone who might be able to help. Write this name and number down. This man has been through it too. He might have some advice for you."

The click of the cassette tape signaled the start of the next call, followed by the familiar dial tone, and then a man's voice broke through the static.

"Hello?"

"Hi, is this Jeffrey?"

"Yes, who is this?"

"This is Cathy. I got your number from a support group for parents whose children have been abducted."

"Ah, yes. Has your child been taken?"

"Yes, my ex-husband took my daughter to Jordan."

"Jordan?" His voice held a mix of disbelief and concern. "Let me find a quieter place. Wait a second."

There was a brief pause as the background noise faded, and then he came back, his voice a little softer but still full of urgency. "Sorry, I'm at work. What's your name again?"

"My name is Cathy. I live in Richardson. My ex-husband has taken my daughter to Jordan."

"Jordan…." I could hear the gravity in his voice. "I can tell you what *not* to do. I live in Dallas. I can meet you if you'd like, but at the very least, I can tell you what I've gone through."

My mom hesitated, her heart pounding in her chest. "Can I ask, did you ever get your child back?"

His response was sharp, tinged with frustration and anger. "No. No, Cathy, I haven't. It's been four years, and I'm still fighting. I paid a lawyer $20,000, and all they did was take my money. Trust me, don't waste your time."

Mom's pulse quickened as he continued. "Grab a piece of paper and a pen. Write this down: Do *not* ask the police for help. Do *not* let the government know what you're doing. Get a passport, but don't tell them what it's for. You will have to find a way to get your daughter back on your own."

When I told my mom about the conversation, she recalled it vividly. "That conversation pushed me deeper into fear. Honestly, I felt like I was spinning out of control." Her words hung in the air, dread playing in her voice as she relived it. The advice she'd received was nothing like what she'd hoped for—no support from the government, no help from the authorities. Just a stark, lonely path ahead, and no easy answers or safety nets to catch her if she fell.

The click of the cassette tape signaled the end of the conversation, but I was no longer on the couch in my living room. I was back in that townhouse, sitting at the kitchen table with my mother, listening to phone call after phone call, each more hopeless than the last. "The United States cannot help you," they had all said, the words echoing time and again like a cold, suffocating certainty.

I closed my eyes, my heart aching for the woman who had fought so tirelessly and for the child—me—lost in the middle of it all. After a deep breath, I turned my attention back to the box. A cassette tape lost in the pile, labeled simply "Ali." The name alone sent a shiver down my spine. Was I ready for this? Could I really handle hearing my father's voice again, especially given everything I now knew?

I hesitated, then braced myself. With trembling hands, I placed the tape into the player and pressed play.

The phone rang, and this time, as the call connected, I immediately recognized the voice on the other end. It wasn't my uncle. No, it was *him*. The deep, thick accent was unmistakable. It was my father.

"Hello?" his voice crackled through the line, a casual greeting that carried an unsettling weight.

My mother's breath caught in her throat. This was the moment she had been praying for, the moment she'd fought so hard to reach. "Hello, Ali. This is Cathy." My mother managed to keep her voice steady despite the torrent of emotions swirling inside her. She had been trying to get through to him for days, each call ending in frustration or silence. This time, he had actually answered, and she was determined to hold it together.

Her heart pounded as the conversation unfolded. Desperate for reassurance, my mother asked about my well-being. My father's response was calm, almost practiced: "Lauren is safe and happy with me." But something in his tone didn't sit right. My mother pressed further, confusion and hurt bubbling up inside her. *Why* had he taken her? What were his motives?

"I believe the United States is a bad place," he explained coolly. "She is better off with me."

My mother's heart shattered at those words. She pleaded with him to let her speak to me, to hear my voice, but he refused.

"It's too soon," he said. "I don't want to confuse her."

She tried again, this time asking if she could visit, but my father postponed it, telling her they could "work something out in the future."

As the days stretched into weeks, the phone calls became a relentless rhythm of hope and despair. Each time, my father shut her out, leaving her feeling more helpless with every refusal.

In the midst of it all, a new rumor surfaced—my father was planning to visit Lebanon, where his sister was about to have a baby. But the news coming out of Lebanon painted a terrifying picture: civil war, violence, and unrest. My mother's fear grew. What if my dad disappeared with me into a country at war, making it even harder—if not impossible—to bring me home?

The longer he stayed silent, the deeper my mom's sense of urgency grew. It felt like time was running out, and with every call that went unanswered, every promise broken, the distance between her and her daughter widened.

Each passing day felt heavier than the last, a slow, suffocating weight of sorrow and uncertainty. My mother's calls to Jordan had become increasingly futile, each attempt met with silence or more lies. No one would speak to her. No one offered any answers. Desperate for any kind of direction, my mother turned to the pages of books and magazines, searching for anything that might guide her in her seemingly impossible mission. In a *Soldier of Fortune* magazine, she found a glimmer of hope—stories of ex-CIA agents, mercenaries, former soldiers, and even rogue politicians who had pulled off daring rescues around the world. The thought crossed her mind: *Could this be the answer? Could someone like them help me bring my daughter home?*

Rick, as always, was determined to do whatever it took. He had made it clear that if there was anyone capable of organizing a rescue mission for me, it was him. He wasn't about to sit back while my mother fought this battle alone.

After days of relentless searching, Rick told my mom he had secured an appointment with the grand jury in Dallas County. His connections, forged during his time as a former investigator with the Dallas County District Attorney's office, might just provide the opening they needed. Rick had seen a lot in his career, but this was personal.

He prepared my mother for the meeting, warning her that the grand jury might not be able to offer the help they were hoping for. "It could be a dead end," he told her. But Mom's resolve had hardened. She was ready to meet anyone who could offer guidance, even if it meant facing more disappointment. Nothing could stop her from trying to bring me home.

Their journey—*our* journey—was filled with a sense of desperation, and at times, it felt like hope was slipping through their fingers. Yet, in the quiet moments between their relentless pursuit, my mother's determination never faltered. Rick's unwavering support kept her going, even when the future seemed bleak. Little did she know that their efforts, this long, exhausting path they were walking, would soon lead them to an unexpected turn—one that might finally bring about the breakthrough they had all been praying for.

CHAPTER SIX

A STRANGE NEW LAND

I had never been outside the United States before. The only trip I had ever taken was to visit my grandmother in Florida with my mom. But now, there I was, standing in my father's family home in Jerash, Jordan. It was overwhelming—this massive, multi-story building felt more like an apartment complex, with each floor housing a separate residence for a different branch of my father's family. I had no idea just how large his family was until then. At the top of the building was an open-air rooftop with an incredible view of the city below.

I was exhausted from the long journey and confused. Why hadn't anyone told me we were going to Jordan? Why weren't my stepmother and siblings with us? The only thing my father would say when I asked was, "Lauren, don't worry. Everything will be fine." But even at seven years old, I sensed that "everything" was very different from what I was used to.

I was about to step into not just a new home but an entirely new culture. My father's home in Jordan was unlike anything I had ever seen. It was more communal than our house in Texas, with so many relatives living in the same building. I wasn't accustomed to this closeness, the feeling of always being surrounded by family. It was nice in some ways, but it also felt like a strange and unsettling new world.

In Jordan, many families live in small one- or two-room apartments, though wealthier families often have larger homes or apartments. These buildings were typically made of concrete, with some constructed from mud and stone, which allowed for additional floors to be added over time. This is how families often expand, with married sons and their families occupying the new floors. The traditional layout reflects the importance of hierarchy within the family structure. In Jordanian culture, men hold the highest honor, and it's customary for the eldest male to live on the top floor, which is the coolest part of the building. The air circulation there is the best, and it's considered a sign of status.

As a seven-year-old, I didn't understand all the details of the culture and religion surrounding me. The roles of men and women were sharply divided. Women generally held a lower status in the family and were expected to take care of domestic chores. Meanwhile, men were seen as the protectors and providers, often with the freedom to go outside and engage in activities beyond the home.

Arranged marriages were common—even between cousins—and the rules around marriage were rooted in Islamic law. Muslim men could marry women of other faiths, but Muslim women could only marry men who were Muslim or had agreed to convert. These cultural expectations were so ingrained that I could feel them in the very air I breathed, though I didn't have the full understanding of why they mattered.

Every evening, the family would gather on the rooftop. The men sat together, chatting and smoking from a long pipe attached to a glass jar, while the women sat separately, deep in conversation. I later learned that they were using prayer beads, moving them along a string while speaking in Arabic. I had never seen anything like it before.

When we first arrived at my grandmother's apartment, I was greeted by a large group of relatives I had never met. They were all excited to see me, and although they spoke mainly Arabic, a few of them knew some English. The women wore long, colorful dresses adorned with gold jewelry, necklaces, and scarves that covered their hair. It was all so different, yet I couldn't shake an unsettling feeling that, somehow, I was supposed to be here.

Trying to remember my time in Jordan is like peering through a fog—some moments are clear, while others blur into confusion. The first few days felt like a series of strange dreams, each one slipping away as my mind raced, trying to make sense of everything. The hardest part was not knowing when I would be able to speak with my mom. I longed to hear her voice, but all I could do was wait and wonder.

My aunt guided me to my room and helped me unpack, her presence both comforting and strange. My father, I soon realized, was rarely around, keeping to a different part of the house. In Jordan, the women took care of the children, while the men seemed distant, preoccupied with their own affairs. This felt so foreign to me. Back in Dallas, my dad was always present in my life. He'd play with me, tuck me in every night, and even make my favorite meal—hamburger steak with grilled onions. But in Jordan, my father's presence was almost nonexistent. When I asked him why, he simply replied, "This is the right way here; you will see." His words were unnerving. I wanted to understand but I didn't.

The rhythms of daily life in Jordan were different, too, especially mealtime. Dinnertime was a flurry of activity, with my grandmother and aunts bustling in the kitchen, preparing a large meal for the entire family. The air was thick with the aroma of spices, hummus, and freshly baked bread. When the meal was ready, a large cloth would be spread out on the floor, and dishes of yogurt, grape leaves stuffed with spiced rice and meat, small plates of hummus, flatbread, and a big bowl of rice would be placed in the center for everyone to share.

In Jordan, eating was a communal affair. While families in urban areas often sit at a table, rural families like ours typically ate while seated on the floor. The food was served from a large common plate known as a *sidr*, and everyone ate with their fingers—specifically, of their right hand, since the left hand was considered unclean and reserved for personal hygiene. The feeling of eating with my hands, without silverware, was incredibly awkward at first. I was used to the structure of American dining: plates, utensils, and the quiet exchange of dishes. But here, food wasn't passed around on plates. Instead, you picked up a piece of bread with your right hand, took a bite, and offered it to someone else, inviting them to do the same. It felt strange, yet somehow intimate, this sharing of food, this ritual of connection.

When the meal ended, everyone would move slightly away from the eating area, say "*al hamdu li lah*" (praise be to God), and wash their hands. It was a process so simple, yet so full of respect for the food, for each other, and for the moment. And after dinner, especially when guests came over, my aunt would bring out a beautifully arranged tray with a silver coffee kettle and small ceramic cups. She would serve Turkish-style coffee, a thick, rich brew, paired with desserts like baklava, the sweetness lingering long after the last sip.

It was all so different from what I was used to, and at times, I felt like a stranger in my own skin pulled in two directions, belonging nowhere. I was trying to learn a new language and new customs, while at the same time wanting to know when I would be able to talk to my mom, or even my stepmother. I longed to have that connection with someone I knew other than my father.

Many nights, I would cry myself to sleep, my own confusion and fear pressing down on me like a heavy blanket. I could still feel the frustration and anger in my father's voice every time I asked, "Baba, when will we go home? When will our vacation be over? I miss my mommy." His eyes would narrow, his patience thinning, and I would instantly know I had crossed an invisible line. He always insisted I speak Arabic, and the first word I ever learned was *Baba*—daddy. But as I spoke it, the distance between us was growing wider.

As the days wore on, my father retreated more, spending long hours in prayer or locked away in his thoughts, leaving me to spend my time with my grandmother and aunts. They were kind, but I was still a stranger in their world, and all I could think about was home—about my mom, my bed, the life I knew. Yet, I was terrified to voice it. Every mention of home seemed to ignite something in my father—a fury I couldn't understand but felt in every nerve of my small body. My mind waged a constant battle, torn between the desperate longing to go back and the fear of making him angry. I was caught between worlds—one that felt so far away, and one that was unraveling before me.

Life in Jordan was full of unfamiliar customs, and adjusting to the most basic routines was harder than I could have imagined. One of the biggest shocks came with something as simple as bathing. In my father's home, I was allowed to bathe only once a week, a stark contrast to the daily showers I was used to back in Texas. But the real challenge came when it was time to use the bathroom. It wasn't anything like the bathrooms I'd known—no running water, no proper toilet. Instead, there was just a hole in the floor with a chain hanging above it. To use it, I had to squat awkwardly and pull the chain when I was finished. And there was no toilet paper—just the expectation that I clean myself with my left hand, a practice that seemed completely alien to me, but one that made sense within the rigid boundaries of their culture, where the left hand was considered unclean.

I struggled to make sense of this. I tried to hold it in, hoping I could somehow avoid using the bathroom altogether. But sometimes, I couldn't make it to the third floor to my Uncle Mohammed's apartment, where he had a regular toilet due to his disability from polio. More often than not, I would have an accident before I could reach it, and when I did, my father's anger rumbled. "How embarrassing to pee on yourself at seven," he would scold, his voice thick with frustration and disappointment.

One day, in a cruel attempt to "teach me a lesson," he made me wear a diaper. He even called my cousins over to mock me, telling them to look at what I was wearing. The humiliation burned in my cheeks as I stood there, small and powerless. I just wanted to go home—to hear my mother's voice, to feel the warmth of her embrace again. But when I asked my father if we could leave, he simply replied, "It's not time yet."

The pain of being separated from my mom was a constant ache, a deep, hollow emptiness that never seemed to fade. But it wasn't just her absence that cut through me. My father was becoming a stranger—a man I didn't recognize. He was changing before my eyes, and with each passing moment, the loving, kind, and protective father I had once known seemed further out of reach. Where was the man who would hold me close, whispering that everything would be okay and that he would always keep me safe? He was disappearing, and in his place was someone I didn't understand… someone I feared. I wasn't just losing my mom; I was also losing the loving father that I once knew.

My aunts and grandmother did everything they could to step into the roles of mother and stepmother, showering me with love and care. But no matter how hard they tried, nothing could fill the emptiness of missing my mother. I wanted to feel whole again, to feel safe, but nothing seemed to bridge that gap. Still, I tried to adapt, even though it felt like I was living in a different world. Slowly, I noticed how my Arabic was improving and how I was becoming more accustomed to the strange routines of my new life. It wasn't easy, but I was starting to find ways to navigate it.

One of the few things that helped pull me out of my loneliness were the big family gatherings. They offered a welcome distraction, providing moments of warmth and a brief reprieve from the tension between my father and me. I'd never experienced anything like it before. Coming from a small family, this was the first time I'd ever been part of something so large and so full of life and noise.

The celebrations were a mix of joy and bittersweet longing. Birthdays, family get-togethers—the women would dress in long, flowing dresses, their arms heavy with gold bracelets and necklaces inscribed with Arabic script and tiny stones that sparkled as they moved. The house would fill with the intoxicating smells of roasting meats and spices, the air thick with the warmth of food being prepared while laughter rang out from every corner. I learned to play the *daf*, a small drum with a round wooden frame and a goat-skin head, tapping out rhythms that seemed to pulse through my chest. The women danced, their eyes alight with joy, while my cousins and I ran around, our feet instinctively moving in time with the music. The tables overflowed with delicacies, and for a brief moment, I could almost forget the pain of missing my mother and feeling like I was losing the father I once knew.

Outside the house, life in Jerash was quieter, but I found small moments of comfort in the afternoons I spent with my younger cousins. We'd wander through the narrow, winding streets, stopping at local vendors to buy falafel—golden, crispy balls of fried chickpeas served in crumpled paper bags. The taste of the hot, spicy flavor would linger on our tongues as we made sure to eat every last bite before heading home, our laughter mingling with the chatter of the bustling streets. Jerash felt peaceful, almost timeless. We would stay out until the sun sank low, the sky turning shades of orange and pink, and the streets still alive with the hum of people heading to shops or gathering at the corner cafés.

But even in the midst of these quiet moments, there was a sound that would always cut through the stillness—the call to prayer. Five times a day, the voice of the *muezzin* rang out across the city, the sound filling the air like an invisible thread connecting every street and building. My father would stop whatever he was doing, unroll his prayer rug, and begin his ritual. First, he would wash his hands and face, remove his shoes, and position himself to face Mecca. Then, he would raise his hands to the heavens, bow low, and touch his forehead to the ground in submission. The movements and chants were so foreign to me, as alien as the culture I was trying to navigate.

At first, I thought they were praying to Jesus, just in a different language and in a different way. After all, I had been taught that I could pray anywhere—whether in the car, at the dinner table, or beside my bed. But my father explained that he was praying to Allah. I didn't fully grasp the difference, but in my young mind, I assumed that *Allah* was just the Arabic word for Jesus.

Everything in Jordan felt different—the way people lived, ate, and prayed, even the air itself seemed heavier, thick with history and meaning I didn't understand. Yet, amid the unfamiliarity, I couldn't shake the feeling that something in me was shifting, changing in ways I couldn't yet comprehend. It was a world of contrasts—both familiar and alien, comforting and terrifying all at once. And every day I spent there, I was caught in a tug-of-war between trying to adapt to this new life and the overwhelming pull to go home, back to what I knew, to the world that felt like mine.

As the days passed, it became clear this wasn't just a vacation. And each time I brought it up, my father's patience seemed to wear thinner. "Don't you like it here? Aren't you having fun with your cousins?" he would ask, as if that should be enough to make me forget about everything I had left behind. But the truth was, I missed my mom terribly.

I remember the day my father finally agreed to let me call my mom. He stood in front of me, wearing his long white robe, his face stern as he looked down at me. He walked toward the phone on the hallway table, his footsteps deliberate, echoing in the quiet of the house. A mix of nervousness and excitement swirled in my stomach as I watched him prepare. His instructions were sharp, his words measured.

"Tell your mom you're okay and having fun. Don't say anything that might make her feel bad or sad," he warned, his voice resolute. He spoke to her first, and although I couldn't understand what they were saying, I could hear the firmness in his tone. His words felt like an invisible barrier, keeping me separated from my mother, from the comfort of her voice. When their conversation ended, he handed me the phone, his presence looming over me like a shadow. He watched me closely as if to ensure I followed his every word.

My heart beat faster as I lifted the receiver to my ear, and I could almost feel the distance between us—the miles, the time, the silence.

Searching through the "Jordan box," I found a cassette tape tucked into another Ziplock bag labeled "Lauren." The moment I saw it, a rush of anticipation flooded me. I couldn't wait to hear my voice from that time, to reconnect with the girl I once was. I hit play, and as the tape began to whirl, my seven-year-old voice filled the room. But when I heard it, it was as if I were listening to a stranger. The thick accent, the coldness in my tone—it was almost unrecognizable. I had expected to hear tears, maybe even joy—a trace of the little girl who had longed for her mother. Instead, all I heard was a quiet, distant version of myself, stripped of enthusiasm and warmth. The voice on the tape sounded small, uncertain, almost scared. It hit me hard: I had changed so much in such a short time, and the little girl I had once been seemed to have vanished, swallowed by the distance that separated me from the life I had known.

"Mom, is it you?" I asked, my voice trembling.

"Yes, honey, it's me," she replied softly, her voice strained in an effort to keep her tears in check. "Do you miss me?"

"Yes, but Daddy said I can't see you right now. Daddy took me on a trip to Jordan to meet my family. It's nice here, but I miss you."

She stayed calm, trying to reassure me, but I could tell her words were carefully chosen to avoid alarming me or saying anything that might risk us being cut off.

"Lauren, I miss you so much. I think about you every day, and I can't wait to see you again." My mom's voice crackled with emotion, a mix of love and longing that only deepened my sense of separation. "Did you know it's Christmas time?" she asked, her voice tinged with sadness.

"No, we don't celebrate Christmas here," I replied, feeling the weight of her words. "No tree. No Santa."

The silence between us stretched before she asked, "Do you want me to send you some gifts?"

Without hesitation, I replied, "Could you send my favorite stuffed animal?" It was the only thing that still felt like home. It felt like the smallest piece of comfort I could hold onto in a world so foreign to me.

She reassured me with her love, telling me again how much she cared and that we would be together soon. But even as she spoke, I sensed the unspoken truth hanging in the air. Deep down, I knew this could very well be the only time we would speak. The distance between us, both physical and emotional, felt wider than ever.

After we hung up, I felt my dad's eyes on me, watching closely. I ran to my room and broke down, overwhelmed by loneliness. I missed my mom, my friends at school, Aunt Joyce, Bev, Rick, Miranda, and the familiarity of home. I missed the comfort of a bathroom that didn't feel foreign. I just wanted to curl up somewhere, to be alone. But if my dad saw me crying, he would only get angry, so I stayed in my room, weeping myself to sleep.

A few days later, my aunt and grandmother told me I would be starting school soon. They took me to visit the school and pick out a uniform. "Why?" I asked, confusion bubbling in my chest. "Why am I going to school here when my home is in Dallas?"

My father walked in just then, and in his usual distant tone, he explained, "While you're in Jordan, you need to learn the language. Don't you want to be able to talk with your grandmother and cousins?"

I felt a lump form in my throat as I asked again, "When can I go home? I miss my mom, and I really want to go back."

My dad's face tightened with anger, and without saying another word, he left the room. The next day, my aunt and grandmother took me to the school for an assessment. After speaking with the teachers, they decided I would be placed in the kindergarten class since I couldn't speak, read, or write Arabic. It was another reminder that I was no longer in control of my own life. I was a stranger in this new world, and all I could do was follow where they led me.

The next morning, my aunt helped me dress in the school uniform—a light-blue, long-sleeved dress and a scarf to cover my hair. I was nervous and confused, but by now, I knew this was not a vacation.

I remember the school vividly, though it felt so alien at the time. It was small, with stark white walls and old wooden desks. Each child sat on a simple wooden bench in front of their desk, while the teacher stood at the front, writing on a small chalkboard. As soon as I walked in, all eyes turned to me. It didn't take long to realize I was the oldest and tallest in the class, an outsider in every sense. The other children spoke to each other in Arabic, and their gazes felt like a weight on my shoulders, but I couldn't understand a word they said. The teacher introduced me with a few quick words and then directed me to my seat.

Here again, the bathroom was just a hole in the floor, an experience I could never get used to. I tried to hold it for as long as possible, but one day, my body betrayed me. I had another accident, and the humiliation was overwhelming. The teacher scolded me in front of the class, and before I knew it, my father was called in. When he arrived, he was furious. I couldn't bear the thought of going back to school, but they insisted I return. The reason, they said, was simple: I had to learn the language.

Every morning, my aunt and grandmother would help me get dressed and walk me to the street to catch the bus. The bus was packed, and each child had their assigned seat. Mine was next to the window, where I sat in silence. A female chaperone sat at the front, keeping a watchful eye to ensure we all stayed quiet and seated. Then, a few weeks into school, another new student joined. She lived farther out, so our bus ride became a bit longer, but in a strange way, I was relieved. At least I wasn't the only new kid anymore.

Over the next two months, I began picking up the language. Slowly but surely, I learned to speak more fluently, and I could even read and write a few simple words. My school arranged for me to use a toilet at a relative's house nearby, which was a small relief. The daily call to prayer, once so strange to me, became a normal part of my life, just like the custom of eating meals on the floor with my hands. Despite these adjustments, there was one thing I couldn't get used to: the overwhelming ache of missing my mom.

I was just a scared, broken seven-year-old girl, stuck in a foreign country, desperately missing the warmth and safety of home. But looking back now, I see how God was already at work, even in the darkest moments. He wasn't just a bigger version of my father, as I once believed.

I didn't know it at the time, but even in that foreign place, God was laying the groundwork for my healing, for the eventual reunion with my mom, and for a transformation of my life in ways I could never have imagined.

CHAPTER SEVEN

FAITH OVER FEAR

I know God because of my mom's faith. It never wavered, even when she wasn't going to church or reading her Bible consistently. No matter the season, she always told me about God, and every night, we would pray together. We'd recite the familiar words: "Now I lay me down to sleep. I pray the Lord my soul to keep. If I should die before I wake, I pray the Lord my soul to take."

In the darkest days of our lives, when everything seemed lost, my mom ran back to Him, desperate for help. And even though a deep darkness settled over her, and though she didn't know what to do, she was resolute. "No" wasn't an option for her.

One quiet Saturday afternoon, with the boys out of the house and my husband absorbed in his computer, I found myself alone, holding an unlabeled cassette. I pulled it from the Ziploc bag and slid it into the player. The now-familiar static of the phone line crackled, and soon Beverly's voice sounded, followed by my mother's. Looking back, I realize this conversation could have easily happened in person—after all, the Lamberts were living with my mom at the time. But on this day, Beverly was visiting her brother, Stan. I know now that God wanted me to hear this conversation for myself, to capture this moment in time so I could share the phone call that changed everything.

"Hello?" she answered quietly, her sadness evident.

Beverly's voice came through, gentle yet concerned: "Cathy, it's me. Are you okay?"

My mom broke down. "No, I'm not okay. I don't know what to do. So many people are telling me different things. I feel like I'm going crazy, and there's just no answer. I'm so worried about Lauren and her safety."

Without hesitation, Beverly responded, "Cathy, we're going to pray." She began praying over my mom, speaking with authority: "Lauren knows You, Jesus; she is Your child. Protect her from any false gods. Keep her safe from anything that is not of You, Lord." In the background, Stan offered Bible verses and recounted stories of miracles from Scripture.

Then Stan picked up the phone. "You're not alone, Cathy. Many people are praying for you. Don't lose hope. As much as you love Lauren, and as much as your heart aches for her, remember—Jesus loves you even more. His heart aches for you too. Trust in Him."

The weight of it all seemed too much for my mom, but Beverly's words were a glimmer of hope. She shared a story from her own life, a moment when she, too, was desperate for answers. "Cathy, I had to be alone. I locked myself in my bathroom, got on my knees, and that's when I met Jesus. That's when everything changed for me."

Through her tears, my mom whispered, "Yes, that's what I need. I need to be alone, away from everyone's suggestions…away from all of this mess." She told Beverly she needed a few days of silence, away from the noise, and that she didn't want anyone to know where she was going—except for her own mother. She knew her mom would pray. Beverly reassured her, "Don't worry. I'll handle everything. I'll tell people you're out running an errand. Just go."

Then, after a thoughtful pause, Beverly added, "Cathy, I remember reading a book during my own difficult time that said fasting brings you closer to God."

My mom's voice broke as she spoke, "Yes…I need to let go of the bad things in my life, all the stuff that's holding me back—like my cigarettes. I need to get away, but I can't until I meet with the grand jury." She paused and Beverly began to pray again. She asked God to grant my mom clarity, provision, and a way to see me again.

The next day was the court hearing that Rick had arranged for my mom. She woke early, her heart racing as she spent quiet moments praying and reading Scripture, seeking peace. Rick drove her to the courthouse, his voice steady but full of concern as he reminded her, "This is just a basic step to file for a warrant for Ali's arrest. But don't expect much from the grand jury. They won't be much help in getting Lauren back."

As my mom stepped into the courthouse, a lump formed in her throat, threatening to choke her, but she forced herself to swallow it down. She clenched her fists, willing herself to stay calm. The air was thick, and every step echoed in the silent halls, but she fought back the tears, determined to speak clearly when the time came. This wasn't just a hearing—it was a battle for my safety, for her peace, and for our future.

Mom stood before the grand jury, her heart pounding as she recounted the painful details of her divorce. "When my daughter was six weeks old, I filed for divorce," she began, her voice composed but heavy. "I have full custody of Lauren." She paused, her gaze shifting as she continued, "Ali, Lauren's father, is from Jerash, Jordan. On November first, he kidnapped her and took her to Jordan."

One of the men leaned forward, his voice sharp with concern. "Have you contacted the State Department?"

As she opened her mouth to respond, tears welled up in her eyes, and her voice faltered. "Yes, sir, I have."

He pressed, "Can they do anything for you?"

Her shoulders slumped as she answered, her voice breaking, "Can I tell you the truth? Not really. All they can do is a welfare check. There are no treaties with Jordan."

Her frustration bubbled over. "The worst part is, the United States spends billions in foreign aid but can't even help us get *our* children back when they've been kidnapped." She broke down, sobbing in a desperate cry for justice. "It's not fair! It's just not fair!"

A heavy silence filled the room. Everyone in the jury nodded, their faces reflecting the gravity of what she'd just shared. "No, ma'am, it's not fair," one of them murmured in agreement.

But then, to my mom's surprise, a man stood up. He pulled out a business card and addressed her with quiet authority. "My name is Al Zapanta. I'm on the board of the State Department. If you don't get satisfaction from them, call me. I'll do what I can." He handed her his card.

As my mom slipped Al's business card into her wallet, she was so overwhelmed by despair that she couldn't even recognize the glimmer of hope in her hand. She couldn't see what God was preparing for us—how He was about to move in ways we couldn't yet understand.

Rick had waited outside the courtroom during Mom's testimony, giving her space but staying close. He met her at the door when she stepped out, visibly shaken and emotionally drained. His eyes scanned her face. "What happened in there?" he asked gently.

Her voice was tired, but there was a slight edge of frustration. "You were right," she said, her words slow. "They told me they can't help because there's no treaty with Jordan. They'll issue a warrant for Ali's arrest. If he tries to enter the United States, he'll be captured and jailed. But they can't help me get Lauren back."

Rick nodded. "Yeah, that's what I expected."

Al Zapanta—the man who handed my mother a business card in the courthouse and opened a door she didn't know existed.

My mom handed Rick the business card she was given in the courtroom. His eyes lit up with the faintest flicker of hope as he saw it. "Al Zapanta. State Department? Hmm. He might actually have some pull." He paused, then added, "Give him a call on Monday. Maybe something will come of it."

When they returned to the townhouse, my mom's footsteps were heavy as she walked through the door. Beverly, waiting anxiously, could see the disappointment on her face before she even said a word. Rick explained the courtroom proceedings, but my mom barely listened. Her thoughts were miles away, consumed with all the things she couldn't control. She turned, walked to her room, and began packing, gathering her Bible, her notebook, and her suitcase.

"I'll be back in a few days," she told Bev, her voice quieter than usual.

With no destination in mind, my mom got into her car and drove toward Fort Worth. She had no plan, no idea where to go, only the feeling that she needed to be alone. After some time, she checked into a motel, the quiet room offering some semblance of peace. There, she pulled out her Bible, the words blurring as her heart poured out to God. "God, if You can hear me…I will do anything to get my daughter back. I can't do this on my own. God, I need You."

As I read my mother's journal, I felt as though I was right there with her in that motel room—alone and desperate, yet faithfully seeking God. Three days without food, only water. Three days of praying, fasting, and poring over her Bible, searching for any answer, any sign of hope. The weight of her isolation and the intensity of her faith hit me as I read her words.

She wrote that on the third day of fasting, God spoke to her through Daniel 10:12 (NIV): Then he continued, "Do not be afraid, Daniel. Since the first day that you set your mind to gain understanding and to humble yourself before your God, your words were heard, and I have come in response to them." In that sacred moment, God was telling my mother, "I see you." He was acknowledging her humility, her surrender, and her shift in focus from her overwhelming circumstances to Him. She had stopped fixating on the problem and had set her eyes firmly on the answer.

In that quiet room, with only the sound of her prayer, she asked, "God, what do I need to do to get my daughter back?" And in her spirit, she heard a clear command: *Quit smoking*. For a woman who had smoked four packs a day since the age of nineteen, this was no small request. And then came the next command: *Confess any areas of unforgiveness*. My mom knew she needed to cleanse her heart.

The passage from Daniel 10 isn't just a historical account; it holds deep spiritual significance. At this time, the Israelites had returned to Canaan after their exile, only to face opposition from the Samaritans that stopped the construction of the temple. Despite everything God had done for them, the people had grown discouraged and abandoned their mission. As a result, God's favor was no longer upon them. Daniel, distraught, fasted and prayed for twenty-one days, seeking God's intervention. But why did it take so long for God to answer his prayers? The angel who appeared to Daniel explained, "But the prince of the Persian kingdom resisted me twenty-one days. Then Michael, one of the chief princes, came to help me, because I was detained there with the king of Persia." (Daniel 10:13, NIV).

The moment Daniel began fasting and praying, a spiritual battle began in the heavens. And the same was true for my mom. The very moment she entered that motel room, set on her path of fasting and prayer, God began to fight for my life. He was about to move in a mighty way, not just because of my mother's sacrifice but also because of her unwavering faithfulness in prayer. God had heard her cries, and He was preparing to show up in ways that only He could.

Her journal made it clear. The weeks leading up to her retreat in the motel, her smoking had escalated—a desperate attempt to cope with the overwhelming stress she faced. At times, she would even light two cigarettes at once, trying to find some relief from the constant anxiety gnawing at her. But in that motel room, everything changed. My mom made a promise to God: *If You bring Lauren back, I will never smoke again.* That vow was not just a commitment to quit a habit; it was a turning point in her spiritual journey.

On her knees next to the bed, she wrestled with the anger and unforgiveness that had built up over the years, both towards others and herself. She confessed it all—every ounce of bitterness and regret—and asked God to help her let it go. As she surrendered, something remarkable happened. When she walked out of that room, she was no longer the same woman. For the first time in what felt like forever, my mother walked with faith, no longer bound by the weight of her past.

When she returned to the townhouse, Beverly immediately noticed the change. "You don't look the same," she said. "Something's different."

My mom smiled, her face reflecting a newfound light. "I'm not the same," she replied, her voice steady with conviction. "God told me that I'm going to get Lauren back." My mother now stood taller, unburdened, her eyes bright with hope for the first time in years.

She began to tackle the mundane tasks she had long neglected—paying bills, getting her car an oil change—all while maintaining an unwavering belief that God was guiding her every step. But the most pressing task of all was contacting Jordan. Three days had passed without any updates, and she was growing desperate. She dialed every number she had, but no one would answer.

Then she remembered Al's business card, the one she had received in the courtroom. With a deep breath, she dialed his office number, praying that this call might be the turning point.

When Al answered, he seemed genuinely glad to hear from her. He shared that just the week before her court hearing, he had been in Washington, DC, having lunch with an old friend—Everett Alvarez.

Everett wasn't just any friend. He was a decorated US Navy pilot and the first American aviator captured during the Vietnam War. After being shot down in 1964, he spent more than eight years as a prisoner of war in the infamous Hoa Lo Prison in Hanoi—known to American POWs as the "Hanoi Hilton." By the time my mother's situation reached him, Everett had become one of the longest-held American POWs in US military history and a respected figure in the intelligence and defense community. His courage and leadership had earned him a powerful network of military and government connections.

During lunch, Everett had mentioned something that immediately caught Al's attention.

A group of veterans from North Carolina had recently started a company called Corporate Training Unlimited (CTU). The company specialized in private security, tactical training, and, most importantly, high-risk recovery missions in the Middle East.

My mom could hardly believe what she was hearing. God's timing had been nothing short of perfect; just as Al had been sitting in the courtroom that day, he had also been hearing about a group that specialized in missions to bring people back from places like the Middle East. The rescue mission was starting to come together in ways she could never have foreseen.

Everett promised to gather more information about CTU and its operations, and true to his word, he wasted no time.

He reached out to the president of CTU, Don Feeney.

The moment Don heard who was on the line, he immediately rose from his desk, instinctively standing at attention out of respect for the man who had endured so much in service to his country.

That single phone call would become the first step in something far bigger than my mother—or I—could have imagined.

What had begun as a desperate search for help was now intersecting with a network of extraordinary people whose lives had been shaped by war, sacrifice, and an unwavering commitment to bring Americans home.

Thirty-seven years later, when I reconnected with Don, he shared the details of that pivotal phone call with me.

As I listened, I reflected on the journey that had brought me to that point. It became clear that my own story, like those of so many others, was shaped by moments of unexpected connection and courage. Around the same time, as I began to process my past, the advice I received about writing a book started to resonate: "Lauren, you need a platform to share your story." At first, the idea of creating such a platform seemed overwhelming, but then a man named Chris Burgess suggested something I hadn't considered—a podcast. And so, I took another leap of faith and launched the *Redeemed* podcast in April 2024.

I had no idea what to expect. I never imagined that *Redeemed* would become more than just a platform to share my testimony. It quickly grew into a space where I could highlight the powerful, life-changing stories of others. And, unexpectedly, it became a bridge to reconnect with people who had played pivotal roles in my life—people I never thought I would see again. One of the greatest blessings came when I had the opportunity to interview the men who were directly involved in my rescue.

Including Don Feeney, president of Corporate Training Unlimited (CTU), a private security firm based in Fayetteville, North Carolina. CTU wasn't just any company; it was forged from the grit and experience of elite ex-Delta Force operatives, and Don was its cornerstone.

Don's résumé read like something out of a military thriller. A founding member of both the Army's elite Delta Force and the 1st Ranger Battalion, as well as a veteran of the 5th Special Forces Group (Green Berets), Don had spent his life mastering high-stakes strategy and counterterrorism. He'd operated in some of the world's most volatile regions, and now, that expertise would be put to the ultimate test—to bring a child home.

Don Feeney during his years of military service before joining the rescue mission that helped bring me home from Jordan.

His wife, Judy Feeney, was just as extraordinary. A specialist in international security and risk management, Judy worked alongside Don at CTU. She had advised global corporations, coordinated crisis response teams, and trained both federal and local agencies in hostage survival and counter-surveillance tactics. Calm under pressure, Judy brought a precision and wisdom that complemented Don's battlefield instincts.

Also at the heart of CTU was Dave Chatellier, a commanding presence with a resume to match. In his younger days, Dave looked like he belonged on a recruitment poster—sharp-eyed, broad-shouldered, and mission-minded. A former US Air Force pilot and decorated officer, his career spanned leadership roles in intelligence, aviation, and operations. He had earned several prestigious honors, including the Air Medal and the Meritorious Service Medal. Dave was the kind of man you trusted when the stakes were life or death.

During my interview with Don, he transported me back to when everything changed. "The week after Alvarez met with Al," Don said, "he showed up at the CTU office to meet with me and Dave. We didn't know the full scope of the mission yet, but I could feel it in my gut—this wasn't just another job."

"I'd never talked to Alvarez before," Don recalled, "but I knew his voice instantly." As Alvarez began describing his lunch with Al, he didn't waste time. He wanted to know CTU's capabilities, what they had done, where they had worked, and if they could pull off the unthinkable. Don laid it out plainly: "We've taken on global contracts—from corporate security to advising on film sets. But we've never rescued a child."

Alvarez didn't flinch. Then came the question that changed everything: "Are you and your team up for the task of getting Cathy's little girl back?"

Don paused as he recounted that moment, the memory still alive in his voice. "When he asked me that, the whole room went quiet. I didn't need time to think. I just said, 'Yes, sir. We can do it.'" He smiled slightly. "When a man like Alvarez asks you to take on a mission like that, you don't hesitate. You just say yes."

That call marked a turning point. What began as a simple phone conversation quickly became the foundation of an international rescue operation. For Don, it wasn't just a decision; it was a promise. A promise to my mother. A promise to me. A promise to risk everything for something far greater than any of them could fully grasp in that moment.

Don leaned forward in his chair as he recalled what happened next. "The following week, Alvarez came to the CTU office to meet with me and Dave Chatellier. At that point, we still didn't know all the details of the mission or the full scope of the situation. But we were already in it. We knew this was no ordinary job." Don's voice grew serious. "Alvarez made it clear this wouldn't be a US-sanctioned mission. No official backing, no guarantees. But there was something about this mission that told me we couldn't say no. We had to meet your mom. We had to know more."

The very next day, Alvarez contacted Al to say that Don and Dave were ready to meet with my mother. It was then that she began to see the promises of God unfold before her eyes— promises she had clung to during her time of fasting and prayer. Weeks earlier, as she cried out to the Lord, He had spoken to her through Daniel 10:12 (NIV): "Since the first day that you set your mind to gain understanding and to humble yourself before your God, your words were heard." That verse had become her anchor. Now, she could sense His hand moving.

As she spoke to Rick and Bev, she felt a stirring, her first glimpse of breakthrough. She asked them to pray with her, not out of desperation, but out of belief that God was guiding every step. She didn't know how this would unfold, but she trusted that the same God who had heard her cry was now beginning to answer.

Don's voice softened as he recalled the next chapter of the story. "After Al and I spoke, I called him back, and that's when we arranged the next steps. Al had booked flights and hotels for us to meet with your mom in Dallas. The meeting was set for just four days before Christmas, two months after your dad had taken you."

As Don spoke, it was clear this mission was no longer just a job. It had become personal. Every detail he shared brought the past to life as I listened. The mission that started with a phone call now had faces, names, and a real sense of urgency. For Don and his team, this wasn't just about the operation, it was about the lives caught in the balance, about the little girl they'd never met but were about to risk *everything* to save.

The day my mom arrived in Dallas for the crucial meeting, she was all business. She checked into a hotel near the airport, already laser-focused on the task at hand. She carried a binder brimming with photographs of me, my dad, and his family. The binder also contained meticulously detailed profiles for each family member, including a rough layout of Ali's home, though my mom couldn't recall the exact address. There was no time for hesitation, no room for uncertainty. She was ready to get straight to the point, to find the path that would bring me home.

As Don recounted that first meeting, I couldn't help but picture the box tucked away in my closet, filled with my mom's journals, binders, and files the physical records of everything she had done over the years. Each page was a testament to her relentless determination and her unyielding search for answers. With no Google or search engines to guide her, she'd gathered information the old-fashioned way, relying on her willpower alone. It was nothing short of remarkable.

Don's voice softened, "Lauren, when your mom walked into the room, she was so confident, so put together, determined to get you back. Right away, Dave and I knew she would stop at nothing to bring you home." The respect in his voice was evident. An admiration had formed over that first meeting.

As they reviewed the photos and notes, Don and Dave were moved. Here was a thirty-two-year-old woman who had been through unimaginable pain, yet still carried herself with a quiet strength, exuding both calm and fierce determination. There was no doubt she was ready to go to any length, with or without their help, to reunite with me.

Yet, Don and Dave were realists. The mission would not be easy. Traveling to Jordan was a dangerous undertaking. It could cost them their lives. As fathers, though, they couldn't ignore the pull of a mother's love and resolve. There was something about my mom's determination that stirred something deep within them. While they were confident in their team's ability to handle the mission, they understood the risks. They laid out the financial reality for my mom—the cost of securing my return would range between $50,000 and $100,000—a price that didn't even cover the full scope of the perilous journey ahead. And with that, Don and Dave asked for time to think it over.

In the days following that pivotal meeting, my mom did what she had always done. She prayed. She reached out to friends and family, asking for their prayers and support. For the first time in weeks, a spark of hope flickered in her heart—just enough to believe a way forward might be possible. But where would the money come from?

My mom could find at least $50,000—an inheritance she had recently received from her father, Buddy Phelps. My grandfather was tragically murdered in 1981, a violent crime that had left our family reeling. He was a well-known boat builder in Niceville, Florida, but his life ended in brutal fashion. He had been brutally beaten and shot, and for years the case remained a mystery—until it was finally solved in 2018. Eventually, Buddy's children received an inheritance of $50,000 each, but the funds were tied up for years before they could be accessed. Only a few months before my kidnapping had my mom finally received her portion of it. Even in the midst of such tragedy, God had provided—and now that provision seemed to be the lifeline that might bring me home.

But it wasn't just my mom who was determined to help. My Uncle Dan, moved by the urgency of the situation, also contributed his inheritance, understanding that the cost of rescuing me might exceed the initial estimate. Together, the two of them had enough money to begin the operation.

But that was in the future. For my mom, this moment was a turning point, an answer to her prayers. With renewed faith and determination, she took the next step. The morning after meeting with Don and Dave, she transferred $18,000 to CTU, the first payment toward the mission that would ultimately bring me home. It was a step of trust, a leap of faith, and a clear sign that she was all in, no matter the cost.

Once Don and Dave received the payment, they immediately assembled a team for the mission. Don reached out to JD Roberts, a seasoned twenty-year Army Ranger instructor and Special Forces team leader. JD and Don had both trained at "The Farm," the CIA's elite training ground and had participated in high-stakes missions like "Operation Eagle Claw" in 1980—an attempt to rescue hostages from the US Embassy in Tehran. Though the mission failed, JD and Don had pulled several people from the flames when their helicopter caught fire, making it a life-defining moment for both of them.

Don knew that JD's experience and unwavering determination made him the perfect person for the mission. When Don explained the details about rescuing a young American girl from her father in Jordan, JD didn't hesitate. "I'm in," he said, admitting that his current job as an insurance salesman felt like "the worst job on earth." Saving a little girl, he added, felt like the righteous task he was meant for.

Jim Hatfield, a skilled firearms instructor and former Special Forces operative, was selected as the team's communication contact. After being medically discharged from the military, Jim went on to work for CTU, leveraging his expertise to support high-risk missions. His military career, especially with the First and 75th Ranger Regiment and as a member of the 18th Airborne Corps, made him an ideal addition to the rescue operation.

In just a few days, my mom's transformation was nothing short of miraculous. From feeling hopeless and paralyzed by fear, she was now encouraged, with a renewed sense of confidence. The moment she had shared her story in the courtroom with Al Zapanta—the first person to offer tangible help, she had seen a glimmer of God's faithfulness. And now, the path ahead was becoming clear.

CHAPTER EIGHT

KEYS TO FREEDOM: PASSPORTS, VISAS, AND A MOTHER'S FAITH

One Saturday morning, a few hours before my family and I had to leave for the first soccer game of the day, I reached for a journal marked "Washington, DC." As I read through the pages, one name stood out—Chris. This was an assistant to Al Zapanta. My mom had written this name repeatedly during her time in Washington, DC. As I continued reading, I came across another crucial detail: During the initial meeting with Don and Dave, the men told my mom something critical—she would need to secure passports for both herself and me, and she had to start that process *immediately*. Without them, the mission couldn't even begin.

Getting a passport and visa for a child who wasn't even physically with you seemed like an impossible task. But for my mom, it was a mountain that had to be moved. And she believed with all her heart that God would make a way.

In 1987, the rules were different than they are today—partly due to cases like mine and other abductions that changed the way authorities handled such situations. Back then, a single parent could apply for a passport for their child as long as the child was present. But now, under current laws, both parents must be present with the child to apply. Still, my mom was facing a complicated, nearly impossible situation.

Not only did she have to navigate the passport process without me being there, my father had already secured an active passport for me—and it had never been reported stolen. When my mom went to the passport office to request a new one, it raised an immediate red flag. She was told multiple times that she needed to bring me with her to even begin the process. The very idea of applying for a passport without me present seemed absurd to the officials she spoke with, and my mother found herself caught in a frustrating web of bureaucracy. She knew that without a passport, the rescue mission couldn't proceed—but how could she obtain one when the system itself was set up to prevent exactly that?

I pulled out a cassette tape labeled "State Department" and clicked play. The familiar hum of the tape machine filled the quiet room. At first, my mom's voice was confident, calm, almost like she was in control. But as the conversation unfolded, her frustration creeped in, turning her tone sharp. "Hello, yes, my name is Cathy Mahone, and I need to speak with someone who can help me get a passport for my daughter."

The woman on the other end of the line started asking my mom about the steps she had already taken to secure a passport, and my mom went through the long list of offices she had contacted. "Yes, I've called all the other numbers, and the last person told me to dial this office—can you please help me?" There was a pause, followed by the sound of the phone line clicking.

Then, a man's voice came on. "Hello, this is Gerald Mann. I understand you need assistance with a passport?"

What followed was a conversation that could only be described as a marathon of repeated explanations. My mom detailed the kidnapping, the flight route, the stops in JFK and Vienna, and the eventual arrival in Amman, Jordan. You could hear the exhaustion in her voice—a woman who had told this story so many times, yet each retelling carried her sense of helplessness. "Ali, my ex-husband, took my daughter Lauren on a Sunday night. The flight left DFW at 9:40 p.m. and landed in JFK. They made a stop in Vienna before continuing to Amman, Jordan."

Mr. Mann was methodical as he asked question after question: Who was Ali? Where did he live? How many other children did my father have? How long had my parents been divorced? His questions probed endlessly, digging into the details of a situation that my mother could hardly bear to relive. "Ma'am, who else have you spoken with? What information have you been given regarding your situation?"

My mom responded, each word heavy with frustration. "I've spoken with the grand jury in Dallas, Texas, and they've issued a warrant for my ex-husband's arrest. If he ever enters the United States, he'll be captured. But that doesn't help me get my daughter back."

There was a long pause on the line before Mr. Mann delivered the blow: "Ma'am, the State Department cannot help secure a passport or visa for a child in another country when their biological father is involved. You will not be able to get a passport for her."

And just like that, another door slammed shut. My mom had hoped for some miracle, some way the State Department could intervene, but instead, she was met with a cold, bureaucratic wall. She wasn't just fighting for a passport—she was fighting against a system that seemed designed to make her impossible mission even harder.

This news was heartbreaking, but it did not deter my mom. As I read through her journal, it felt as though I was following a detailed road map of every step she had taken in her relentless pursuit to bring me home. With unshakable determination, my mom called Al Zapanta.

She poured out her struggles to Al, explaining her repeated failures to secure a passport and how the bureaucratic roadblocks were threatening to stop her in her tracks. Sensing the urgency in her voice, Al reassured her. "Cathy, let me make a few calls and see what I can do." Al, with his extensive connections in Washington, DC, wasn't about to let this stand in their way. The odds were stacked against them, but he also knew that, with the right push, rescue could still be possible.

At the time, Al wasn't just any civilian. He had deep ties within the military and government. He'd served in both the 63rd and 97th Army Reserve Commands (ARCOMs), and from 1978 to 1987, he was the Battalion Commander of the 3/160th Infantry Battalion in the 40th Infantry Division of the California Army National Guard. He had returned to the US Army Reserves and worked at the Pentagon. Al had the expertise and the connections that might just make the impossible, possible.

A few days later, Al's assistant, Chris, reached out to my mom with instructions. She needed to gather all the necessary documents—photos, birth certificates, applications—and book a flight to Washington, DC. She would need to apply for the passport in person. My mom had no doubt that Al could open doors no one else could, and with that confidence, she packed her bag, knowing this trip would not bring her back to Dallas. From Washington, DC, her next destination would be Jordan, where she would meet up with the rescue team.

As I continued to read Mom's journal, her words struck me with a force that stole my breath, crashing over me like a tidal wave. Amid the chaos and urgency to bring me home, she had taken a step that sent a chill through my bones. She met with a local attorney and drafted her will. I paused, the journal trembling in my hands, and set it down on the table, needing a moment to steady my racing heart. My fingers sifted through the box of papers beside me, the rustle of pages the only sound in the quiet room, until they landed on a stapled document—Last Will and Testament. Seeing the title in stark black ink made my heart sink. As I read through the pages, the reality of her sacrifice unfolded—she had appointed my Aunt Joyce, the woman who had taken Mom and me in when I was an infant, as my guardian should anything happen to her during this perilous mission. She knew the very real possibility that she might not return alive, yet her love for me propelled her forward, a fierce determination that left me in awe. In that moment, I saw the depth of her courage, her willingness to risk everything—not just for me, but for the chance to bring me back to safety, her faith in Jesus giving her the strength to face even the darkest fears.

That courage carried her into the next leg of her journey, though the road was far from smooth. On January 6, 1988, Mom was scheduled to fly to Washington, DC, a trip that held the promise of progress in my rescue, but a severe ice storm, one of the worst Dallas had seen in a decade, brought everything to a grinding halt. I imagined her standing at the airport, watching as flights were canceled one by one, the icy wind biting at her cheeks as she clutched her coat tighter, frustration mounting with each delay, feeling like every time she took a step forward, another storm—literal or metaphorical—rose to block her path, testing her resolve. After what must have felt like an eternity of waiting, the skies finally cleared enough for her to board a flight, and on January 7, she landed in DC, exhausted. Her nerves were frayed but her determination remained unshaken.

Chris, Al's assistant, met her at the airport, his familiar face a small comfort amidst the uncertainty, and drove her to the Mayflower

Hotel—a grand, historic building that had stood as a Washington staple since 1925. I pictured her stepping into the opulent lobby, the chandeliers casting a golden glow over marble floors, her eyes wide with surprise at the luxury she hadn't expected, especially since she was footing the bill herself.

Sensing her hesitation, Chris explained, "Cathy, this is no ordinary trip. The people you're meeting are high-level political figures. Staying at the Mayflower puts you in the heart of it all." His words underscored the gravity of her mission, and as I read, I felt a surge of anticipation, knowing she was exactly where she needed to be, God's hand guiding her toward the connections that might bring me home.

As I traced my mom's journey through her journals, the depth of her resolve gripped me, pulling me into the moment she unpacked her belongings at the Mayflower Hotel. I imagined her carefully laying out photos of me—my smiling face a bittersweet reminder—alongside critical documents and the paperwork she carried like a reminder.

The weight of her situation crashed over her, and I felt a lump rise in my throat as I read how tears began to fall, her whispered prayer breaking the silence, affirming God's plan and asking for my safe return. Her vulnerability struck me, a mother's love laid bare.

She wiped her tears with a trembling hand, tucking the pictures into a drawer to shield her heart. Though sleep eluded her that night, the room's opulent stillness was a stark contrast to the storm within her.

The next day, however, brought a new challenge. Thanks to the lingering grip of that brutal ice storm, government offices remained closed, forcing Mom to wait until January 9, 1988, to visit the passport office. She likely paced the hotel room, her nerves stretched thin, the ticking clock amplifying her desperation to reach me in

Jordan. When the day finally arrived, Chris stood by her side, and together they endured hours in a crowded passport office, the air thick with tension and the murmur of impatient voices. My heart raced as I read how, when her name was called, she approached the counter, her pulse pounding in her ears.

Chris explained the unusual situation—my absence—but the woman behind the counter cut him off, her impatience a sharp edge. "Please step forward." Her expression hardened.

Mom took a deep breath, steadying herself, and spoke with as much calm as she could muster: "I'm sorry, I know you're very busy." She handed over the application and photos, her hands shaking slightly, her silent prayer to Jesus a lifeline as she braced for the next hurdle.

That hurdle came swiftly when the woman picked up my paperwork, a shadow of doubt flickering across her face. My breath caught as I read Mom's account—her dreaded question hung in the air: "Where is your daughter?"

Mom's heart skipped a beat, suppressing the panic, she stammered, "She's sick at home." Her voice wavered, but she held the woman's gaze, praying silently that her lie would hold. Each time the woman seemed ready to probe further, a ringing phone or a colleague's interruption broke the moment, and I could almost hear the suspenseful silence between those interruptions, each one a divine distraction orchestrated by Jesus.

Finally, the woman looked up, her face softening just enough to offer hope. "It should be ready in about an hour." A wave of relief crashed over Mom, and I shared her exhale, a release after days of holding her breath. It was as if God had timed every interruption perfectly, guiding her through this fragile moment when everything could have unraveled. She clung to that sense of divine timing, her faith deepening with every answered prayer, a victory that fueled her hope.

Later that afternoon, when they returned to the passport office, the documents were waiting—two passports that felt like keys to my freedom. I could hardly believe it as I read her words: "We have a passport for Lauren."

Her conviction rippled through the pages, her belief that she was on the path to reclaiming me, no matter the cost. Yet, as I turned the journal page, the reality settled in—visas were still needed, and with no updates from Dave, Don, or JD, the urgency intensified. She'd be in DC longer than planned.

Determined to stretch every dollar, Mom checked out of the Mayflower's lavish embrace, its chandeliers and marble floors no longer fitting her mission's humble needs. She gathered her belongings, the rustle of papers a quiet resolve, and she found a more affordable hotel, its modest walls a practical choice amid the expensive restaurants surrounding the Mayflower. She opted for McDonald's meals, the scent of fries a stark contrast to the hotel's luxury, a sacrifice that spoke to her resourcefulness. I admired her grit, evident even in the smallest decisions as she prepared for the next battle to bring me home.

In her downtime, she continued her relentless pursuit for information. She called Jerash, Jordan, over and over again, hoping to catch my dad or anyone in his circle who could provide a lead. She was on edge, every phone ring stretching the tension taut. Don, Dave, and JD had advised her to keep her actions as "normal" as possible—to maintain the facade of routine so as not to raise any suspicion. So, she called at all hours, trying to figure out when my dad might be home. More often than not, he refused to take her calls, and when I listened to the cassette tapes, I heard the distance in his voice, his refusal to engage fully with her.

While my mom navigated her prolonged stay in DC, each failed call to Jordan deepened her unease, prompting her to reach out to Bev and Rick for updates. There was an urgency in her journal—a need to know if my dad or his brother Amir, who lived just a short drive from our townhouse in Richardson, had tried to contact her while she was away. Bev and Rick had become silent sentinels, guarding the home where my toys, clothes, and memories waited, ever vigilant in case someone from dad's family showed up unexpectedly. They were ready to cover for my mom, their loyalty a quiet fortress around the life I'd left behind. I imagined them peering through the curtains at every unfamiliar car, their hearts heavy with the weight of their role, and I felt a surge of gratitude for their steadfast presence.

I'll never forget how Beverly described the pain of living in that townhouse during those long weeks while my mom was in DC—and later Jordan—waiting for any scrap of news about me. During our *Redeemed* podcast interview, Bev's voice wavered. "Lauren, I tried so hard to focus on my job and family, but it was nearly impossible with your home surrounding me—every room a gallery of happier times." I pictured her walking past my bedroom, the door ajar, my stuffed animals and Barbie dolls on the floor, each a dagger of memory piercing her heart. She fought to suppress the growing fear that I might never return—or worse, that my mom might not make it back either.

The tension seeped into every corner, even touching young Miranda, who sensed the heaviness despite her innocence. Bev said, "Even Miranda knew something was wrong. Not only were we living in your house, but she kept asking, "When will Lauren come back? When will Miss Cathy come home? When can we go back home?" Her questions, so pure yet so piercing, mirrored the ache in everyone's hearts, a wound that refused to heal. The house wasn't just empty—it was a hollow shell, echoing the unbearable quiet of waiting, the uncertainty a weight we all carried in our own way.

Miranda and me as little girls.

Flipping through my mom's journal, I paused at her detailed account of a phone call with Beverly, a moment that shifted the darkness with a flicker of light. While in DC, Mom had called Bev to request clothes because her stay had stretched longer than expected, and the city's chill seeped into her bones. Bev readily agreed, but then her tone shifted, a spark of excitement breaking through. "Hey, I need to tell you something."

Mom, ever attuned to the smallest change, instantly sensed the shift. "What is it, what's going on?" Her voice tightened with anticipation.

Bev's words came like a sunrise. "Well, you know how Rick and I have been trying to have another baby, and it's been so difficult? I took a pregnancy test, and I'm pregnant, Cathy. We just found out this week." A lump formed in my throat as I read, tear stains smudging the page where my mom had written. Beverly, one of her dearest friends, was pregnant again after years of longing, a miracle unfolding in the midst of despair. Mom had cried on the phone, her tears ones of joy—a rare emotion after weeks of grief—and that joy rippled through me, a testament of hope when it was needed most.

Unable to contain my excitement, I snapped a picture of the journal entry of the story, new to me despite all I'd heard, and sent it to Beverly. Minutes later, my phone rang, and Bev's voice, emotional and bright, filled the line. "Lauren, I can't believe your mom wrote about this in her journal."

My heart raced. "Do you remember this day?"

Her voice softened, choked with emotion. "Of course, I remember every detail of that conversation. Those days when you and your mom were gone were some of the darkest of our lives. Sitting in that townhouse, day after day, not knowing what was happening. It was so hard. But then, in the midst of it all, the goodness of God showed up. I found out I was pregnant—a light in such a dark time. I knew it would encourage your mom."

In the deepest pit of their despair, there was a spark of hope—new life. It was a beautiful paradox, joy emerging from pain, and nine months later, Rick and Bev welcomed their son, Luke Lambert. They chose the name "Luke," meaning "light in the darkness," a fitting tribute to the hope he symbolized, a reminder that even in the bleakest moments, God was weaving light into the world.

Yet, even this glimmer of joy couldn't fully ease my mom's mounting anxiety, as I read in the next pages of her journal. The unanswered calls to Jordan left her feeling more overwhelmed, fear creeping back with a vengeance, its icy grip tightening with each passing day in DC. The longer she stayed, the more her already tight budget drained, the city's costs eating away at her limited resources. I could picture her counting the dollars in her wallet, the weight of delays pressing heavier on her shoulders, each tick of the clock a reminder of the stakes. With no visas secured for either of us and no updates from Dave, Don, or JD, the urgency intensified. The road ahead loomed with uncertainty.

Al Zapanta sensed her strain and introduced her to Romey, a kindhearted woman who worked in the senator's office. Romey quickly became a calming presence, offering Mom a rare reprieve from the relentless pressure. I could imagine her weary face softening as Romey guided her on a tour of the House and Senate, even leading her through the hidden underground tunnels beneath the Capitol—a secret place that felt worlds away from her mission. That simple act of showing her a different side of Washington, a glimpse beyond the chaos, helped her breathe a little easier.

The real escape, though, came when Al invited Mom and Romey to a movie premiere. It was a moment that left me in awe as I turned the pages of her journal, reading how she was swept into the glamour and pressure of the evening—the chatter of the crowd buzzing in my ears and the clink of champagne glasses a sharp contrast to my mom's quiet determination. Al knew this wasn't just about making connections with influential people who might hold the key to navigating international law and the border crossing ahead. It was a mental break from the stress that had consumed her.

I pictured her unpacking a few nice dresses, unsure of what to expect, and my heart swelled with pride at how she selflessly lent one to Romey, who had nothing suitable. After the movie, they stepped into an exclusive after-party, surrounded by high-profile individuals who could potentially shape the mission's success, all of them flickers of hope that the night might turn the tide.

My mom wore a gold chain necklace with a Krugerrand—an old gold coin her boyfriend had given her as a token of value, but a man approached Al, his tone urgent. "She needs to take that off. Now," he said, pointing to the necklace. Embarrassed and confused, Mom quickly removed it and stuffed it into her purse. I felt a pang of sympathy for her, caught off guard by a cultural misstep she couldn't have foreseen. Later, she learned the coin's weighty significance—a symbol of apartheid, racial segregation in South Africa—a meaning far removed from its intended worth. The irony struck me deeply: This coin, given in a time of peace, would soon symbolize the sacrifice she was willing to make, its value later helping pay our rent amid the mission's costs. It would cost her everything she owned to get me back.

At that same event, Al introduced my mom to Everett Alvarez, a man whose name leapt off the page and filled me with gratitude—a pivotal figure in her journey. He was the one who had first mentioned CTU to Al and connected Mom with Don Feeney and Dave, the architects of my rescue. I could picture her standing in the crowded party, shaking hands with Mr. Alvarez, her heart racing with a mix of awe and appreciation, words of thanks catching in her throat as she tried to express how much his help meant. My admiration swelled as I read her account, seeing how far she'd come, yet still deep in the trenches of this mission. Alvarez, ever humble, simply nodded, his eyes reflecting the fierce determination in hers. He didn't seek credit, but he understood the stakes. He shared her faith that, against all odds, this mission would succeed.

As I turned the page of my mother's journal, my eyes landed on the words "January 10th," written in bold, dark ink—just eighteen days before my rescue. Chris and my mom made their way to the Jordanian embassy, where they were scheduled to meet with Al. The passports were in hand, but the next hurdle loomed even larger: securing the visas. The embassy was notorious for its tough, bureaucratic barriers. They were about to face a battle she wasn't ready to fight. As they neared the imposing building, a cold sense of dread settled in her chest. In Jordan, women had few rights, and men controlled most of the power. It was a world that felt miles away from her own.

Clutching a small piece of paper in her pocket with a verse that had become her refuge, my mom silently prayed, seeking comfort from the words that had carried her through the storm: He said: "The Lord is my rock, my fortress, and my deliverer: my God is my rock, in whom I take refuge, my shield, and the horn of my salvation. He is my stronghold, my refuge and my savior—from violent people you save me." (2 Samuel 22:2–3 NIV)

Once inside, Chris advised her to stay quiet and let Al do the talking. My mom, exhausted and anxious, agreed. Al approached a man who barely acknowledged my mother's presence and proceeded to explain the situation. The man listened briefly but offered no reassurances, dismissively stating that he couldn't make any promises and that he would "get back to them." My mom's hope slipped away as the words hung in the air. It was as though the walls of the embassy were closing in around her.

Sensing her frustration and exhaustion, Al gently suggested a break. "You've made great progress with the passports, Cathy," he said. "Go clear your mind. Visit a museum. Relax for a bit."

Following Al's advice, my mom headed to the Space Museum, but the exhibits meant little to her. Her thoughts were too consumed with what lay ahead. As she wandered through the halls, her mind kept spinning. Is this really happening? Is my daughter really in Jordan? Am I actually about to try and rescue her? Overcome by the enormity of it all, she found a quiet corner and prayed. "Jesus, guide me. Show me what to do. I need You to bring Lauren back."

Later that day, Al called her back to his office, a smile breaking across his face as he handed her the visas. Overcome with emotion, my mom's knees buckled, and she burst into tears. She hugged Al fiercely. It was a small victory in the grand scheme of things, but it was a victory nonetheless. She carefully wrote down another Scripture in her journal: "And David inquired of the Lord, 'Should I pursue this raiding party? Will I overtake them?' 'Pursue them,' he answered. 'You will certainly overtake them and succeed in the rescue.'" (1 Samuel 30:8 NIV)

It was a promise my mom held onto tightly, knowing that with each step, the mission was inching closer to the moment when she would finally be reunited with me. But the road was far from over, and the hardest battles were still ahead. With renewed strength and determination, my mom pressed forward, holding on to the hope.

CHAPTER NINE

PLOTTING THE ESCAPE

The "Jordan" box—a weathered container brimming with my mother's journals and cassette tapes—had been my compass, guiding me through the intricate details of my kidnapping and rescue. But as I sifted through its contents, I noted something was missing. The box held my memories, the fragments of a little girl's fear and hope, but it couldn't capture the perspectives of the men who were vital to my escape. Each member of the rescue team held a key piece of the puzzle, and their voices were essential to tell the full story.

Dave Chatellier, for instance, was the first to travel to Jerash and was tasked with locating me and mapping an escape route out of Jordan, a mission fraught with danger. His perspective was the missing link that would bring the narrative to life. A surge of anticipation moved me forward, an eagerness to uncover the untold chapters of my own story through his eyes.

Rick Lambert had connected me with JD, who then shared Dave, Don, and Jim's phone numbers, a chain of links that felt nothing short of miraculous after thirty-seven years. I was on the verge of speaking with the people who had put their lives on the line for me, and my mind raced with a thousand questions. *What if they don't want to talk? What if they don't want the story told? How will I handle that?* The uncertainty loomed, but I paused, took a deep breath, and prayed, trusting He would lead me through this delicate journey with the same care He'd shown all those years ago in Jordan.

One summer evening after work, I found a quiet moment during my son's swim practice (because, as any busy parent knows, that's often when you steal time for the things that matter most). I slipped away to a corner of the bleachers, the distant splash of water and laughter fading as I dialed Dave's number with my heart pounding. "Dave, this is Lauren Burns—well, you would have known me by a different last name." My voice rose as I tried to bridge the decades between us.

Before I could finish, Dave's voice broke in, warm and steady. "Lauren, I know exactly who you are. I was hoping you would call."

My heart skipped a beat, a rush of emotion flooding me. He'd been expecting this moment, perhaps as much as I had. I poured out my gratitude, telling him how honored I was to finally connect after all these years and how deeply thankful I was for everything he'd done for me and Mom. I even apologized for taking so long to track him down, my words tumbling out in a rush of nerves and excitement.

But before I could say more, Dave interrupted, his voice slow and sincere, and I held my breath, eager to hear what he'd share about the mission that had changed my life forever. Dave's words hit me like a wave, their sincerity echoing through the phone. "Lauren, what you and your mom went through was so traumatic. Honestly, I didn't expect to ever hear from you again. People who experience something like that often need to move on and never look back. You don't owe me anything."

His humility struck me deeply, a reminder that he didn't need gratitude. He just needed to know his actions had mattered. I felt a swell of admiration for this man who had risked so much, his selflessness a testament to the kind hearts placed in my path all those years ago. Dave quickly shifted to ask about Mom, his voice warm with respect as he shared how much he admired her unwavering faith and incredible bravery. "And how about you, Lauren? Tell me about your life now, your family." A brief pause hung between us before he added, "You know, I never really got a good look at you. I only saw you for a brief moment when we moved you from one car to another. In my mind, you're still that seven-year-old little girl. It's hard to believe you're all grown up now with children of your own."

Tears welled as I struggled to compose myself, his words painting a vivid picture of that fleeting moment in my own mind in 1988. "Dave," I managed, my voice thick with emotion, "because of you, I have an amazing life. I have a fulfilling career, I'm a wife and a mother, and I still have a relationship with my mom. Thank you for risking your life to save mine, for bringing me back to my mother and back home to the United States."

Dave Chatellier with my mom in my bedroom after I was taken—
my toys still on the floor, my life frozen in place.

Ever humble, he didn't want the focus on himself—he eagerly turned the conversation to my rescue story, his curiosity a bridge to the past I longed to explore. I began asking about his role in the mission, and he replied thoughtfully, "I'll pull out my old journals and notes. Let me go over everything, and I'll try to explain it the best I can."

Then, almost as an afterthought, I ventured, "Would it be okay if I interviewed you for my podcast?"

Dave hesitated, a hint of uncertainty in his voice, "I don't know how we would do that, but sure, whatever I can do to help, I'm happy to."

I felt a spark of excitement, sensing Jesus opening another door for this story to reach others. The next morning, I woke to a long, detailed email from Dave, my heart racing as I read that he'd stayed up late, unable to sleep, his mind revisiting the mission. After poring over his notes, I knew the interview had to happen. Dave was the only one who could reveal this part of the story—the details even Mom didn't know.

The evening of our podcast interview, I set up my microphone, my nerves buzzing as I welcomed Dave. "I'd love for you to share your side of the story, the details of your mission and anything you feel comfortable sharing." As he spoke, I hung on every word, determined to capture every detail of the story that had shaped my life.

Dave, an expert in his field with a lifetime of experience, was also one of the most selfless men I'd ever met, his wisdom far beyond what I could fathom. He began with a reflective tone. "Lauren, I've thought about your mission many times over the years. I'm eighty-five now, so I've had a lot of time to reflect. There were so many mistakes we made, so many moments we could have been captured. But God had a plan for your life, and that's why the mission was a success." His words carried a weight that anchored me. I felt a deep reverence for how God had moved through every risk they took.

Dave took a deep breath, his voice steady as he delved into the mission's challenges. "It wasn't just a logistical challenge. It was a journey full of unexpected twists, moments of desperation, and glimpses of divine intervention. I was the first sent to Jordan. With my background in military intelligence, I knew how to navigate dangerous terrains, but what lay ahead wasn't something I could have prepared for.

The task seemed simple: Locate your father's house, find you, and secure an escape route out of Jordan. But the complexity hit me as soon as I arrived." He paused, his tone growing reflective. "I flew into Amman under the cover of being a tourist. Blending in was crucial. Too much attention could unravel everything. I rented a car and drove toward Jerash, where I knew you were being held. Your mother had given me photos and details, but as I neared the city, I realized the Jerash in those photos was gone, its landmarks buried beneath new development, the town expanded in ways I wasn't prepared for."

I could feel the tension in his words, picturing him gripping the steering wheel, the road to Jerash alive with the activity I remembered—cars, trucks, people moving in every direction, the chaos amplifying the weight of his mission.

His voice grew more intense as he continued. "The closer I got to Jerash, the more the pressure pressed down. What had seemed a clear path back home now felt like a tangled web. My mission was still clear—find an escape route, find you, find your father's house—but if I failed, there'd be no rescue. Everything hinged on that."

Dave's urgency pulled me in, and a shiver of fear for him, knowing how high the stakes were, rippled over me. He paused, his eyes distant as if reliving the moment, then added, "I called Judy Feeney at the CTU office. The situation was critical, and I needed help fast, more than just my team on the ground. 'The photos are outdated,' I told her. 'The town is bigger than we expected, and it's changing fast. Cathy needs to pull every contact she has. But quietly. We can't afford to alert the Jordanian military.'" As I listened to Dave, I could almost hear the familiar crackle of the phone line as he spoke to Mom, the urgency in his voice.

Dave's tone softened as he recalled the broader strategy. "Judy relayed the message to your mom, who was in Washington, DC, waiting anxiously for any word. Judy told her the situation was more complicated than we'd realized, and I needed all the help she could muster—connections, favors, anything." He gave me a knowing glance, a flicker of admiration in his eyes. "Your mom wasted no time. She wrote a letter to Queen Noor."

My heart skipped a beat as I interrupted, "I have that letter." Emotion welled up as I spoke, the memory of Mom's strength and desperation vivid in my mind. Queen Noor, the American-born wife of King Hussein of Jordan, was known for her humanitarian efforts, and Mom had taken a leap of faith, pleading for her intervention to secure my safe extraction.

Dave nodded, acknowledging the significance of her actions, but his voice grew somber. "As you know, Lauren, time wasn't on our side. We couldn't wait for a royal reply. Every second counted, and I had to keep moving, even as the situation grew more desperate."

Dave's days in Jerash were a grueling test of endurance, as he shared in vivid detail. "Each morning, I left my hotel before dawn, using those early hours to survey roads and potential escape routes. I drove the highways stretching from Jerash toward Syria—narrow, chaotic roads where large trucks raced by, overtaking each other, turning one-lane paths into a hazard. Dead camels littered the roadside, as common in Jordan as deer on Texas highways, a grim reminder of the dangers lurking even in routine journeys."

I tried to recall Jerash, my memories hazy: snippets of narrow dirt roads, hills dotted with olive and lemon trees, the beautiful countryside blending with crowded marketplaces, mosques, and schools. The images blurred, but Dave's words brought them into sharper focus, painting a picture of a city both vibrant and perilous.

He continued, sharing a daring moment that left me on edge. "I drove all the way to Aqaba, the Jordanian port city on the Red Sea, and stood at the edge of the Gulf of Aqaba, staring across at Eilat, Israel's southernmost city, less than a mile away. For a fleeting moment, I entertained a wild idea. What if I swam across with you on my back?"

My breath caught, eyes widened, imagining the dark, somber atmosphere of Aqaba, with military patrol boats lining the shoreline, contrasted with Eilat's laughter and sunlight, a vacation paradise just out of reach. But reality hit hard.

"But, the Jordanian military presence was overwhelming. Those boats weren't there to keep people out. They were there to keep people in. Swimming across would have led to certain capture—or worse."

A wave of relief released as he crossed Aqaba off the list, but the stakes grew even higher as he turned north, driving ten hours to the Syrian border, only to find a war zone—checkpoints, armed guards, signs of conflict everywhere. Smuggling a child through that insanity was impossible. The Syrian border was no option either.

With options dwindling, Dave's focus narrowed to the Allenby Bridge, the sole, official crossing between Jordan and Israel, but even this route brimmed with risks. "The bridge was heavily monitored by both Israeli and Jordanian forces, and without proper documentation, crossing would be impossible." The clock was ticking, each route more perilous than the last, the tension mounting.

Meanwhile, Mom received Queen Noor's response—a brief, devastating letter declining to help, citing political backlash from a past case. Mom's heart sank, one of her last hopes evaporating, and I ached for her.

Yet, Dave's resolve gave me strength. "Judy relayed the message, and though I wasn't surprised, I knew there was no turning back. The risks of staying in Jerash were growing by the day." He took meticulous precautions—changing rental cars, never staying in one place too long, blending in at the Roman ruins near the King's Highway, a UNESCO World Heritage site known as the "City of 1000 Pillars." I pictured him among the ancient statues of Artemis, kids digging for coins in the strata, his monocular telescope scanning the city below, hoping to spot Dad's house, all while the Jordanian police began to ask questions....

Dave's quick thinking saved him. "I told them I was scouting for a movie—an upcoming project. It was believable because it was partially true—Don and I had worked on security for the Stallone's Rambo films, and Don was in Israel managing security for *Iron Eagle II* with Louis Gossett Jr."

I smiled, marveling at how Jesus even provided a credible cover story through seemingly random connections, a divine thread weaving through the mission.

Dave paused, then looked at me with a quiet intensity. "Lauren, if you haven't interviewed Don yet, you really should. Don and JD have pieces of your story I can't share, and you'll want to gather that information too."

"Actually," I was able to say, "I've already spoken with Don and JD—they've both agreed to do an interview."

Dave's face softened, approval in his eyes, his voice carrying genuine satisfaction. "Good. Each conversation is a puzzle piece bringing your past into focus." I felt a thrill of progress, knowing I was on the right path.

In the weeks that followed, I dove into interviews with everyone who played a role in my rescue, though balancing full-time work with evening calls was no easy feat. Thankfully, Don and JD were flexible, always willing to talk whenever I found a spare moment, their generosity a blessing I didn't take for granted. Dave's interview had connected so many dots, especially around the escape route, while Don's insights into Allenby Bridge's security measures added even more clarity. Slowly, the full story unfolded, each conversation a brushstroke painting the larger picture of my past.

When it was finally time for my interview with Don, I could hardly believe it was happening. "Don, I can't believe we're talking, and I get to learn so much about you," I said, my voice thick with emotion. "I feel like I've known you and Judy my whole life. I owe my life to you."

Don's response was gentle but weighty. "Your rescue mission was unforgettable. So much happened in our lives after that mission that you and your mom don't even know about. Did you know you were the first child we ever rescued? When we brought you home, news of your rescue broke all over the United States. Phones at the CTU office were ringing off the wall with other parents desperately searching for help to get their children back."

My heart swelled with awe, realizing the ripple effect of my rescue, a testament to God's broader plan, touching lives far beyond my own. "No, Don, I had no idea," I whispered, feeling the enormity of his words.

"After your rescue, we went on about ten more missions, rescuing other children. Your story was the catalyst that led to more children being brought to safety." Don leaned in, a smile in his voice, pulling me back to the moment. "We could talk about that for hours, but let's get back to *your* story." He then shared the pivotal day he met Everett Alvarez at the CTU office in North Carolina. He painted a vivid picture of how that encounter set the wheels in motion for my rescue.

From there, Don's narrative flowed into the invaluable connections he'd forged, a thread that deepened my admiration for him. His work providing security for *Rambo* and *Iron Eagle II* had opened doors to critical conversations with high-ranking Israeli commanders, figures who held the keys to navigating the mission's complexities. I could almost hear the hushed intensity of those discussions.

My excitement grew as Don introduced another crucial player, David Halevy, an Israeli journalist and correspondent for *Time Magazine*, who also served as a Lieutenant Colonel in the Israeli Defense Force Reserves. When Don mentioned my rescue mission, Halevy's expertise in high-stakes operations kicked in, and he knew exactly who to contact: Colonel Digley, a former commander of Israeli military intelligence and a renowned counterterrorism expert.

Colonel Digley's background was truly astonishing, his story unfolding like a page from history. He had commanded an elite branch of Israeli military intelligence, specializing in counterterrorism, with credits including the 1972 rescue of a hijacked Sabena airliner in Tel Aviv. His expertise shone even brighter with his role as ground force commander in the 1976 Entebbe raid—Operation Entebbe—a daring mission to rescue hostages hijacked on an Air France flight from Tel Aviv to Paris, and diverted to Uganda after stops in Athens and Libya. I pictured the tension of that operation, the precision it demanded. This man's skills would prove invaluable in orchestrating my own rescue.

His secret counterterror operations laid a foundation for the plan ahead. Don's voice grew animated as he recounted telling Colonel Digley about the American girl kidnapped in Jordan and detailing the mission to grab me and get me out over the Allenby Bridge. Digley's response was immediate. He looked at Don and JD and, of all things, invited them to his house for dinner in Tel Aviv.

That evening, as Don and JD stepped into Colonel Digley's crowded house in Tel Aviv, surrounded by Israeli military men, I could almost feel the air thicken with purpose. Digley introduced them to his friends, high-ranking figures like the first fighter pilot, the first tank commander, the first Israeli special operations commander.... It was a lineup that left me breathless with its weight. Don's voice carried a hint of surprise as he realized the danger of the border had been underestimated, and Digley's determination to gather these experts for a plan filled me with gratitude.

I imagined the room buzzing with rapid Hebrew, the tension palpable, until one man spoke up in English, his voice cutting through the silence. "There is only one way you can do this mission. You must get a bridge pass for the Allenby Bridge and use it for the crossing out of Jordan."

Don's recollection shifted to earlier discussions with Dave, a transition that deepened my understanding of their planning. They had initially dismissed the Allenby Bridge as too difficult, the necessary documentation seeming out of reach, but Colonel Digley's insight changed everything. Don's resolve grew as he realized they couldn't rule out the route yet. They needed to dig deeper and find a way to secure the proper papers for the crossing. I felt a surge of determination mirroring his as the bridge (known today as the King Hussein Bridge, built in 1918 and spanning the Jordan River near Jericho and Al-Karameh) emerged as the critical link between Jordan and the West Bank, a lifeline in the mission's heart.

Reflecting on this, God's fingerprints were visible everywhere, the Jordan River's deep symbolism resonating with me. It was where John the Baptist baptized Jesus, the main water source for the Sea of Galilee, the setting of Jesus's miracles—feeding the 5,000, walking on water, calming the storm—and I felt a shiver of faith, knowing Jesus was about to calm the storm in my life as we crossed that bridge.

The biblical connection grew stronger as Don's story unfolded, pulling me into a deeper sense of wonder. One of Jesus's messianic miracles occurred near the region of Gerasenes—modern-day Jerash, my father's town and my prison—where He cast demons out of a mute man, driving them into a herd of pigs, as told in Mark 5:1–20 (NIV). The healed man begged to follow Jesus, but He said, Jesus did not let him, but said, "Go home to your own people and tell them how much the Lord has done for you, and how He has had mercy on you," (v. 19) pointing across the Sea of Galilee toward the Decapolis. The man obeyed, and people were amazed.

I felt a call in those words, a purpose in writing this book to share God's goodness and power, using ordinary people like me to bring hope amid brokenness, just as that man did.

The next day, Colonel Digley escorted Don and JD to the Allenby Bridge border, pointing out the dangers: landmines, booby traps, barbed wire fences, anti-tank traps, and minefields. He even provided them with a firearm and paperwork to carry it.

Border passes remained elusive, however.

After regrouping with Dave, Don and JD shared their findings, and Dave agreed the Allenby Bridge was the best option, especially after exploring other routes like Aqaba and Syria, which had proven too risky. With Israeli soldiers eager to assist, the plan seemed viable, but the question loomed—how would they obtain a bridge pass?

Yet a Scripture echoed in my own heart: "See, I am doing a new thing! Now it springs up; do you not perceive it? I am making a way in the wilderness and streams in the wasteland" (Isaiah 43:19 NIV).

God was making a way, just as He had through the surprising connections with *Rambo* and *Iron Eagle*, David Halevy's introduction to Colonel Digley, and the involvement of Israeli soldiers—a stream in my dry wasteland, bringing life, hope, and freedom where none seemed possible. This wasn't just a physical escape route; it was a spiritual reminder that no situation is too desperate for God to intervene through every twist and turn.

CHAPTER TEN

BLUE EYES

After my rescue, my mother and I would lie awake at night, talking quietly in the dark. In those moments, she shared pieces of how she brought me home and gently asked about my time in Jordan. Some memories surfaced easily. Others stayed hidden.

But one moment always hovered between us.

It was the day a stranger saw me on the streets of Jerash.

For thirty-seven years, that moment existed in my mind only as fragments—a man in a crowd, a glance, and a rescue set in motion. I didn't know his face or his thoughts. I only knew that in a place where I had learned to disappear, someone finally saw me.

Years later, that moment came into focus in an unexpected way—through a microphone.

When JD Roberts agreed to sit down with me on the *Redeemed* podcast, I knew I was about to hear the story I had carried my whole life, told by the man who'd lived it from the other side. As we talked, I realized this wasn't just an interview. It was the first time I would hear, in full, what had been unfolding around me while I was in Jordan, unaware that rescue was already closing in.

JD Roberts during his years of military service before the mission to rescue me.

As JD spoke, the distance between past and present collapsed. His voice pulled me back to those streets, and suddenly I wasn't a woman behind a microphone anymore. I was a little girl again, in Jerash, waiting to be found. "Lauren, you'll have to bear with me," he said. "It's been a long time since I've shared your story, but it's one I can never forget."

JD cleared his throat, and I leaned in as his words pulled me back to December of 1987. "Dave was the first one to hit Jerash searching for you. But he was having a hell of a time—three weeks in, visa clock ticking, and no sign of you. He needed help." JD's voice steadied, thick with the urgency of those days. "Meanwhile, Don and I were crisscrossing Jordan and Israel, tapping military contacts—Colonel Digley, Israeli soldiers, even producers from *Rambo* and *Iron Eagle*—hoping for intel to plot your escape across the border."

The tension coiled as he laid out the stakes. "Jerash was small, but your dad's family was big. We wore disguises—robes, headscarves—to blend in, but eyes were starting to linger. People wondered why we kept circling the streets. It was getting desperate." JD paused, letting the weight settle, and I scribbled faster, pulse racing. *All this, while I was trapped, oblivious.*

"The Jordanian police were sniffing around," he went on. "We couldn't keep dodging them without tipping someone off. That's when we knew we needed your mom; Jerash had changed since she had been there. What had once been dirt roads were now paved, and the city had changed so much that the buildings and layout no longer resembled anything in her photos, so they were useless. Dave called your mom and asked her to gather any information about your whereabouts, but without alerting your dad. We were in a race against time."

As JD spoke, I sat, amazed, my mind reeling. He was confirming everything Mom had told me over the years, right down to those faded, useless photos. "I went to the ruins where your mom had been years before," he said. "I recognized the spot from a photo she'd given me. She told me she and your dad stood there once, him pointing out his family home from that exact vantage."

I couldn't hold back. "I've seen those photos—Mom and Dad on camels, laughing, long before I was even a whisper in their minds."

"I had those photos in hand as I climbed the hill, monocular pressed to my eye, straining for a better view. But nothing matched. The city had sprawled too far—ruins, landscape, buildings—all different, like the past had been erased.

"That's when I started praying. Right there in those ruins. 'God, show me where Lauren is,' I begged. 'I can't do this alone.' The city's growth had swallowed every clue—your father's home, you—it was impossible without Him." Desperation pulsed through his words. This hadn't been just a mission to JD. It was personal, a cry from a man lost in the unfamiliar, reaching for divine light.

"We had to move fast. Every scrap of info from your dad could be the key. Were you in school? Hanging out in certain spots? Talking to his family? We were grasping for anything to pin you down. That's when your brave mom stepped in." He leaned closer, eyes alight with admiration. "I've faced desperate missions worldwide, worked with tough folks, but your mother? Her faith, her grit…unmatched. Nothing was stopping her."

My pen stilled, a lump rising in my throat. I'd always known Mom was strong, a rock of independence, but hearing JD—my own hero—lift her up like that? It was a revelation. She wasn't just my mom; she was a warrior.

JD's tone sharpened, clear as a bell. "Dave called her, coaching her through it. 'Ask Ali this: Is Lauren in school? Made any friends? How's she communicating?' Every question was a calculated jab, hunting for a crack in his wall." I nodded, my mind flashing to a dusty cassette tape I'd found in the Jordan box. Before I could mention it, JD fixed me with a look. "Lauren, have you heard this before?"

"No, but I might have a recording of that conversation. I have a whole Ziplock bag full of cassette tapes, and one is labeled Conversation with Ali."

"When we're done here, listen to it. Hear what your mom did for you." My heart thudded—his words lit a fire to uncover that moment myself.

He pressed on. "Your mom's amazing, Lauren. She held it together. She got on that call and pulled the intel we needed." He paused, savoring the memory. "She called Dave back. 'He's got her in a private school.' That was it—our breakthrough. Proof you were in Jerash, and not just any school, but a private one. That shrank our haystack to a needle's point." Relief washed through his voice, and I felt it too—the light piercing the fog of those lost months.

"From there," JD said, "we tracked down that school. Found out elementary kids rode little orange buses—girls only, each with a chaperone. Finally, something solid. We hit the streets, eyes peeled for every orange blur rolling by, praying one would carry you."

My breath caught, picturing them—tired, relentless, chasing buses through Jerash's dust. This wasn't just a clue; it was a nudging of puzzle pieces into place, one desperate prayer at a time.

JD's words still burned in my ears, and I couldn't shake them. "Listen to that tape, hear what she did for you." I hadn't been ready before, but after JD's interview, I knew I had to face it. That evening, with my boys tucked in bed, I dug out the cassette player and pressed play. My dad's voice hit me, thick with that familiar accent yet distant as a ghost. My heart slammed against my ribs, fear and trauma roaring back, every wound he'd left splitting open anew.

Then came Mom's voice, calm but edged with steel: "What does Lauren do all day?" she asked, her tone masking the urgency I knew simmered beneath.

Dad answered fast, too smooth. "Don't worry, Cathy. She's in school, taken care of—she's fine."

But Mom wouldn't bend. "What school?" she pressed, voice quickening. "She doesn't even speak Arabic."

His reply was firm, a wall going up. "A new private school—small classes. They're teaching her Arabic. She's doing well."

I sat, frozen, the tape spinning out a life I could barely recall, each word peeling back layers of a world hidden from me. Hearing JD's story snap into place was a strange comfort, like bits of a shattered past mending under God's quiet hand.

I'd been gone ten and a half weeks by then, a number that hit harder hearing my mother fight for me on that crackling tape. Needing her side of the story, I reached for her journals.

I found January 14—the date of her flight from Washington to New York to see Uncle Dan. He'd always been my rock, steady through every milestone, and for Mom, he was a pillar of trust and love she couldn't leave without embracing one last time.

Tears blurred the ink as I read, her words torn between resolve and dread. She knew this goodbye might be final; Jordan loomed, a gamble that could trap her forever if it went wrong. Yet beneath her fear burned a mother's fierce hope, tethered to Jesus. Two days later, January 16, marked her next leap: a flight to Cyprus. Uncle Dan and his friend Bob drove her to the airport, and before she boarded, Dan pressed the book *Not Without My Daughter* into her hands—a story of escape too close to her own. On the long leg to Rome, she barely cracked it open, teetering between terror and faith in the plane's back row.

She wrote every detail in her journal, capturing the moment she peeled the plastic wrapper off that book. She confessed a gnawing fear: What if someone sees the title and guesses I'm sneaking my own daughter across foreign borders? She tried to read, tracing the story of a mother like her, but the parallels overwhelmed her—it was too much, too soon. She tucked it away again, her thoughts a storm of what-ifs, yet her resolve held firm.

January 17 brought my mom to Cyprus, her journal entry glowing with a faint spark. Don, a steady anchor in the storm, waited for her at the airport. They settled into the Sun Hall Hotel in Larnaca.

(Its white walls and Mediterranean shimmer hid a shadow I'd only later uncover—it was rumored to be a terrorist haunt.) I pictured my mom there, unflinching, her focus locked on the team, on me. JD's words from our podcast painted her resolve in vivid strokes. Dave held the line in Jordan, while Don and JD rallied around Mom with Jim Hatfield, each step pulling the mission's threads tighter.

That night, Don brought JD to my mother's room. Their first meeting crackled with urgency. JD's voice echoed in my ears as he recounted it: "Jerash is four times bigger now, Cathy. Your photos? Relics. Finding Ali's house—finding Lauren—it's a maze."

I imagined Mom's heart dropping, her thoughts spinning, as JD's grim truth sank in. Then, JD paused and shifted to steel-edged focus as he talked about Jim Hatfield. "That's where Jim Hatfield stepped up. Dave had called your mom to Cyprus to wait for our signal, and Jim was our linchpin. He would stick by your mom's side, get her to Amman's airport when the moment hit, handle the cash, and all of our luggage."

JD's unraveling web hooked me deeper. I frantically took notes: "Cash only—cars, hotels, supplies—no traces. Jim locked it down."

The enormity of it sank in as JD kept going. "Every ticket was one-way—flexible, untraceable. Jim handled the gear too. Day of the mission, we'd move light—no luggage, nothing to slow us down. In and out, like ghosts, leaving no evidence behind."

My pulse quickened, and the tension in his voice wrapped around me. This wasn't just a rescue, it was a chess match—every move calculated, every risk weighed—all for one desperate shot at bringing me home. Mom's faith had carried her this far, but now I saw the machine behind it—Dave, Jim, JD, Don, and Judy—a team stitched together by sacrifice and strategy.

JD's voice grew somber. "When we first hit Jerash, we figured your mom needed to be there when we found you; we thought you'd trust us more seeing her face. But time was slipping fast, and we still hadn't pinned you down." I scribbled his words, feeling the clock tick through his tone.

My mother's journal carried me to January 19, and the stakes sharpened immediately. JD had flown back to Amman to link up with Dave, leaving my mom and Don behind in Cyprus. The distance gnawed at her. With each entry, I could feel her nerves fraying, the hours stretching thin.

That night, she picked up the hotel phone and called my father, steadying her voice as she asked to speak to me.

"She's asleep," he said.

The next evening, January 20, at 8:00 p.m., she called again. This time, he refused. I heard that call years later on a cassette tape.

Then I turned the page....

Her words turned raw. She wrote that she snapped, desperation spilling over the margins. "You wimp!"—a line I recognized the instant I read it. "Hiding behind your mother and sisters. Keeping my daughter from me. You dirty dog!"

On the tape, the line went dead.

In the journal, silence followed.

I pictured her collapsing in that hotel room, sobs shaking her body, wondering if those words had burned the last bridge to me.

Don heard my mom yelling and crying through the walls of his hotel room. "Your mom was breaking," he told me. "She was exhausted and terrified, but she was still unbowed. Nothing was going to stop her from getting you back."

His words sank deep. What would my life have been without her fight? What had it cost her, day after day, facing those giants of fear? But Mom's battle wasn't hers alone—Jesus was her shield and her strength, towering over the fear that loomed like a goliath, guiding her through every trembling step.

My mom stayed in Cyprus with Jim, while Don boarded a flight back to Amman to support JD and Dave. By then, I'd been gone nearly eleven weeks—a number that stood out to me now as I pieced this story together. The mission was getting close.

Dave had been searching Jerash for three of those weeks, scouring for me and my dad's house, but every lead fizzled. The longer he stayed "in country," the more eyes lingered. His face was too familiar, his cover thinning. Fresh blood was overdue, and Don's arrival was the spark they needed to shake things up. In Jerash, he linked with JD, and they quickly agreed—Dave had to fade back. His time in the spotlight was a ticking risk.

Reading the journals had pulled me close to those days, but hearing JD and Don—my rescuers—relive our story just hit different. I'd shared my story with those I loved but talking to the men who saved me? That was new ground. Each conversation unfurled details I'd never grasped. Every word, every move was no accident.

JD and Don painted Jerash in stark strokes. Don told me, "We swapped rental cars constantly. Couldn't let the locals pin us down. Days bled into each other, driving street after street, hunting for you. We grew beards, draped ourselves in robes and headscarves. Anything to melt into the crowd."

I felt the pulse of their danger, the sacrifices piling up just to inch closer to me.

"After days circling that town, JD and I hit a wall," Don said. "We were nowhere, and the risk was climbing. We pulled off onto a side street, ditched the car, and slipped into the market's bustle, hoping to vanish in the chaos. The longer we lingered, the tighter the noose. Desperation was choking us."

JD echoed that weight in our interview, frustration etching his words. "We'd thrown everything at it—every trick we knew—and still nothing. Three weeks, no you, no house. That's when I knew: We'd run dry without God. I prayed right there: 'Lord, we're lost. We need You. Show us Lauren, or this falls apart.'" He paused, then shared the verse that anchored him: "You said to me, 'I will point out the road that you should follow. I will be your teacher and watch over you.'" (Psalm 32:8 CEV) Sincerity cracked through his grit—a soldier humbled, turning to the only guide left.

Listening to JD, I was overwhelmed with emotion. In a moment when everything seemed lost, when their training and experience couldn't find a way forward, they turned to faith—and it was in that moment that God revealed the next step.

My whole life, people have always commented on my eyes. Strangers would stop and say, "You have beautiful eyes; I'm sure you hear that all the time." As I've gotten older, I've realized those comments aren't just about appearance. They're a reminder of God's perfect design, and in this story, my *eyes* became a key part of the mission. Even in the chaos of Jerash, those eyes would help guide my rescuers to me.

As JD and Don laid out their pieces of this puzzle. "We were out of moves," he'd said, "but not out of hope."

Don chimed in, his tone tight. "Every dead end pushed us harder, praying Jesus would light the way." I sat there, pen trembling, marveling at JD's plea and Don's determination, all leaning on the One who'd never lost sight of me.

Then, in the midst of it all, something incredible happened. As JD stood on a street corner, an orange school bus rolled up. He glanced up, and through the window, he saw me. My bright blue eyes stared back at him. A rush of excitement flooded him as he bolted to Don, grabbing his shoulders. "I saw her!"

Don, jolted by JD's fire, stammered, "You saw who?"

"Lauren—in that bus!" JD's voice danced between disbelief and joy.

"How do you know?" Don pressed, surprise tangling with doubt.

"Her bright blue eyes—I'm sure!"

Don's heart raced. "Where? Where'd you see her?"

JD pointed as the bus pulled away, and without a beat, they ran towards the car. But it was too late—the bus had vanished in Jerash's twisting streets. But when JD recognized me by my eyes, it was the turning point. It was God's answer, loud and clear. They were on the right track. Despite impossible odds and fading hope, Jesus had guided them straight to me.

The men had confirmed what my father had told my mother was true, I was in Jerash and attending school, a breakthrough that flipped their plan: Intercept me on the bus, not at my dad's house. JD's voice crackled with urgency in our call as he recounted chasing that orange blur through Jerash's maze of twisting, narrow streets, swallowing it whole. "We couldn't keep up without eyes on us."

Don chimed in, "But it was enough. Knowing you weren't locked away gave us a shot."

They lingered near the school that day, watching buses, clocking drop-offs and pickups, praying for another glimpse of those blue eyes.

Talking to Dave, Don, and JD, I felt the weight of what they carried—hope tangled tightly with desperation. They had finally seen me. After weeks of searching, a single moment on a school bus confirmed what they had only dared to believe.

I was in Jerash.

But seeing me wasn't the same as finding me.

"That bus was our lifeline," Don told me later. "But it wasn't the endgame. We still didn't know where your dad was keeping you."

Finding the school was one thing. Home was the key.

For days, my mom tried calling my father's house, desperate to hear my voice. Every call ended the same way—shut down, silenced.

Then Dave called again. "Cathy, we need your memory."

They had reached the edge of what they could do alone.

If the rescue was going to move forward, it would require the one thing they didn't have—a mother willing to walk back into the place she had once tried to escape.

CHAPTER ELEVEN

HIDING IN PLAIN SIGHT

The ancient city of Jerash buzzed with life as my mom stepped into its narrow and winding streets. Stone arches and dusty paths framed a town that seemed frozen in time, but underneath the charm, a silent mission pulsed.

I was in Jerash.

But one critical piece still eluded them—the location of the house where I was being kept. Without it, the rescue mission couldn't move forward. And now, it was up to my mom, armed only with courage and a mother's relentless love to walk into the unknown and find it.

During one of our long phone conversations, my mom vividly relived the moment Dave called her.

"I'd been waiting in Cyprus," she said. "Every minute stretched like a month, though it was only days. And then Dave's voice on the phone—'We saw her.' Lauren, when he said that, my heart raced so fast I could hardly breathe. Joy and fear collided inside me. They were so close. But so much could still go wrong: failure, capture, jail time…it all loomed over us."

I could hear her heart breaking through the phone. "I was anxious," she admitted, "but I couldn't crumble. I had to keep my eyes locked on Jesus, like Peter walking on water in the storm. When Peter looked away, he sank. I knew if I let fear pull my gaze off

Jesus, I would sink too. I had to trust God's guidance, even when the turmoil roared around me."

For the next three days, she called my father's house over and over again, hoping to hear my voice, to confirm what her heart longed to believe. But every time, he blocked her. He was cold and kept stonewalling, offering no chance to even hear me breathe on the other end of the line.

Then another call from Dave came, this one urgent. "We've seen Lauren once, Cathy, but that bus sighting is our only hit. We need you to find Ali's house."

"What did that day feel like?" I asked.

Her voice cracked as she answered, tears spilling through the line.

"If it's too painful, we can stick to your journal," I offered.

She immediately replied. "No, Lauren. It's okay. It's good to remember what God has done."

She told me how she gathered her things in a frenzy, mind racing three steps ahead, barely breathing in the moment. In the middle of packing for the most dangerous mission of her life, she called Beverly Lambert, asking her to send pink sponge rollers.

"My curling iron wouldn't work in Cyprus or Amman." She told me, laughing through her tears. "And I thought…what if I see you? I want everything to be perfect. Even my hair."

That detail hit me harder than I expected. She wasn't thinking only about my rescue; she was thinking about being a mom, about comforting her daughter, and about reclaiming some sense of normalcy in a situation that was anything but normal.

"I was on the next flight to Amman," she said. "My heart was pounding, but I trusted God to finish what He had started."

I sat there, piecing the story together in my mind. Flying into Amman made perfect sense. Queen Alia International Airport, just outside the city, was the closest major gateway to Jerash, only about an hour's drive away. But it wasn't just a geographic choice; it was also a strategic one. Don, Dave, and JD needed a safe place to regroup with my mom, to finalize the plan, and to prepare her so she wouldn't walk into Jerash alone and exposed.

Carrying only what she needed and the weight of a mother's fierce, unbreakable love, my mom boarded that plane from Cyprus to Amman. When she landed, the team was waiting. Don, Dave, and JD—three pillars of strength handpicked to fight for her and for me.

They stayed together that night at the Hala Inn Suites, a small hotel where the anticipation was thick enough to choke on. Every hour that passed wound the coil of hope and fear tighter in Mom's chest.

She described that night to me. "I was so close to you, Lauren. But the 'what-ifs' clawed at me. What if your dad saw me? What if we were caught? What if you leaving Jordan hurt you more?"

Fear stalked my mother's every step. But she fought it the only way she knew how: scribbling Scriptures in her journal, whispering prayers under her breath, and clinging to the promises of God.

As the sun crept over the hills of Amman, the tension from the night before lingered like a shadow. My mom stood silently at the window of the hotel room, watching the city stretch awake, her mind spinning with memories and fear. She clutched her scarf tightly, bracing herself for the day ahead. JD methodically checked his bag one last time, scanning maps and reviewing notes from Dave's detailed briefing. Don moved with quiet confidence, his military instincts sharp—today demanded precision, nerves of steel, and unshakable focus. No one spoke. There was nothing left to say. After a whispered prayer, they slipped out of the hotel and into the rented sedan. My mom sat up front beside Don, who took the wheel, while JD slid into the back seat, eyes fixed on the road like a sentry. As they left the city behind, the rising sun cast a warm, golden light over the hills. But inside the car, the mood was heavy. Every mile toward Jerash pulsed with dread. They weren't heading there to visit Roman ruins. They were searching for the place where I was being hidden. Each turn of the road felt like a countdown to something irreversible.

My mom's nerves buzzed under her skin, but she summoned a deep resolve. "I'd walked the streets of Jerash with your aunts before your dad and I got married," she told me. "The town was smaller back then, but I believed I could find your father's house. I knew I could."

Before leaving Amman, she dressed in a long black jilbab, pulling a scarf over her hair to blend in with the local women. The men dressed in robes, too, trying to disappear into the background. "Your father's family was well-known in that town," she said. "They had a pharmacy, a doctor's office…there were eyes everywhere. We couldn't risk being recognized."

The forty-five-minute drive to Jerash stretched like a lifetime. My mom sat tensely beside Don, who gripped the steering wheel, his jaw tight. JD remained quiet in the back, scanning every street sign, every storefront. "I could barely breathe," my mom told me. "My nerves twisted tighter with every turn."

When they finally rolled into Jerash, nothing looked familiar: new roads, taller buildings, a town transformed. Doubt crashed over her like a wave.

"Cathy," Don asked, breaking the silence, "do you recognize anything? Any landmarks?" JD leaned forward, eyes locked on her, waiting. Overwhelmed, she slid to the floorboard.

"Father," she cried aloud, "You didn't bring us this far to fail. Show me Lauren. Show me the way."

Her prayer hung in the air like a tremble.

As the car labored up a steep hill, God answered. Memories flooded her mind—walking those same streets with my aunts years ago, arm in arm, laughter in their steps. Her voice came, faint but sure. "Turn left…go straight…then left again."

Don glanced through the rearview mirror at JD, eyebrows raised. Had she lost it? But he obeyed, turning the wheel. Step by step, God retraced her footsteps from years past.

The car wound through the hills, then slowed. My mom lifted her head—and froze.

"I saw his car," she whispered.

There it was. My father's white Mazda, shipped from Texas, still bearing the original plates. He had maxed out his credit cards to buy it before fleeing to Jordan. Weeks earlier, a skip tracer—someone hired to find people who don't want to be found—had even called my mom, asking if she had any information on my father.

She told him, "If you find him, let me know. I'm looking for him too."

When she told me that, she broke down. "God used even that," she said.

In a sea of dusty local vehicles, the white Mazda gleamed in the sun, impossible to miss. It stood out like a beacon.

Don didn't hesitate. He slammed the wheel into a hard turn, the tires gripping the road as the car spun around. "Hide your face—now!" he barked, eyes flicking to the rearview mirror, scanning for any sign they'd been spotted.

They approached the white Mazda again, slower this time, tense. Don's eyes locked on the opposite side of the road…and there he was. My father, unaware, stepping casually out of the building. It was only a second, but it was all they needed. The confirmation. The connection. The target.

That was the moment my mom knew—they were one step closer to finding me.

As I listened, chills went through me. I couldn't deny it—nothing in this rescue mission had moved forward until someone prayed. Not the forming of the team, not JD spotting me on the school bus, and not this moment when my mom located my dad's house in Jerash. God was in every detail, every detour, guiding her shaking hands and lighting the path toward a miracle.

Isaiah 42:16 burned in her then: "I will lead the blind by ways they have not known, along unfamiliar paths I will guide them; I will turn the darkness into light before them and make the rough places smooth. These are the things I will do; I will not forsake them." (Isaiah 42:16 NIV)

Having spent time interviewing each person who fought for my rescue, I uncovered details I'd never have known otherwise. Only my mom could paint that prayer in the car. Only JD could relive spotting my blue eyes on that bus, a jolt of divine clarity. Dave highlighted the details of finding the escape route, and Don unfolded the details of Colonel Digley and the border crossing. Every one of them played extraordinary roles with danger in every step. Piecing their stories together, I saw the whole breathtaking tapestry, too vast for any human hand alone. "God made sure we knew," Dave told me. "This was *His* mission. It was beyond us, every bit."

After my mom pinpointed my dad's house on January 25th, she retreated to the hotel, nerves frayed but hope flickering. The men stayed behind, eyes on the prize. Don recalled, "We saw your aunt lift you off the bus that afternoon, a chaperone hovering. You were right there. So close, but not ours yet."

The next morning, they were back before dawn. Dave's call replayed the whole scene for me. "At 7:45, that bus rolled up, with your aunt and you waiting. They tailed the bus, noting a stop at a farmhouse on Jerash's edge, then slipped back to the hotel, details in hand.

I sat with those accounts, heart pounding, as my mother said, "While they watched you, I was fighting my own battle—fear clawing at me, faith my only grip."

Back at the Hala Inn, on the afternoon of January 26th, the men huddled over maps and timings, voices low, plotting the grab. Don dropped a detail that stuck with me. "We had a code word, 'the Son is shining,' to signal all clear."

I asked JD later, "Why a code?"

"Phone lines could've been tapped, US to Jordan. It kept us safe—meant the mission was on."

My mom's call echoed in my mind. "When Don said it, my mom broke down—'The Son, Jesus, shining!' It was God, not just a word." She had told me this part of the story over the years, but we never knew who came up with the code words.

Alone in her room after that meeting, my mom paced. "They were out there risking it all," she said, "and I had to hold the line with prayer—trusting God to knit us together."

Thirty-seven years later, in the fall of 2024, my mom and I met Judy Feeney at our first *Desperate Rescue* reunion as I started this book and learned *she'd* birthed that code. "I came up with 'the Son is shining,'" Judy said, eyes bright. "Don taught me caution—'Son' for Jesus, not 'sun,' signaled safety. I told Don to pass it to Cathy."

All those years, Mom thought it was Al or someone else on the team until Judy's story cracked the mystery open. "I prayed day and night," she added, "knowing nothing's impossible for God."

"Mom never knew," I marveled, sitting around a table with Judy, feeling like she'd always been family.

Judy wasn't alone. She and Beverly, and Grandma Barbara Phelps—all warriors on their knees Judy reminded them of the simple command in Scripture: "Pray continually" (1 Thessalonians 5:17 NIV) alive in her voice. I choked up, seeing God weave their prayers with Mom's and the men's into my rescue. Back in '88, my mom's tears at "the Son" weren't just born of relief. They were born of faith. She may have been blind to Judy's hand in it, but she remained locked on God's. Every detail sang His name.

"Lauren," my mom told me over the phone, her voice quivering like it was yesterday, "I'd prayed all night. And when I walked into that room, JD grabbed my arm. 'Cathy, tomorrow's it. We're taking her.'"

Her words stirred something deep—but it was Dave who ultimately filled in the blanks I never knew. "We'd mapped that bus—7:45 sharp. But the escape?" He let out a breath. "That was the beast, gnawing at us day and night."

Then came another piece, "'Twelve weeks gone. Your dad's shadow is everywhere.'" The tension in the hotel room must have been unbearable, but Dave painted the scene so clearly, I felt like I was there.

"We were all in," he said.

I could almost smell the stale coffee in that hotel suite, see the curled edges of maps spread across the table, and feel Jesus hovering in that space not just in their prayers, but in the very structure of the plan.

The men had laid out their notes—escape routes stretching across the table like lifelines drawn in pencil. Dave's voice dropped into a slow, steady rhythm as he recounted their options. "A plane out of Amman? Too risky. Too many eyes—guards, passports, tickets, checkpoints. No way. A boat from Aqaba? Smugglers' turf. Pure chaos."

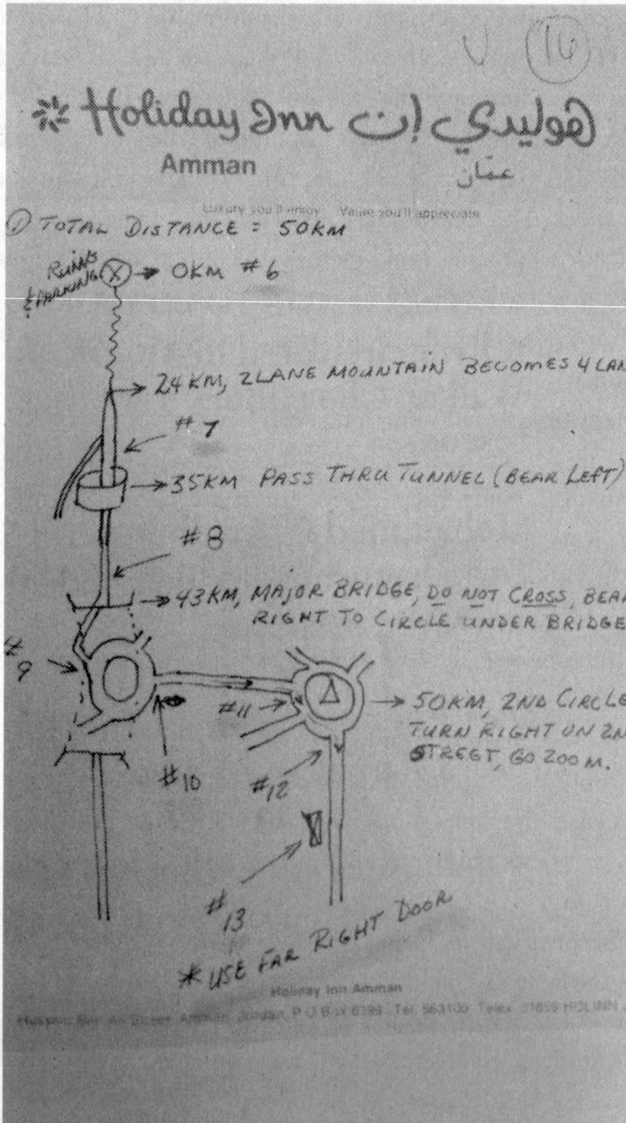

The handwritten escape route, sketched on a hotel notepad
as the team planned how to get me out of Jordan.

He paused before continuing. "We even considered sneaking you out on foot—forty kilometers to the Israeli border in the dark. But Lauren, it was a prayer with no legs. Patrols were everywhere. You were too small. No way you could make that run."

Hours ticked by, tension coiling, until Don slammed a fist down: "The bus—it's our shot."

Hijack it mid-route, scoop me off, barrel to the Allenby Bridge. It was bold and probably reckless, but it could slide through Jerash's bustle unnoticed.

"We'd walked that border with Colonel Digley," JD added. "Israeli brass with a hawk's eye. For two days, his men had pointed out every mine, every sniper nest. We knew it cold."

Still, the plan hung on fragile threads: bridge passes, my passport's Jordan stamp—my mom's foresight in Washington with the help of Al, a silent miracle.

Don's embassy story hit me like a punch. "Lauren, you've seen *Desperate Rescue*—that yelling bit?" he asked, grin sharp.

"A million times," I said, "my boys too—they know it by heart."

"Well, buckle up." He chuckled. "Here's the uncut version." He and JD had stormed the US Embassy in Amman days earlier—January 25—chasing a legal lifeline. "Thirty, forty minutes in line," he said. "Sweat sticking my shirt to my chest, JD fidgeting beside me. I finally hit the plexiglass. 'How do we get an American kid home? She's with her Jordanian dad.'"

The officer behind the glass didn't blink. "My job's to notify him you're trying to snatch her. She's Jordanian now. Born here or not, doesn't matter."

Don's temper flared, "like a match to dry grass," he said. "I slammed that window, yelling, 'What kind of soldier are you? She's ours!'"

Boots shuffled, security loomed, but Frank Baker, Assistant Regional Security Officer, cut through. "Cool it—not here, not now. Coffee later."

That afternoon, in a cramped Amman coffee shop, steam curling from chipped mugs, Don and Dave met Frank, spinning a tale to hook him. "We painted your dad dark," Don told me. "Car theft, fraud back in the States, using you as his bargaining chip. Half-true. Enough for him to bite." They didn't mention the rescue, probing instead for intel. "Local cops? Border tricks?"

Frank leaned in, voice low. "The embassy's a dead end. Jordanian officials won't budge. But I've got a guy—Adil Abbadi." He was a Jordanian ex-officer and embassy fixer—Frank called him gold. "He's navigated worse," he said.

Don and JD exchanged a glance. They knew the stakes. Trusting a local, especially one with ties to the system they were trying to outmaneuver was a gamble. Abbadi could just as easily play both sides, turn them in, or disappear with their plan. But with no other door open, they followed their gut and said yes.

Abbadi met them the next day—January 26—all ears as they fed him the car-theft line. "He bought it," Don said. "We promised to get your dad for importing stolen goods. Boom. Leverage."

My jaw dropped. God had turned my dad's own mess in the United States into our edge in Jordan.

"But the bridge passes? That was the real fight," Don said. He and Abbadi went to the Ministry of the Interior. Passes for Don and JD were easy to get. Abbadi's charm greased the wheels, but the entire time, they braced for the possibility that the man beside them might flip.

Dave, set to fly home, did not need a bridge pass, but my mom and I needed to claim ours in person. "January 28," Don told me. "I took her there."

My mom's voice cracked over our call. "I was a wreck—shaking and praying Jesus would hold me up." They'd rehearsed a cover: Don was my uncle and my mom was taking a weekend trip in the middle of a spousal rift.

At the Ministry, desks piled with papers, air thick with cigarette smoke, Don led her to the counter. "I started," he said, "but the official waved me off. 'Her story, not yours.'" My mom's moment to shine or fail.

"I took a breath," she told me, "deep as I could, and let it out. 'My husband and I are at odds; I just need time away with my daughter and her uncle.'" Her voice held, but when the official grabbed the phone to verify, her wall broke. Tears streamed, real, raw. "I couldn't stop," she said, "but it wasn't acting. It was you, Lauren."

Don watched, stunned. "That flood hit him. She wasn't faking. The official hung up and slid the passes over, no questions." They walked out of the building, passes in hand.

"Oscar-worthy," Don said, "but it was all Jesus. She trusted Him to carry her through."

I felt those tears sting my own eyes, her courage a fire I could touch.

Don turned to Mom. "Book flights. Tomorrow's the day we have been waiting for." January 28 loomed, the plan locked: Stop the bus at 7:45, grab me, and tear across the Allenby Bridge.

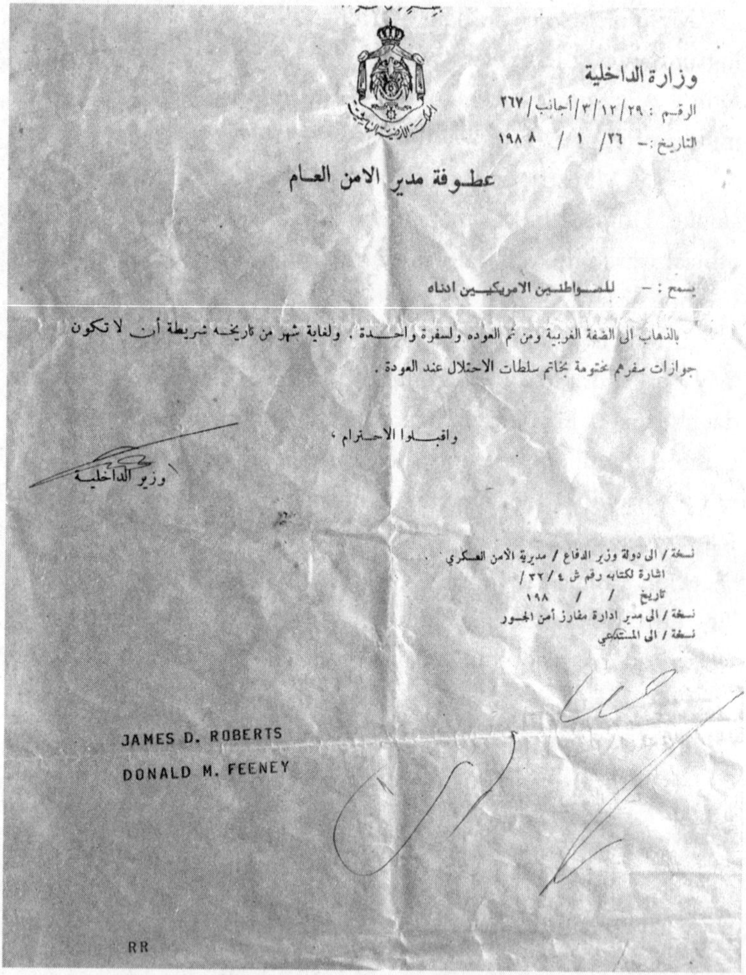

وزارة الداخلية
الرقم : ٢٩/١٢/٣/أجانب/٢٦٧
التاريخ :- ٢٦/ ١ / ١٩٨٨

عطوفة مدير الامن العام

يسمح :- للمواطنين الامريكيين ادناه

بالذهاب الى الضفة الغربية ومن ثم العوده ولسفرة واحدة . ولغاية شهر من تاريخه شريطة أن لا تكون جوازات سفرهم مختومة بخاتم سلطات الاحتلال عند العودة .

واقبلوا الاحترام ،

وزير الداخلية

نسخة / الى دولة وزير الدفاع / مديرية الأمن العسكري
اشارة لكتابه رقم ش ٤ / ٣٢ /
تاريخ / / ١٩٨
نسخة / الى مدير ادارة مفارز أمن الجسور
نسخة / الى المستدعي

JAMES D. ROBERTS
DONALD M. FEENEY

RR

The actual border pass paperwork required to cross the Allenby Bridge during the rescue mission.

JD's voice was steel in our call. "It was high risk: capture, jail, or a bullet if it went south. We'd trained for this—years of it—but this was different."

Dave added, "Even with Colonel Digley's maps, Abbadi's pull, all the planning…it was still a coin toss."

My heart hammered, their words painting a tightrope over a pit.

"Lauren," Mom whispered, "I saw Jesus everywhere. Don's fist on that glass, Frank's nudge, Abbadi agreeing to help…."

Faith wasn't their backup. It *was* the mission, the pulse driving us to that bus at dawn.

My mom with Judy Feeney—the voice behind the words, "the Son is shining."

CHAPTER TWELVE

THE SON IS SHINING: A DARING RESCUE AT DAWN

January 28, 1988. Mom's eyes snapped open at 5:40 a.m., heart hammering against her ribs. "I'd tossed all night in the tangled sheets. Fog smudged the Hala Inn's windows. Three months of begging God, and there it was: the day." She'd painted it so raw I could feel it—her bare feet on the cold tile, hands trembling as she reached for her Bible, its leather worn from Fort Worth motel nights. "I flipped to Psalm 18," she told me. "Back in Texas, I'd scribbled in the margin, 'Jehovah is my rock, my fortress, my savior.' I read it slow, letting Jesus steady my breath."

I pictured her in that dim room, pulling on the Dishdasha, which was long, brown, and rough against her skin. She tied a scarf tight over her hair.

"I splashed water on my face," she added, "and stared in the cracked mirror, whispering, 'Today, Lord, bring her home.'" Every move pulsed with, "My God will supply all your needs…."—a promise she clung to as she descended the creaky stairs to meet JD, Dave, and Don. The men were waiting in the lobby, drinking coffee and reviewing last-minute details.

After hearing my mom and the men describe the day of the rescue, I could see the full picture in my mind. The lobby hummed with tension: JD hunched over a chipped mug of black coffee, steam curling up; Dave thumbing a wrinkled map; Don pacing, boots scuffing the faded rug.

"We sat your mom down and walked her through it," JD told me in our call. "'We're taking Lauren off the bus at the farmhouse, just on the outskirts of Jerash. There are no police in that area, and it's nowhere near Ali's home. It's the safest play we've got.'"

My mom's relief spilled out in her retelling of the same story. "I told the men, 'No shootouts. I want to keep my baby safe. Please don't use guns unless you have to.'"

Dave had clocked me boarding the bus at 7:45 the day before as he watched from a red Nissan, and my mom had secured flights from Amman to Dallas as a decoy, knowing we would never make it through that super secure airport.

Don's voice cut through, "I've never done a mission without a prayer first, and I'm not about to start now. We need God on this."

My mom's nod was instant. "He'd carried us this far; we couldn't move without Him."

After leaving the hotel, they split up. Mom, Don, and JD piled into a white rental car, its vinyl seats cracked and warm; Dave peeled off in the red Nissan, dust kicking behind him. "My job was to scout your dad's house," Dave told me. "To make sure you got on that bus."

At the farmhouse rendezvous a mile out, the white car idled, and the engine ticked. Fog draped the olive groves. Don gave last minute details to my mom. "Your mom sat in the back seat, her hands clasped tight. I sat in the driver's seat with JD in the front passenger seat."

"We prayed right there," my mom said of those moments. "With heads bowed, I said, 'Jesus, guide our hands, shield us from harm, and bring Lauren home safe.'"

Judy Feeney's code, "The Son is shining," hung in the air.

The day before, Dave had spotted me getting on the bus at 7:45, but now it was 8:15 and there was no signal from him that I was on the bus. My mom could tell that JD and Don were starting to worry. A few minutes later, they saw Dave driving the red car down the road. He pulled up beside them and said, "The Son is shining."

Don said, "When the little orange school bus arrived, I swerved the white rental car to the left, deliberately blocking it in."

I could almost hear gravel under the tires and see a haze of dust as he described it.

I still carry the memory of that chaotic moment as Don's voice replayed it for me, steady and clear during our interview. "I leapt out of the white rental car, my boots crunching against the gravel, and strode toward the driver's door with purpose." He paused, then added, "I spoke to the bus driver in English to grab his attention and sow a bit of confusion, giving JD the time he needed to secure the bus's keys."

My heart raced as I reimagined the scene—dust moving around the chipped and faded school bus, its exhaust puffing black plumes into the chilly fog. Meanwhile, JD moved with precision, flanking the right side toward the accordion-style door of that old bus. In his hands, he held a bright white envelope that my mom had stuffed the night before with newspaper cut into dollar-sized strips.

She told me later, her voice soft with memory, "I sliced that paper while the men planned, my fingers shaking with every cut. Abbadi wrote on the envelope in Arabic: 'To Ali, him alone.'"

Inside the envelope, Mom's note: "You took my daughter. I have her back. Your brother and wife are safe in the States—for now. Don't follow. The eyes of Texas are upon you."

Her courage was a testament to her faith.

My mom hurried toward the bus, her eyes scanning the windows, searching for me through the fog. Then, in a blink, she froze. "I saw you," she told me, her voice catching, "in the very front row, your blue eyes as big as moons, staring out at me."

I'll never forget that instant, gazing through the grimy bus window into *my mother's beautiful, calm, blue eyes.* Blue eyes like mine. A foreign sight in this foreign land. A sight that rooted me to my vinyl seat in shock. It was surreal. My mind reeled. *Mom? Here? She's supposed to be in Texas!* Her smile pierced the haze of my confusion, but my legs locked with fear and disbelief—what about all the things my father had said about my mother. He kept telling me Mom wanted me to be happy and knew I was happier with him…that work was keeping her busy, but she'd visit when she could. Then, after all this time, she was standing right in front of me. What would my father do? Was he here? All these thoughts brought confusion and fear, pinning me in place. *Is this a dream? Can it really be her?* I longed to believe it was true, yet doubt held me captive.

As my mom stood there, JD waved the envelope, his Arabic crisp and commanding. "I've got an urgent message for Ali, please open the door." The chaperone—a young, stern woman—narrowed her eyes but cracked the door open, the creak echoing in my ears. Mom shoved past JD, weaving through the rows of chattering children, her determination unyielding.

"You wouldn't budge," she recalled, her voice thick with emotion. "You just looked up at me with those big, shocked eyes." She crouched down, her knees pressing into the metal floor, and scooped me up, snagging my small backpack in one swift motion. "Baby, it's me, your mom," she whispered, her arms warm around me. "We're going home."

Everything blurred into a whirlwind—my face buried in her chest, the scent of her scarf filling my senses as she carried me off the bus. But as we stepped down, the chaperone lunged, jumping onto Mom's back, forcing her to let go of me. I stood still, fear spiking, and watched as Mom swung her fist, striking the woman's nose. Bright red blood streamed down the chaperone's face, a stark contrast against the dusty ground. I stood frozen.

While my mom fought with the chaperone, JD acted fast. He ripped the brass keys from the ignition, the metal glinting in the weak light, and hurled them into the tall, dew-damp grass. I asked him later why he didn't keep them.

"I knew that if I took the keys, the bus driver and chaperone would run for help immediately. My hope was that they'd waste precious time searching for them instead—giving us the chance to slip away." He nodded. "Let them scramble…and that's exactly what happened."

A few seconds later, Don's sharp eyes caught movement. "Car. Four people inside. They are slowing," he said, his voice tense. "Stay calm," he ordered, locking his arm around the chaperone's shoulders to spin her away, masking her blood-smeared face from view. The dusty black car crawled past, but as Don steadied my mom and the woman, the car picked up speed and vanished down the road.

JD said, "I saw your mom struggling with that woman, so I moved in. 'This is Mamma,' I told her. 'She's taking her baby home. Do you understand?'"

The chaperone glared, blood dripping from her nose. "Mamma?"

"Yes, Mamma." JD guided her back toward the bus. "Let's move!" he yelled, his tone brooking no argument.

My mom lifted me into the footwell of the white car's backseat, draping rough wool blankets over me, their weight a strange comfort while I was practically paralyzed with fear and shock after seeing my mom after months apart.

Mom whispered, "Quiet. Stay still. Everything's okay."

My temperature started spiking, my vision blurred into a haze, and my small frame became unsteady on the car's gritty floor. My heart raced, yet I didn't fight or try to flee. Instead, I withdrew into silence. All I could do was trust Mom to shield me, her presence a lifeline as we sped away, wrapped in God's unfailing care.

Still in shock, I tried to speak; my voice wavered, but Mom told me later that every word came out in Arabic except for a few in English that broke through: "Mommy, I love you, and you are so beautiful." By then, we had cleared the crowded streets of Jerash and were far enough away that the men finally said it was safe for me to come out from hiding. Mom pulled the blanket back and lifted me into her lap. Tears filled my eyes as I reached for her hand, gazing into her familiar blue eyes, a mirror of my own. "Mommy, you're so beautiful," I whispered again, the words a lifeline in my haze.

Mom shared with me how, in that moment, peace washed over her like a warm wave. "After three months of fighting, I was exhausted and overwhelmed, but God's light shone through, steadying my heart."

"Everything will be okay," she whispered, her breath warm against my forehead, "but you have to stay quiet and very still." Mom kept her hand on my shoulder, a gentle anchor reassuring me I was safe. Even so, I could sense the tension in the car as Don and JD drove down the winding dirt road, their silence heavy, their focus locked on the escape.

A few blocks later, we pulled over to switch cars with Dave, his red Nissan idling in the fog, so local police wouldn't know which vehicle we were in. Once we'd swapped to the Nissan, everyone shed their disguises, trading robes for plain jackets to avoid recognition.

While the men changed, mom used the blanket to shield us and quickly helped me of out of my green plaid school uniform. The buttons slipped through her fingers as she worked quickly. When she finished, she wrapped her arms tightly around me.

I don't remember much of that car ride. My mom told me later, "You went into shock, Lauren. Your skin was burning, your eyes were glassy, and you were completely disoriented." Lost in a fog of trauma, I didn't speak for most of the drive. Mom had been prepared for it. "JD and Don had warned me that shock might hit me hard." Though she knew we were still in danger with police possibly on our trail and my dad's network lurking, she kept her hands on me, gently repeating, "Everything's going to be okay." I could feel her fingers tracing circles on my back, her touch a quiet prayer as we sped toward safety.

My next words broke were in Arabic again, a desperate refrain: "Mommy, I'm scared." I said it over and over, my voice small and trembling. She didn't understand the Arabic, but she knew my fear. She could feel it in the way I clung to her.

Later she told me, "I just held you tighter, wishing I could take it all away." Then she pulled me close, her arms a fortress around me. I could hear her heart racing, and the familiar scent of her perfume—lavender and rose—filling the air. I stared into her beautiful blue eyes, so like my own, and felt a flicker of realization. *This is real.*

My fear melted away as the truth sank in. This wasn't a dream; it was really her. I threw my arms around her neck, and tears streamed down my cheeks, soaking into her scarf. She held me tight, her lips brushing my face as she kissed my cheeks, whispering over and over, "You're safe. I've got you now, and I'll never leave you." I buried my face in her shoulder, her warmth a balm to my trembling heart, and felt God's peace settle over us both.

I learned later that as Mom and I sped toward the Allenby Bridge with Don and JD, Dave had taken on a critical role after we left the farmhouse and switched cars. He told me during our first meeting at the Desperate Rescue reunion in September 2024, "I drove the white Toyota back to Jerash to watch the bus and make sure you all had enough time to escape." I pictured him pulling into a dusty gas station on the outskirts of town, the air heavy with the scent of petrol, topping off the tank as he kept his eyes on the road. Seven minutes later, the orange school bus came roaring down the narrow lane, its engine rattling.

Dave, acting as our decoy, honked sharply at the driver, pulled out in front of the bus, and drove toward town before doubling back toward the bridge. "I kept the car moving at a steady pace on that narrow two-lane road—slow enough not to attract attention, but fast enough not to lose them." I could feel the tension in his words, and I could see how Jesus guided his every move to buy us those precious minutes.

As Dave entered the Jordan Valley, the thick fog wrapping around his car like a shroud, he glanced in the rearview mirror and froze. Flashing red lights pierced the gray. A police car loomed behind him. Officers hung out of the windows, waving frantically for him to pull over. Dave shifted to the center of the road, blocking their path to keep them at bay.

A voice boomed over a loudspeaker, commanding him to stop, but he set his jaw and ignored it. The police shouted more orders, their voices crackling with urgency. Finally, Dave eased over, rolling to a halt and blocking the right lane, the car's tires grinding over loose stone. Six officers swarmed his vehicle, shouting in Arabic, their boots kicking up dust. Dave munched on a Snickers candy bar, its chocolate melting in his hand. "I'm a tourist on my way to the Dead Sea," Dave said in English. I couldn't help but smile at his cool-headed response, a testament to God's peace in the storm.

"No! No! No!" the commander screamed, his face red with frustration. "Passport! Passport!"

Dave repeated, "I'm a tourist, going to the Dead Sea." His voice remained steady despite the chaos.

The police kept yelling, "Passport! Passport!" their demands growing louder. Dave reached into his jacket and pulled out his passport as two more carloads of police screeched to a halt, boxing him in from behind and alongside. Now, more than two dozen officers surrounded him, their shouts a cacophony in the foggy valley.

The school bus driver arrived, peered through the window at Dave, and shook his head. He hadn't seen this man during the hijack. The police rummaged through Dave's rucksack, tossing out a Pepsi can with faded Arabic writing, a small glass jar of Jerash sand—a souvenir—and a pile of dirty clothes.

I held those very items in my hands at the reunion, tears streaming down my face as Dave handed them to me on the second day.

With warmth in his voice, he said, "I've kept these as mementos of your rescue. This Pepsi can and this jar of sand—they were with me that day. I think you should have them."

My voice cracked as I hugged him. "Dave, are you sure? You've kept these for thirty-seven years. Are you sure you want me to have them?"

He nodded, smiling. "Absolutely. I was saving them for you."

I reflected on that moment, wondering where I'd be if I'd ignored God's whisper to write my book, share my story, and start a podcast. Would I have ever met Dave, had this monumental conversation, or held these relics of my past—these tangible reminders of the miracle God had worked in my life? I've learned that your reward lies on the other side of obedience. You must take a step out in faith.

Dave kept this Pepsi can all those years—a small reminder of the day everything changed.

The police weren't done with Dave. "License! License!" one officer shouted, banging on the open window. Dave handed over his driver's license and the rental car agreement, registered in Abbadi's name, his hands steady despite the pressure. Traffic backed up behind them, drivers honking their horns in frustration, the sound echoing through the valley.

The officers argued among themselves, their voices rising as they tried to decide if his car matched the description they had just heard over the radio. The color and model were enough to raise suspicion, but there Dave sat, grinning, eating his candy bar like a carefree fool.

They ordered him out of the car, motioning for him to open the trunk. He complied, popping it open to reveal nothing but empty space. No trace of us. More than thirty-five minutes passed, each second a prayer answered, when Dave heard the police radio crackle. The word "Alia" was repeated several times—my mom's alias on the fake flight reservations.

Without warning, the officer threw Dave's papers back at him, and the police piled into their cars, racing toward Amman airport, where they *thought* Mom and I were boarding a plane. They'd found the reservations my mom had made as a decoy, and now they were shutting down the entire airport to hunt for us. This carefully laid misdirection would give us, hopefully, the window we needed to cross into Israel.

As Dave drove away, he spotted two Jordanian policemen hitchhiking down the road, their uniforms dusty from the valley's grit. "I figured having them in my car would help me get past roadblocks," he told me, "and I was right." Every time he approached a roadblock, soldiers would see the officers in the passenger and rear seats and wave him through without a second glance. He continued his drive, passing through half a dozen roadblocks, his heart pounding as he craned his neck at each tall antenna marking a police or army post, anxiously scanning for the red Nissan which would mean Don, JD, Mom, and I had been caught. He told me, "I was praying the whole time, 'God, keep them safe. Let them cross.'" In his role as our decoy, he risked his own life to save ours.

Meanwhile, as Dave navigated his escape, the rest of us were headed toward the Allenby Bridge, the tension thick in the car. My mom's arms tightened around me, her silent prayers a soft murmur against my ear: "God, protect us. Get us into Israel safely, and let no harm come our way. In Jesus's name, amen."

The car rumbled along as Don drove us toward the Jordanian-Israeli border, the sky darkening with heavy clouds. A thick fog descended as we wound through the valley, cloaking the landscape in gray, and no one spoke a word. We all understood the danger closing in and how close we were to freedom. The silence stretched, heavy with fear, until my mom looked up.

"What is that bright light in the distance?" She pointed through the front window, her finger trembling.

"There, beyond the mountains," Don responded, "is Israel." Its hills glowed as the sun broke through. The sun was shining over Israel.

My mom let out a sigh of relief as she said the code words. "The Son is Shining." It was a powerful reminder that God's light shines even amid our fear. He'd never left us.

God was with my mother in the motel room when she was fighting on her knees in prayer. God was with her in the courtroom. God was with me on the bus when JD saw me. And God was with them in the car through the streets of Jerash, pointing the way to my dad's home.

But God was not done yet. He was with us in the valley of Jordan amid the fog as we approached the border of Israel.

My mom slipped a blue coat over my shoulders—the one Aunt Joyce had bought. Its soft wool still carried her faint lavender scent. Mom whispered, "Aunt Joyce, Rick, Bev, and Miranda are all waiting to see you back home." The car grew quiet again, tension humming beneath the surface as we drove through the thick fog toward Israel, the windshield wipers squeaking rhythmically.

JD leaned forward, his voice low. "Cathy, hand me our clothes." He rolled down the window just enough and tossed our disguises, my green plaid school uniform included, to families living in tents along the roadside. Their children's eyes widened with curiosity as they ran to see what treasures we dropped. "We can't leave any trace. Not with the checkpoint ahead."

The drive from Jerash to the Allenby Bridge took about an hour and twenty minutes. It's the southernmost crossing over the Jordan River, one of five land borders between Israel and its eastern neighbors. We passed through two military checkpoints along the way, my heart pounding with each one, but the soldiers waved us through without hesitation, a quiet miracle.

The Allenby Bridge loomed ahead. Originally built during World War I as a simple wooden structure for British forces crossing from the East Bank to the West Bank, it had grown over the years into one of three major bridges spanning the river. Now, army bunkers and tall posts flanked it. Jordanian soldiers stood guard, their rifles crossed over their chests, barrels glinting in the dim light.

Don parked the car, and the engine hummed as we stepped out onto the damp ground. Abbadi approached, the one who'd secured our bridge passes. He greeted Don calmly, shaking his hand and assuring him, "Everything is in order."

Meeting Abbadi, Don handed him the rental car keys, saying, "Mr. Chatellier will be here shortly. He'll pay you and bring the other rental car." Abbadi nodded, shook Don's hand again, and carried our passports and passes into the old, run-down building. Its peeling paint and bullet-pocked walls were a stark reminder of past conflicts.

Steady and calm, Don turned to my mom and me, guiding us toward an old, worn-down bus. Its rusted sides creaked as we climbed aboard. JD took the front seat, his eyes alert, while Don instructed us to head to the back. My mom pulled me close, her scarf brushing my cheek, and whispered, "Stay quiet—everything will be okay." The bus was hot, and the air was thick with the smell of diesel. We sat on torn seats, our hair still covered, Mom's arms a shield around me. Time crawled as we waited for the bus driver and Abbadi to return with our passports.

Abbadi could hand our identities to the Jordanian soldiers at any moment, so all Mom could do was pray, trusting God to protect us and grant safe passage into Israel. Minutes stretched into what felt like hours, the tension mounting as we sat exposed, knowing the police could find us any second. Then Abbadi climbed aboard, handing our passports to the men with a calm, "Everything is fine."

Don pressed, "Where is the bus driver?"

Abbadi replied, "It's lunchtime; everything is okay. Don't worry."

JD urged Abbadi, "Get the driver. Let's go."

He and Don strategized quietly, plotting an escape if the border turned against us.

Diesel fumes hung in the air, shrouding the bus from prying eyes. Hard vinyl bit into my legs as the world outside passed like a dream I couldn't wake from. Every instinct said: *Be small, be silent*. My mother's arm locked around me, and I pressed my face into her chest, my body feeling hot. I stole quick glances: the men with my mom whose faces looked intense; soldiers at the checkpoint with rifles across chests. The engine idled as we sat on that bus—forever in my mind. "You're okay," my mother whispered, steady even when I wasn't. I matched my breathing to hers and didn't move, didn't speak, knowing the safest thing I could do was disappear into her arms and wait for the moment to pass.

The bus driver finally stepped on, his boots scuffing the floor, and pulled us out of the parking lot. The engine groaned as we passed shattered ruins and buildings destroyed in one of the Arab-Israeli wars, their crumbling concrete a silent witness to the conflict.

A two-story bunker loomed nearby, its heavy-caliber machine guns aimed at the Israeli side of the river, a chilling sight. JD's gaze locked on three soldiers, noticing their assault rifles lacked magazines. He caught Don's eye, tilting his head toward the bunker, signaling: "I'll jump off, overpower them, and take the bunker if needed."

The bus inched forward across the narrow bridge. A Jordanian soldier walked ahead, setting our pace agonizingly slow. We stopped mid-river, and Mom held me tighter, her heart pounding against my ear, a rhythm of hope and fear. The Jordanian driver stood and stepped off, and an Israeli man took the wheel while the Jordanian soldier swapped with an Israeli counterpart. The bus crept on, crossing the Jordan River at the soldier's deliberate stride.

As we crossed, Jordanian police waved frantically at the border, trying to stop the bus, but it was too late. Once over, they couldn't touch us.

When we passed the blue and white Israeli flags, their colors vibrant against the gray, Don and JD turned to Mom with smiles of relief. We had crossed into Israel. We had made it to safety!

The bus parked at the terminal, and its doors hissed open. Don and JD hugged Mom, their voices warm. "You can breathe now; we are safe."

Mom broke down, tears streaming as she kissed my face, looking into my eyes with a promise. "We are safe. It's okay; we are going home." It had been three months since Dad took me to Jordan—months when Mom feared she'd never see me again, but she pushed forward, trusting God to bring me back.

A group of women visiting the Holy Land noticed the commotion. JD explained, "She was kidnapped by her father; we just escaped into Israel to reunite her with her mom."

The women lifted their hands to the sky, singing, "Praise you, Jesus. We have come to the Holy Land, and we have seen a miracle. Hallelujah!"

Though *we* had reached safety, Dave lagged forty-five minutes behind due to his encounter with the Jordanian police. I learned later that, as we crossed, he pulled up to the Allenby Bridge, where Abbadi was waiting to take our rental car back. "Abbadi met me and asked what had taken me so long," Dave told me at the reunion, his tone light despite the memory.

I could picture the scene as he described it. Dave stepped out of his rental car with dust on his shoes, paid Abbadi for his help, and asked, "Can you get me out of Jordan? The bridge is too big a risk now." Abbadi nodded, calm as ever, and both men jumped into their rental cars—Dave's white Toyota and Abbadi's tan sedan—speeding away from the border as I crossed into Israel.

Halfway to Amman, Abbadi veered off the main road into a rundown village, its streets lined with crumbling mud-brick homes. Dave followed, his heart pounding, with no choice but to trust. "I kept my distance," Dave said, "watching as Abbadi parked and entered a dilapidated building." Moments later, Abbadi emerged, a live chicken tucked under his arm, its feathers ruffling in the breeze. Puzzled, Dave rolled down his window and asked, "What are you doing?"

Abbadi grinned. "This is the best place to buy chicken at the best price."

After securing the chicken, Abbadi led Dave back toward Amman, pulling up to his modest concrete house with a sagging roof.

Dave's frustration boiled over. "I have to get out of town as fast as possible."

Abbadi replied, "I need to grab something. It'll just take a minute." When he returned, he wore a Royal Jordanian Airlines jacket with a faded logo and carried a handful of credentials, IDs and badges galore.

"I'm a Royal Jordanian airline pilot," he told Dave, climbing in. "I fly 747s for the airline."

Dave hadn't known. Don forgot to mention Abbadi's military pilot role, but those credentials proved to be Dave's salvation, guiding them past blockades.

They hit checkpoints far from the airport, but Abbadi flashed his papers, and each time, soldiers waved them through. At Amman airport, chaos reigned. Police had locked it down, suspecting Mom and me on the grounds. They checked paperwork and rifled through luggage. Abbadi walked Dave past every checkpoint, leading him to the Royal Jordanian Airlines counter, where he knew the ticketing agent and the gate guard.

Dave asked, "Are there any flights going out today?"

The gate guard responded, "Yes, but only one."

Dave's pulse quickened. "Are there any seats?"

"One first-class seat."

"I'll take it."

She handed him a ticket, then called over the intercom to hold the flight. As Dave headed down the gangway, a police officer stopped him.

Realizing he hadn't paid the "airport tax," he pulled out 200 Jordanian dinars. "Will this cover it?"

The officer grinned. "Oh, yeah, absolutely." He rushed Dave to the plane. Dave boarded, unaware that he was on a nonstop flight to Paris.

In France, Dave handed over his passport to customs, but he had no luggage.

The officer frowned. "You don't have a visa."

"No, I'm not staying here. I'm going to America. My ticket is for the United States."

The officer shook his head. "No, your ticket is for Paris, France, and you don't have a visa. You must go back to Jordan."

"Wait, let's talk about this for a minute...."

American Airlines had just opened a Paris-to-New York route, and Dave suggested, "Call American Airlines and have someone bring me a ticket. I'll stay in the airport. I won't go anywhere."

"No, we can't do that. You must go back to Jordan."

After a lot of back and forth, an American Airlines representative arrived. They agreed to let Dave stay in a locker area with secured flight items, where he spent the night. The next morning, they put him on a plane to New York.

In a recent *Redeemed* podcast interview, Dave told me, "I knew it was an act of God back then. After reflecting, I see it now. God had a purpose for you. He used me as a simple tool to get you out of Jordan. The Lord led us through this entire rescue. You can see where He reached in, touched someone, and made it possible for you to escape—on His time schedule."

After returning home, JD called Mom to share some sobering news: Abbadi had been arrested and put in jail for helping us escape.

In the aftermath of my rescue, the fallout did not fall evenly.

Abbadi did not serve significant jail time. When questioned, he gave investigators the name of Frank Baker, the Assistant Regional Security Officer at the US Embassy in Amman. Baker was subsequently removed from his position while the State Department launched an internal investigation.

Investigators alleged that Baker had knowingly assisted—directly or indirectly—in the abduction of an American child and had illegally aided and abetted the efforts of American citizens attempting to violate host-government law. The accusation was severe and the consequences swift.

What *never* happened was just as telling.

Don and Dave both offered to submit sworn written statements, under penalty of perjury, affirming that Frank Baker had no knowledge of the true rescue mission in Jordan. They made it clear that Baker had never been informed of any plan to abduct a child and that any information he shared was given under false pretenses. The State Department never contacted them. There was no follow-up. No request for clarification. No interest in hearing their account.

Frank Baker agreed to take a polygraph examination regarding his knowledge of the abduction. One was never administered.

In the end, Baker returned to the Marine Corps without public exoneration, and Abbadi was released.

In an Israeli bus station, I curled into Mom like a backpack, my ear on her heartbeat. My Mom kept whispering, "Almost there."

I didn't understand words like *checkpoint* or *border*—I just knew we weren't in Jordan anymore and we were going home. Home was my bed with the pink pillow, the door that clicked, the house that knew my footsteps. We were going there. We'd done the unthinkable. Against the odds, we'd crossed a border—an invisible line I couldn't see or understand—and we slipped past a trap. We'd made it out of Jordan.

But rescue isn't resolution. The next chapter waited on US soil: healing from the trauma, learning to live life without my father, and figuring out how to live quietly when your name has been in the news. Each step felt uncharted and heavy with questions.

Still, I carried what I'd learned on that bridge and in that terminal. We were not alone. The same light that cut through the fog at Allenby would meet us back in Texas. We were heading home—and this was not the end of my story.

It was the beginning.

CHAPTER THIRTEEN

WELCOME HOME BABY GIRL

Seeing my mom again for the first time after the kidnapping was like stepping into a dream I wasn't sure I believed. I was caught between two worlds—shocked, disoriented, and unable to make sense of all that had happened. For the first three days, I only spoke Arabic. I kept waiting to wake up and find Mom gone again. The confusion and trauma of being taken—ripped from my mother, my home, my country—had buried the truth under layers of fear and manipulation. My father had filled my head with promises that she'd be coming soon, that everything was fine. But now, with her arms wrapped around me and her tears soaking into my hair, I didn't know what was real and what was imagined.

The miracle of our escape felt like a gift from God—but it was only the beginning. That embrace, as fierce as it was fragile, marked the end of one nightmare and the start of a new journey. A journey of healing, of rebuilding trust, of learning how to be a daughter again—not to the father who had stolen me, but to the mother who had never stopped fighting to bring me home.

I couldn't understand why my world had been shattered by the one person meant to protect me—my father. Wrapped in my mother's love, I couldn't yet see the long road stretching ahead. What followed wasn't a simple return to normalcy, but a winding path through pain, marked by questions that pressed heavy on my young heart:

Why me? How could he? But God took my hand through years of hurt, healing the wounds my earthly father left behind, and led me toward peace.

Our identity is deeply intertwined with family—their history, their names, and the legacies they carry. Since ancient times, we've been defined by who our parents are, by the roots of their families, and by the weight of our surname. It's a truth as old as the Bible itself: You are known by your name, by your bloodline. But for me, that foundation crumbled the day my father took me. The man I once called father transformed into a stranger who forever changed my life. I was left adrift, my sense of self fractured, and forced to question everything I thought I knew.

For three endless months, I had been torn away from my mother, and fear had wrapped itself around me like a shadow. I'd lie awake, wondering if I'd ever see her again. I felt like the disciples in Matthew 8:24–26, trapped in a boat as the storm raged, waves crashing over the sides while doubt screamed louder than the wind. Would God hear us? Could He still the chaos tearing through my life? But just as Jesus stood and rebuked the storm, silencing the tempest for His trembling followers, God answered prayers with my return, teaching me to trust Him even when the waves towered high.

We weren't home yet. Safety was just the first step. When we stepped off the bus at the terminal, the world felt strange, like waking from a dream I couldn't shake. The air carried the sharp tang of the sea, a whisper of freedom cutting through the haze. Emotions swirled around us. Don's shoulders relaxed, and his breath steadied as he saw the border behind us. We were safe—not home—but close enough for hope to bloom.

After that tear-streaked reunion, soldiers arranged a vehicle to carry us onward. As we drove through unfamiliar streets, I pressed my face to the window, watching the landscape shift—each mile a stitch pulling us closer to a new beginning. Soon, we reached a hotel by the beach, where the sound of waves hummed softly against the shore.

Israeli soldiers approached, their boots clicking sharply on the pavement, eyes narrowing as they studied us. "What's your purpose in Israel?" In a nation braced for threats, strangers were a risk.

Don stayed calm. "Call Colonel Digley," he said.

At the name, the soldiers' tension eased, their shoulders squared with recognition, and their tones softened with respect. Colonel Digley, a trusted figure in their ranks, was a key that unlocked their trust. They radioed him, and within moments, they returned. "We have transportation ready," one said. "It's been a long journey, but you're safe now." Those words landed like a lifeline, pulling us from the edge of chaos into a fragile calm.

Don and his team gathered for a debriefing to piece together the mission that had set us free. I wasn't there. My mom and I were resting, still shaky from the ordeal, but later, I heard about an unexpected visitor.

Louis Gossett Jr., the actor whose movie had served as the clever disguise for our rescue, had caught wind of the operation. He showed up at the hotel, his presence larger than life, and tracked down Don in the lobby. With a firm hand on Don's shoulder, he asked, "So, when were you going to tell me about the American mother and daughter you rescued using my movie as the cover story?"

Don fumbled for words, caught off guard. "Man, I'm sorry—I couldn't tell you. If it all fell apart, I didn't want you tangled up in it."

Mr. Gossett's face softened into a smile. "I get it. But can I meet them?"

Don's grin lit up the room. "Yes, sir. Of course, you can meet them."

That night, the film crew threw a dinner in our honor, and the energy in the room was electric. White linens draped the tables, candlelight danced across smiling faces, and the air hummed with laughter and the clinking of glasses raised in toast after toast to freedom, to bravery, to us. Mr. Gossett made his way to my mom first, pulling her into a hug that seemed to say more than words could.

Then he knelt in front of me with a single rose in his hand. "I'm so glad you're with your mom again," he said, his voice warm and steady as he handed me the flower and wrapped me in a hug. I held the rose tight, its soft petals brushing my fingers, a small piece of beauty after so much fear. The night unfolded into a celebration—music filled the space, and even the Israeli soldiers, usually so serious, kicked off their boots to dance with us. For a little while, I forgot the weight of everything and just felt alive.

Members of the rescue team with actor Louis Gossett Jr.,
whose film helped provide cover for the operation.

But the joy couldn't erase the toll it had all taken. My mom and I stayed in Israel for two nights at a hotel near the beach, the rhythmic crash of waves outside our window a soothing contrast to the chaos we'd left behind. The next day, we wandered down to the shore. The sand was warm under my feet, and the ocean stretched out wide and blue, like it could swallow our worries if we let it. We splashed in the waves, chasing each other and laughing, trying to outrun the shadows in our minds.

This was me on the beach in Israel just days after being rescued from Jordan.

Yet beneath the playfulness, my mom was unraveling. Her eyes were heavy with exhaustion, her spirit drained from months of strain. I wasn't much better. My thoughts jumbled and my words slipped between Arabic and English as I tried to make sense of it all. She didn't press me with questions. She just stayed close, her quiet presence telling me I was safe, loved, and that maybe, step-by-step, we'd find our way back to ourselves.

After three days in Israel, it was finally time for us to go back home to Texas. The airport buzzed with unfamiliar faces, and my mom couldn't shake the nagging fear that we were still being watched. Every hurried step, every sidelong glance from a stranger felt like a potential threat. We finally boarded the plane with Jim and JD at our side. My heart was still racing as the plane's engines roared to life, and as we took off, the shimmering blue of the Mediterranean Sea faded beneath us. For the first time in months, a weight begins to lift. We were leaving the danger, the tension, and the fear behind in Jordan and heading toward safety, toward home.

The flight to Dallas stretched on for hours, a haze of fatigue blurring my restless thoughts. I pressed my forehead against the cold window and watched the endless sea of clouds stretching out below like a dream I couldn't quite grasp. A mix of excitement and weariness churned within. My mom had promised that Aunt Joyce, Miranda, Bev, and Rick were waiting for us back home. Their familiar faces were a beacon pulling me forward.

I clung to Mom, my anchor in the storm, and she patted my back gently. "Lauren, everything will be okay," she whispered. "We're going home."

Her words wrapped around me like a blanket, and as I closed my eyes, safe in her arms, I still wasn't sure if I was dreaming. Nothing felt real yet—not the plane, not the escape, not even this fragile peace—but deep down, a quiet certainty took root: We were going to be alright.

When the plane finally touched down in Dallas, my stomach fluttered. The cabin filled with the rustle of passengers gathering their belongings, but I sat frozen for a moment, gathering the courage to step back into the world I'd left behind. As we disembarked and made our way up the entry ramp, my eyes darted through the crowd.

Then I saw Miranda, my blonde-haired best friend, barreling toward me with all the energy her four-year-old legs could muster. Her hair flew behind her like a golden banner, and before I could brace myself, she crashed into me, wrapping her tiny arms around my waist. She'd been staying with her parents at our townhouse the whole time I was gone, and though she was so young, her hug carried a heft of understanding that stole my breath. We held each other tightly, smiles breaking through the exhaustion, and together we walked toward the terminal where more familiar faces awaited.

Reunited with my best friend Miranda at Dallas–Fort Worth Airport—
a moment of comfort in the middle of so much unknown.

JD and Jim flanked us as we moved, their presence a steady comfort amid the commotion of the airport. They'd gotten us out of Jordan, but even here, in the supposed safety of Dallas, they remained vigilant. My father's family had roots in the area, and the possibility of retaliation kept them on edge. JD veered to the left and Jim to the right, searching for any hint of trouble.

I noticed Rick standing near Aunt Joyce and Bev, his own gaze sweeping the terminal. He didn't know JD or Jim, and their intense, no-nonsense demeanor clearly set him on edge. When JD's eyes locked with Rick's, the air crackled with unspoken tension, each man sizing up the other like soldiers on a battlefield.

That tension shattered when my mom stumbled forward, tears streaming down her face, and collapsed into Bev and Rick's arms. Her sobs echoed through the terminal, raw and unrestrained. JD and Jim realized Rick was one of us. The atmosphere shifted, the suspicion dissolving into relief.

Rick stepped toward them, a wry smile tugging at his lips. "Well, I'm guessing you two are safe," he said, his voice warm but cautious.

JD chuckled, breaking the last of the strain. "Yeah, but I wasn't too sure about you."

Rick grinned. "Man, I was thinking the same thing about you two!"

Then Aunt Joyce was there, a massive teddy bear tucked under her arm. The moment she saw me, she let it fall to the floor with a soft thud and pulled me into the biggest hug I'd ever felt. Her familiar scent, lavender and the smell of our home wrapped around me, and I melted into her embrace. Rick and Bev joined in, lifting me off the ground as their arms encircled me. We stood there, a messy tangle of limbs and tears, the joy of being together again mingling with the lingering shadows of what I'd escaped. Relief washed over me in waves, but beneath it, a quiet fear still pulsed. Would this safety last?

After we untangled ourselves, Aunt Joyce wiped her eyes and smiled. "I have a surprise waiting for you at the house," she said, her voice bright with promise. That spark of excitement pulled me forward, a reminder that life could still hold good things, even after everything.

We piled into Rick's surveillance van, its worn seats and faint hum a strange comfort after the sleek sterility of the plane. As we drove toward the townhouse, JD and Jim filled Rick in on pieces of the mission. Their voices stayed low, but I caught fragments—close calls, daring moves, the sheer audacity it took to get us out.

At one point, JD glanced at Rick. "When I got off that plane and locked eyes with you, I knew you weren't just some ordinary cowboy."

Rick's laugh filled the van, a sound laced with both relief and respect. "Well, that is a high honor coming from the man that just saved my best friend's daughter."

But beneath the growing camaraderie, a sobering truth lingered. My father's family was still out there, and their reach might extend even to Dallas. Rick, ever the protector, handed JD and Jim a pair of weapons, his expression serious. "Just in case," he said quietly. They nodded, his words settling over us all. They knew the next step was to confront that threat head-on, to ensure my father and his family would never come for me again.

After we landed in Dallas, the whirlwind didn't stop. JD, Rick, and Jim wasted no time getting us back safely to the townhouse before driving straight to my uncle Amir's house, determined to draw a line in the sand. I wasn't there, but I heard later how Rick stared Amir down, his voice low and steady. "If one hair on Lauren's head is harmed, or if anything happens to her, some very bad things are going to start happening in your world."

Amir flinched, his face paling as he stammered that he was glad I was back with my mom. He swore that my father meant me no harm, but he admitted that my father had messed up big time by taking me to Jordan.

Back at Aunt Joyce's, life took on a surreal glow. She loved Christmas more than anything, and while I'd been stuck in Jordan where the holiday didn't even register, she'd kept every tree twinkling, every decoration in place, waiting for me to come home. I'd missed the holiday entirely, lost in a haze of fear and survival, but on January 31, we made up for it

The living room sparkled with lights, the air thick with pine and cinnamon, and I tore into gifts my mom had picked out weeks before the rescue, as if she'd known I'd be back. Aunt Joyce had wrapped them in Washington, DC, while she and Mom clung to hope, waiting for news. That day, Miranda and I sprawled on the floor, giggling over my new toys—dolls, games, little treasures that felt like a bridge to normalcy.

I was happy, lighter than I'd been in months, but I recognize even now that a part of me still floated outside myself, unsure how to land. Mom sat nearby, recounting our escape to Rick, Bev, and Aunt Joyce, her voice a mix of triumph and exhaustion. I didn't grasp how long I'd been gone or how close we'd come to losing everything, but the love in the room wrapped around me like a shield.

The world outside wasn't so gentle.

News of our rescue exploded, rippling across the country faster than I could process it. Reporters hounded my mom's family in Florida, digging for photos and details about the kidnapping. Uncle Dan called from New York, warning us that journalists were calling everyone we knew, hungry for a piece of me and the story. Soon, they were camped outside our townhouse in Richardson, their cameras flashing. Headlines screamed from *The New York Times* and *The Paris Review*: "Rambo Mom Rescues Daughter." I'd catch glimpses of the reporters through the curtains, my stomach twisting. Home was supposed to feel safe, but this felt like another kind of siege.

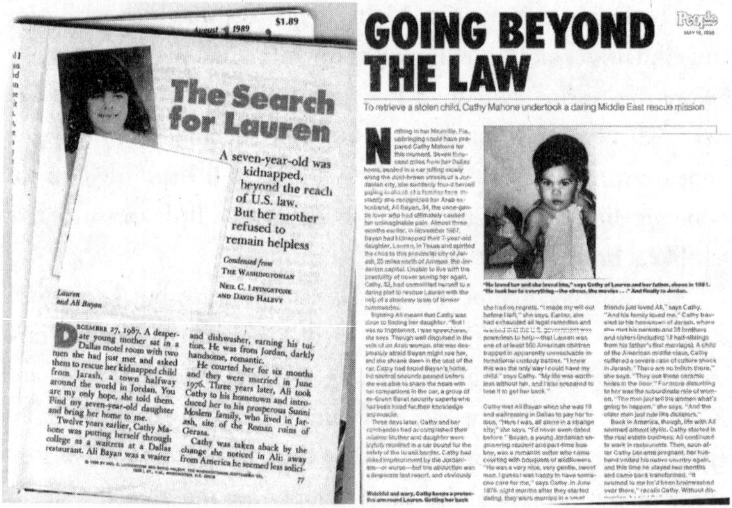

August 1989 $1.89

The Search for Lauren

A seven-year-old was kidnapped, beyond the reach of U.S. law. But her mother refused to remain helpless

Condensed from THE WASHINGTONIAN

NEIL C. LIVINGSTONE AND DAVID HALEVY

Lauren and Ali Bayan

DECEMBER 27, 1987. A desperate young mother sat in a Dallas motel room with two men she had just met and asked them to rescue her kidnapped child from Jarash, a town halfway around the world in Jordan. You are my only hope, she told them. Find my seven-year-old daughter and bring her home to me.

Twelve years earlier, Cathy Mahone was putting herself through college as a waitress at a Dallas restaurant. Ali Bayan was a waiter and dishwasher, earning his tuition. He was from Jordan, darkly handsome, romantic.

He courted her for six months and they were married in June 1976. Three years later, Ali took Cathy to his hometown and introduced her to his prosperous Sunni Moslem family, who lived in Jarash, site of the Roman ruins of Gerasa.

Cathy was taken aback by the change she noticed in Ali: away from America he seemed less solici-

77

GOING BEYOND THE LAW

People

To retrieve a stolen child, Cathy Mahone undertook a daring Middle East rescue mission

My story made national headlines after I was brought home from Jordan... but the real story was only beginning.

And safe wasn't a word my mom could lean on yet. She was a live wire, jumpy at every phone ring, every loud noise from the TV. My uncle Amir lived too close, and the shadow of my father still loomed large. What if he tried to take me again? I'd sometimes see her eyes dart to the windows, her hands clenching, and it made my own chest tighten.

Rick sensed it too. One day, he called her up. "Cathy, I need to teach you to shoot. Come out to my place. I've got a range."

So we headed to Van Alstyne, to Rick and Bev's house, where the air smelled of grass and gunpowder. Rick was in his element, hauling out pistols, shotguns, and AR-15s like a kid showing off his toys. Upstairs, Mom was pulling on tactical pants and camouflage, yelling down to Bev, "Do you have a banana clip?"

Rick's voice boomed from his gun room, brimming with excitement. "Do I have a banana clip? Yes, I've got at least twenty-five banana clips!"

Bev laughed, cutting through the chaos. "Rick, she needs one for her hair, not her gun!"

I couldn't help but giggle, seeing Rick's crestfallen face. For a moment, the tension broke, and I felt a spark of lightness—like maybe we could laugh our way through this after all.

But that lightness shattered a few weeks later. A sharp knock rattled our door, and my heart leapt into my throat. Mom grabbed the .357 Magnum Rick had given her. With hands trembling, she edged toward the entrance. I froze, the room tilting around me.

Every sound, every shadow felt like danger creeping back in. She flung the door open, gun raised, and there stood Amir with another man beside him. "Why are you here, and who is that?" she demanded, her voice steel wrapped in fear.

My uncle stepped back, hands up. "Cathy, this is my uncle. He just had surgery and came from Jordan."

The man shifted, revealing a hard plastic brace around his chest and waist.

Mom wasn't buying it. "Remove the brace," she ordered, her eyes sharp, searching for a hidden threat.

He did, proving it was just medical gear. No weapons.

Amir's voice softened. "We just want to make sure Lauren's okay. Ali made a mistake. The family's sorry."

I stood behind her, my breath shallow, torn between wanting to believe him and the icy dread that wouldn't let go.

Mom didn't waver. "Leave now, or I call the police." They backed off, and the door slammed shut.

Mom's voice trembled as she called Rick, the phone pressed tight to her ear. We scrambled to stuff clothes into bags. The townhouse, once my haven, now felt like a trap closing in. That night, we sped to the Lamberts' house. I can still remember the sound of tires humming against the road as darkness swallowed the streets behind us.

Rick didn't sugarcoat it. "It's not safe there anymore. You need to move."

I watched Mom's shoulders sag, the weight of the past three months crashing down on her. The rescue had cost $80,000, every penny scraped together while she fought to find me, and now she faced starting over.

I was wrestling with my own storm. I'd found relief being back with familiar things: my friends, my language, a bathroom I knew, and food that tasted like home. But beneath it, confusion and hurt churned, a gnawing ache that safety could still slip away. As Mom steeled herself to return to work, to rebuild a life for us, I struggled to piece together what had happened. The world wasn't the innocent place I'd once believed it to be, and my father, once my protector, had become someone I could no longer trust.

When we returned to Richardson, survival pressed down hard. I carried a storm of emotions I didn't yet know how to name—deep love for my mother, sharp hurt and anger toward my father, and questions that had no safe place to land. Would I ever see him again? Did I want to? And if I did, could I ever trust him again?

My mom had nothing left but a handful of gold coins and a small box of jewelry that rattled when she shook it. She sold every piece, her fingers trembling as she handed them over, to scrape together a deposit for a new apartment in a different neighborhood. It wasn't much, but it was ours. Our chance to disappear. Our chance to rebuild.

Beverly, with her experience as a private investigator and a knack for finding missing people, was more than eager to help us. "If my job is to track people down," she told my mom with a steady gaze, "then I know I can hide you and Lauren." She dove into action, guiding us through the maze of concealing our identities—new names, new stories, a fresh start. My mom was a little fearful to get me back into school, but she was also convinced that a normal routine was what I needed to move forward. I wanted that too—classrooms, crayons, the buzz of a life I used to know. But normal felt like a far-off dream. Honestly, I was so afraid to leave my mom again.

My mom went to the new school to register me, but her nerves got the better of her, and she scribbled my real name on the forms, forgetting the fake one Bev had crafted. For three months, we settled into the apartment. I'd started to breathe easier, tracing the familiar shape of a desk, the chatter of kids at recess. But the media found us out through the school records, their relentless hunt shattering our fragile peace. We packed again, boxing up everything we owned and moving into another apartment.

One day, while I spent time with my Aunt Joyce, my mom was at our new apartment unpacking and getting things organized. My mom heard a strange clatter from the roof—a sharp, scraping sound that made her stomach drop. She grabbed the gun Rick had given her and dialed him in a hushed panic.

Minutes later, Rick burst through the front door, his boots pounding as he swept through the rooms, clearing each one like a soldier on a mission. When he kicked open the bathroom door, there was Mom, perched on the toilet, gun still clutched tight. "Cathy, what are you doing? I told you to hide!"

She shrugged, sheepish. "Well, I had to go to the bathroom."

Later, Rick climbed up to check the roof and found the culprits—not my father's family, but reporters, their cameras clicking trying to get photos of us.

The rescue had brought me home, but it couldn't erase the scars. I'd come back from Jordan a tangle of fear and confusion, wrestling with questions too big for my seven-year-old mind to answer. Why had this happened? Why me? And my father had torn that trust apart when he took me. He'd lied, not with small fibs but with a betrayal so deep it shattered the ground beneath me. I'd always thought parents were good—a safety net I could fall into. Now, that net was gone, replaced by a gnawing ache. How could a father cause so much pain?

What I couldn't see then was the journey waiting ahead. God was already weaving a path for me, one where I'd come to know the love of my heavenly Father, a love that wouldn't break. But first, I'd have to stumble through the dark, wrestling with Him, with the hurt, and with lessons that would shape me in ways I couldn't yet imagine.

CHAPTER FOURTEEN

NEW IDENTITY

When we first returned from Jordan, nighttime was my enemy. I couldn't bear the thought of sleeping alone, haunted by the echoes of my time away. At eight years old, I'd crawl into my mother's bed, clinging to her as if she might vanish too. She turned those restless hours into moments of healing, using bedtime as a sanctuary for us both. We'd kneel together, reciting prayers that felt like a shield against my fears, and then we'd lie side by side, talking about anything—my cats, her day, or sometimes the harder things, like Jordan.

One night, as we chatted, her voice softened. "Did you ever go to the mosque while you were there?" She explained what it was, who Allah was, her tone gentle and curious.

A wave of guilt crashed over me. "No, Mom, I didn't pray to Allah," I said quickly, my heart racing. But the lie gnawed at me, and as she pressed my unease, I broke. "I lied," I sobbed. "I did go. I prayed on the rug like Daddy showed me, but I thought it was to Jesus, just different." Tears streamed down my face. Fear that God would turn away twisted inside me.

She pulled me close. "Lauren, God knows your heart. He sees your love, and He forgives you." As she prayed over me, her words wove peace into my trembling soul, and I drifted to sleep, lighter than I'd felt in months. Those nights didn't erase my fears, but they built a bridge between us, a foundation of trust that held me steady.

I slept with her until I was eleven.

Those bedside moments were precious, but my mother knew healing required more than whispered reassurances. The previous six months had drained us emotionally, financially, and physically. And our ordeal lingered as we struggled to keep afloat. One evening, as I traced patterns on her quilt, she said, "I think it's time we go to Grandma's."

She'd reached out to my grandmother in Niceville, Florida, where she'd grown up, craving the support of family to help us rebuild. Money was tight after so many moves, and the idea of being surrounded by loved ones felt like a lifeline. So, we packed our lives into boxes once more, loaded the car, and drove twelve hours down I-10 through Louisiana to the beautiful beaches of Florida. I didn't mind the cramped ride; the promise of my grandmother's embrace and my cousins' laughter fueled my excitement. We were chasing stability, a chance to stitch our lives back together with the thread of family.

Stepping into my grandmother's gray and white house was like entering a different world. The air carried the sweet scent of her baking brown sugar nut cookies that I'd devour by the dozen, and the front yard bloomed with elephant ears towering over me, a jungle of green welcoming us home. Our bedroom was cozy, just a queen bed and stacks of moving boxes for our clothes, but it felt right.

Life settled into a rhythm that soothed my jagged edges. Mornings began with Grandma's eggs sizzling, bacon crisping, and grits steaming on the stove. I'd perch on a stool, helping her stir collards or flip pork chops, her hands guiding mine with quiet patience. Afternoons melted into lazy hours of *Murder, She Wrote* and

The Andy Griffith Show, the TV's drone blending with the click of her sewing needle as she pieced together quilts. She made one for each of us kids, bold patchwork squares that wrapped me in warmth, and I'd mimic her, crafting tiny versions for my dolls. With my uncle, aunts, and cousins nearby, the house buzzed with life. For the first time since Jordan, safety wasn't just a word; it was the creak of the porch swing, the chatter at the dinner table, the feeling that I belonged. These simple joys were the glue binding my broken pieces, proof that happiness could grow again.

As we settled into this new adventure, my mother kept an eye on the shadows of our past. She worried that my father or his family might track us down, unraveling the peace we'd found. About a year after our return, sometime after we'd settled in Niceville, she decided to officially change our last names to have a new identity. "We're changing our last name to Elliott," she told me, a nod to her favorite uncle, James Elliott, a man whose name carried kindness and strength. Back then, it was simple: a notice in the local paper, a few signatures, and it was done. I never realized it was that easy to change a last name. Was it really that easy to erase my past? The only thing left of my father had been his name, and now that was gone too.

When I saw "Lauren Elliott" inked on the forms, my chest tightened, a flicker of loss for the name I'd known, but there was a rush of relief too. It was a shield, a way to slip into this new life without looking back. "This means we're safe," Mom said, her smile steady. "A fresh start."

I turned the name over in my mind, testing its weight. It felt like stepping out of a worn-out skin into something new—something mine. With that change, the world opened: I enrolled in my third new school, my backpack emblazoned with my new identity, and Mom started a job, her confidence blooming alongside mine.

Each "Elliott" we wrote was a brick in the foundation of our rebuilt lives. It was also another way that I could separate myself from the person that caused me so much pain—my father.

My first day of school was a whirlwind of nerves and possibility as I stepped into Rocky Bayou Christian School, a small, quiet place where my mother hoped I could find safety and a semblance of normalcy. She had met with the principal and my teacher, her voice steady as she explained our past, instructing them to call her immediately if anyone came looking for me.

I gripped my backpack, "Lauren Elliott" stitched neatly across it, and stepped through the gates. Kids chattered around me, oblivious to the journey that had brought me here, and for once, I was just another student and not the girl who'd been kidnapped, not a survivor, just Lauren. After school, Mom waved from the car in the pick-up line, her eyes bright with pride. She'd landed a job, a small victory that mirrored my own. We were finding our footing, piece by piece.

As I walked those unfamiliar halls, I felt the stirrings of hope. The road from Jordan to Niceville, Florida had been long and paved with fear, but here we were standing taller, breathing easier. My mother's love, my family's warmth, and a new name had carried us through. The scars of my past hadn't vanished, and healing was still a quiet, ongoing work, but for the first time, I believed we could truly start over. Together, we'd gathered the fragments of our shattered lives and begun to build something new.

The name change was meant to protect me, but it also left me wondering who I really was. Was I Lauren Elliott now, or was I still the girl I'd been before everything fell apart? That first year, I struggled to catch up, having missed nearly a full year of school while in Jordan. My teachers, aware of my situation, arranged extra tutoring, their kindness invaluable as I tried to reclaim what I'd lost.

School became a proving ground, but peace was fleeting. One day, a lady entered my classroom, whispered to my teacher, and escorted me to the principal's office. My stomach twisted as I saw the principal's tight smile.

"Everything's going to be okay," she said, her words hollow against the worry in her eyes. "Your mom's on her way."

Sitting there, my heart raced not just from the fear that my father might have found me, but from the sinking realization that my new name couldn't shield me from the past. Memories of Jordan crashed in—the mosque's echoing calls, the unfamiliar prayer rug, the confusion of a life I hadn't chosen. When my mother arrived, she whisked me home, explaining that the police had spotted someone resembling my father entering the United States.

Panic overwhelmed me. Would he come for me again? Why couldn't I just be a normal kid, free from this shadow?

Hours later, relief came with a phone call. It was a false alarm; the fingerprints didn't match. My mother held me close, her arms a fortress against my fears. "He'd be arrested if he tried," she assured me, her voice calm yet firm. "God brought us back together, and the school did the right thing." But the incident had torn open old wounds, leaving me shaken.

My father believed we were living in Dallas—the last place his brother, my uncle, had seen us before we disappeared. After our return from Jordan, my mother made it clear to my uncle that if my father ever wanted to write to me, he could do so through letters sent to a PO Box in Florida. It was a carefully calculated decision, one meant to protect us and keep our true location a secret.

To deepen the deception, the letters and photographs from my father were forwarded to my grandmother's house. It was safer that way—neutral ground. Every envelope that arrived felt like a landmine. He had no idea we were no longer in Dallas. As far as he knew, we were still there, living a life just out of his reach.

But I wasn't at peace. Each letter ignited something inside me—a surge of emotion I couldn't name. My heart would pound with every delivery, torn between longing and fear, between wanting to hear from him and wishing he would stop. A storm of curiosity and fear churned inside me. Part of me ached to rip it open, to glimpse the unfamiliar faces in the pictures and absorb his words, while another part begged to bury it all, to erase him and pretend none of this had ever happened. Yet, with every letter, I was pulled back into an emotional chaos I couldn't outrun. "I took you because I love you," he'd write, but those words didn't soothe. They stung like salt rubbed into a raw wound, leaving me more confused than comforted.

I began to question what love was supposed to be. His version seemed built on broken trust, lies, selfishness, and harm. Even through his letters, he couldn't acknowledge his mistakes, refusing to own the pain he'd caused. At ages eight, ten, and even fourteen, I held onto a fragile hope: If he would just say the right thing, if he could answer the questions that haunted me, maybe this deep ache would heal, and I'd finally feel free.

It took years to see the truth. My earthly father didn't hold the answers I craved.

That false alarm at the airport lingered like a storm cloud, a reminder that normalcy was a fragile illusion. I longed for a father I could trust, for a family like the ones my classmates had. As I wrestled with faith and forgiveness, my mother became my rock. She'd been fighting to rebuild our lives since the rescue, moving us five times in two years, each relocation a fresh start stitched with hope. She took a job at Cellular One selling cell phones—those bulky gray bricks with car antennas—and her charisma shone. Within a year, she was a top salesperson, saving enough to rent our own townhouse just twenty minutes from my grandmother's. It was small, but it was ours—a testament to her grit and love.

As we settled into our new home, life began to take on a comforting rhythm. I attended Rocky Bayou Christian School, slowly closing the gap with my studies. We found St. Andrews Church in Destin, Florida, where my mother joined the choir. I'd sit in the auditorium and listen to her voice rising with the worship songs, wrapping me in peace. Church became our refuge, a place where the past felt distant.

In Florida, surrounded by family and the familiarity of my grandmother's house, I started to feel like Lauren Elliott. The name, once foreign, began to fit like a jacket I was growing into. Singing hymns beside my mother, I glimpsed a belonging that went beyond names, rooted in faith and the steady love we shared.

Our days grew sweeter with routine. Saturday mornings meant cartoons, followed by housecleaning with my mother, music blaring as we scrubbed and laughed. Then came the fun—strolling through the mall with no intent to buy, just soaking in the bustle, ending with a warm cookie from the American Cookie Company. I usually ended up with icing smeared on my fingers. We'd hit the Tom Thumb gas station with reusable cups, snagging fifty-cent sodas or ice cream, and shop at Walmart or Ross for bargains. At home, we cooked simple meals, though sometimes we'd sneak Kentucky Fried Chicken into the movies, giggling as the scent wafted through the theater and heads turned to find the culprits. These moments, small as they were, wove a tapestry of joy, teaching me that happiness didn't need extravagance, just us.

Through every challenge, my mother stood tall. A single mom post-divorce, she was a resilient force, hardworking and endlessly resourceful. She showed me how to stretch a dollar, but more than that, she showed me how to thrive after loss. Watching her, I began to see my own identity taking shape, not just in my new name or the echoes of my past, but in the strength she'd passed down to me. The false alarm had rattled me, but it also highlighted how far we'd come. I wasn't just "the kidnapped girl" anymore; I was Lauren Elliott, survivor, daughter, believer. My story bore scars, but it also carried healing, faith, and the quiet power of starting anew. With my mother by my side, I could face whatever came next. My sense of self grew stronger with each step.

Our church, St. Andrews, was more than a place of worship. It was a second home where bonds grew strong and lasting. One of those bonds was with Miss Linda, a choir member whose warm voice matched her welcoming spirit. She and my mom hit it off instantly, their friendship blooming over movie nights filled with *Anne of Green Gables*, the scent of sizzling pizza, or the comfort of a lasagna fresh from the oven. Those evenings wrapped us in a sense of belonging, a rare and precious gift.

Then came the day Miss Linda announced she'd been accepted into Christ for the Nations, a Bible college in Dallas, Texas. Her excitement was contagious, and for my mom, it lit a spark of possibility. After four restorative years in Florida, she felt the tug of Texas calling her back. It wasn't just nostalgia for old friends driving her; her job was unraveling. The company she worked for was shifting ownership, and with it, her income was set to plunge by half. The uncertainty gnawed, pushing her to search for a new beginning. Miss Linda's move felt like a bridge back to a place we'd once called home.

After nights spent in prayer, wrestling with doubt and hope, my mom found her answer. A new job with a cell phone company in Dallas emerged, promising stability, and she secured an affordable apartment just ten minutes from where Miss Linda would be studying. It was as if the stars aligned, urging us westward. Florida had been our sanctuary, a healing ground after years of turmoil. For me, Rocky Bayou Christian School had been a divine help, easing me back into learning, while living with my grandmother and chasing my cousins through sunny afternoons had restored my childhood. Those days of laughter and love were a balm allowing me to be a kid again—free, unburdened, and safe.

For my mom, Florida was a season of renewal. With family nearby, she rebuilt her strength, saving every dollar to reclaim our independence. But by the time I turned eleven, change loomed once more. We boxed up our lives, stacking memories into a U-Haul truck, and pointed it down I-10 toward Texas.

I watched the familiar fade in the rearview mirror, a knot tightening in my chest. Moving wasn't new to me. I'd grown used to the rhythm of packing and leaving. Yet each time, it chipped away at my sense of security. Just as I'd start to feel settled to build friendships that felt like roots, we'd uproot again. I clung to my worn stuffed animal, its faded fur a quiet constant in a world that wouldn't stay still. Would I ever find a place to belong? A home that didn't slip through my fingers?

The road stretched long and quiet as we crossed the bridge in Mobile, Alabama. My mom's hands gripped the wheel, her thoughts spilling out in a whisper: "Am I making the right choice? Can I do this alone?" Then, as if the sky itself heard her, she looked up and gasped. A double rainbow stretched across the horizon, its colors bold against the gray. It was God's promise, vivid and alive: *I am with you always.* Tears shimmered in her eyes as peace settled over her, a quiet strength I could feel from the passenger seat.

In moments like that, she'd quote Scripture, her voice soft but sure. "For I know the plans I have for you," declares the Lord, "plans to prosper you and not to harm you, plans to give you hope and a future." (Jeremiah 29:11 NIV) *Those* words were more than a verse; they were our refuge. They reminded me that my identity wasn't tied to a zip code or a house, but to a foundation that couldn't be shaken. No matter how many times we moved, that truth held me steady, a rock beneath the shifting sands of my life.

As the rainbow faded behind us, my mom reached for my hand, her smile bright with resolve. "We're going to be okay, sweetheart," she said, her voice firm. "Texas is our new beginning." I nodded, wanting to trust her, to believe the road ahead held promise. But a question lingered in my mind, tugging at my heart: Would Dallas be the haven we needed, or would the echoes of our past find us there?

The highway rolled on, carrying us toward an answer I couldn't yet see, a story waiting to unfold.

CHAPTER FIFTEEN

WOUNDS OF A FATHER

"Father wounds" are a quiet ache that many of us carry, though they manifest differently for each person. Some bear the scars of physical abuse, others the sting of emotional neglect—words unspoken, love withheld, or trust shattered. These wounds burrow deep, shaping how we see ourselves and the world.

Emotional wounds from a father can take countless forms. For some, it's the silence of a father who never said, "I love you." For others, it's the rejection of being unwanted or the ache of navigating life between divorced parents' homes, weekends spent with a father who has a new family where you don't quite belong. It might be a father who wounded with harsh words, battled addiction, or betrayed your mother through infidelity. The list is long, and the pain is personal.

In my case, the wounds were carved by a father who took me to Jordan, immersing himself in a world that, to me, felt foreign and frightening. He left me with relatives I barely knew, scared and confused, while he became a stranger lost in his faith. The trust he broke, the childhood he stole, and the "father"—the security of one who is supposed to protect you at all costs—he took from me left scars that ran soul deep. I mourned the loss of our bond, even as he lived on, because the father I knew was gone. Healing felt impossible until I learned that only my heavenly Father could fill the void and mend what was broken.

In Priscilla Shirer's Bible study titled *Elijah: Faith and Fire*, she likens this process to winemaking: Grapes are gathered, pressed, and fermented. During purification, the wine is poured from one vessel to another, unsettling it to remove impurities. Each relocation refines it, preparing it for its purpose. Moving to Texas felt like being poured into a new vessel—uncomfortable, uncertain, but necessary for growth. God was about to shake up my world, and with it, my relationship with my mom would change in ways I couldn't yet see.

Back in the Dallas area, we were ready for the next adventure. We settled into Mount Vernon Apartments in DeSoto, Texas, and I enrolled at Trinity Christian School in Cedar Hill, a twenty-minute drive from home. My mom started her new job with a cellular company, but within a month, reality hit hard. Sales were down and her income wouldn't cover our bills. Doubt crept in, and fear stirred. Had she been reckless, moving us away from family, forcing us to start over? But she knew better than to let fear win. She prayed, asking God to calm her heart and guide her steps.

Her resilience was a lesson in itself. She didn't have all the answers, but she had faith and that was enough. As I watched her navigate uncertainty with grace, I began to understand that healing from my father wounds wasn't just about forgetting the past. It was about building a future rooted in trust—trust in my mom, in God, and in the strength He was growing within me.

The next week, my mom walked into the leasing office of our new apartment complex, her heels clicking with purpose on the tile floor. She was on a mission to find a job as a leasing agent, a role she'd mastered years before and one that promised the comfort of working just steps from our front door. She handed over her resume with a hopeful smile to the beautiful blonde leasing agent sitting behind the front desk.

Within days, Suzanna, the apartment manager with a warm voice and a clipboard always in hand, called her for an interview. My mom got the job on the spot. The very next day, she quit her job at the cellular company, and by the following week, she was settling into her new desk at the apartments. This job was a true miracle. Free rent lightened our financial load, and her flexible hours meant she could shuttle me to and from school. Once again, her laughter filled the car as we sang off-key to the radio.

While my mom carved out a fresh start, I was thrust into my own upheaval, once again the new kid in a sea of strangers. That first day, I stepped into the classroom, the air filled with the scent of pencil shavings. Unfamiliar eyes sized me up. My stomach twisted as I scanned for an empty seat, while the chatter pulsed of judgment, or so it felt.

I was furious with my dad for uprooting my world and angry at God for letting it all unravel. At night, I'd collapse into bed, the mattress creaking under my weight, and let out deep, wrenching sobs that shook my whole body. "Why, God?" I'd whisper into the dark. "Why does my life have to be this hard?"

Part of me ached to call my dad, to demand answers to the questions clawing at my mind. *Why did you leave? Do you miss me?* By then, it had been four years since I'd seen him or my siblings. Did they even know why I'd vanished from their lives?

That loss cut deeper than I could name. It was not just my father; my stepmother and siblings, too, had been erased from my world like a chalkboard wiped clean. I'd lie awake, picturing a day when we'd all sit around a table again, laughing like nothing had happened. But then fear would slink in, tightening my chest. Could I even trust the man who'd shattered me?

We continued to live in shadows, guarding our address like a secret code. Letters from Dad still arrived via my grandmother's post office box, each envelope a tiny grenade. I'd hold them, hands trembling, torn between ripping them open to see photos of my family and shoving them under my bed where the pain couldn't touch me. The move to Texas hadn't just changed my scenery; it had cracked open a vault of grief I didn't know how to close.

Yet, amid the hurt, I'd dream of a different future. What if Mom remarried? I could have a dad again, maybe even siblings to bicker and bond with. Then Mom wouldn't have to do everything alone. But then I'd think of our quiet nights, just the two of us, sharing cocoa and secrets, and wonder how a stranger would fit into that sacred space. I scribbled these hopes in my journal, the pen scratching against the page as I prayed. "God, heal my heart. Lift this sadness and mend my family." Even when my faith faltered, those words tethered me to something bigger.

School became my proving ground, a place where I could shine or stumble. I'd mastered the art of making friends, a skill honed from too many fresh starts. I'd flash a grin, crack a joke, and soon I'd have a crew like a military kid, fearless and fast to connect. But while friendships clicked, schoolwork didn't. Math and spelling were my kryptonite. I'd sit in class, heart hammering, slumping low in my chair as the teacher's chalk squeaked across the board.

Once, she called me up to solve a problem. My legs wobbled, the numbers blurred, and I stood there, mute, as snickers rippled behind me. After school, I'd trudge to tutoring, and at home, Mom would sit down with me at the kitchen table, her voice steady as we tackled homework. Tears would fall. Mine from frustration, hers from a quiet ache I didn't yet understand, but she refused to let me fail.

Mom first blamed my struggles on the chaos of our past—missed school in Jordan and the shaky year after we returned. But as we pored over worksheets, she saw something more. She booked an appointment at Scottish Rite for Children, a hospital in Dallas.

After tests that felt like puzzles I couldn't solve, I got my answer: dyslexia and dyscalculia. In the early nineties, those labels were mysteries to most and to me; they screamed "dumb." Another hurdle in a life already stacked with them. But my mom stood firm, meeting with teachers and counselors, her voice unwavering as she fought for the tools I needed. The move to Texas hadn't just tested my heart; it revealed a mind that was wired differently, and she was determined to help me conquer it.

Life felt like a gauntlet: hiding from my past, bouncing between homes, losing friends as fast as I made them, and now wrestling with a learning disability. I'd slump at the kitchen table, head in my hands, sobbing over fractions and spelling lists. Why was everything so hard? Why did I lug this rage at my dad around like a backpack full of bricks? The pressure would build until it burst, tears soaking my notebook. I craved "normal," a word that mocked me. Now, as an adult, I see we all carry scars beneath the surface, but back then, staring down middle school, I felt like the only kid with a fractured family and a brain that betrayed me.

Our story wasn't invisible, though. It had splashed across headlines. *People*, *Reader's Digest*, and *The New York Times* ran articles of my kidnapping and rescue. Mom had stayed silent then, but after Texas, she chose to speak, starting with *Good Morning America*. Letters poured in, desperate pleas from parents in her shoes. She knew God could weave our pain into purpose, but sharing meant baring our souls. Was she ready to relive it? Was I? The move had settled us physically, but emotionally, the ground still shifted beneath my feet.

Now twelve, through it all, I learned hiding my hurt only fed it. God wanted it laid bare, to heal what I couldn't. One night, as Mom and I talked over the hum of crickets outside, I spilled it all: no normal childhood, no dad, and a last name that was not really mine. She handed me my journal, urging me to write. Years later, and like mom's journals brought me clarity, my own journals, reread again as an adult, reminded me of that time where I wrote prayers like this one: "God, I'm lonely, and Mom is too. Send her a husband, me a dad, maybe a sibling." That journal held my chaos, a map of a heart still finding its way through the wreckage of our moves and the hope of what might come next.

I'd sit cross-legged on my bed, the springs creaking beneath me, with tears streaming down my face as I longed for a father who truly loved me. The sting of my earthly father's betrayal, the abandonment and the chaos he'd sown, cut deep, leaving me to wrestle with a heavy question. How could my heavenly Father love me when "father" felt like a word dipped in pain? I couldn't feel God's arms around me, couldn't climb into His lap or hear His voice soothe my fears. The Bible calls Him "Father" over and over—thirty times for God, one hundred and fifty times as Jesus's Father—but for me, that word conjured hurt, not healing. Was God distant and wounding too? My heart ached with a fragile thread of faith that frayed more with every sob.

During one of our late-night talks when the kitchen light cast soft shadows, life shifted again when Mom broached a new possibility: "What if I started dating?" She'd tried once in Florida, a single date that fizzled, but this felt different.

"I'd love for you to be happy," I said, meaning it, though my stomach fluttered. A father figure sounded like a dream—someone to cheer at my basketball and volleyball games, to ease Mom's load—but fear nibbled at me too. What if he didn't like me? What if he left? What if he changed the quiet magic of just Mom and me?

That trust felt tested as I pedaled my bike around our new complex, the Texas sun hot on my neck, tires humming against the pavement. That's when I met Mark, a weekend visitor whose dad lived in our building. Divorced parents meant he split time between them like I'd once imagined, and we bonded fast—racing bikes and weaving through parked cars. His dad, Richard, welcomed me with a grin, his apartment a cozy chaos of movie nights and bad puns that left us snorting with laughter. I'd sprawl on their worn couch, popcorn in hand, soaking in the ease of it all, a flicker of what "normal" might feel like after years of upheaval.

Mark's older sister, Tammy, was the spark at the leasing office—the twenty-three-year-old blonde with a contagious laugh who'd greeted my mom that first day. She radiated her dad's warmth, and one afternoon, Mom dropped a surprise. "Tammy and her dad are coming for dinner."

My eyes widened. "Richard?"

She blinked, startled. "How do you know him?"

"My friend Mark invited me over to watch movies." I shrugged, oblivious to her raised brow.

"You went to someone's house without asking?" she pressed, her tone sharp with that protective edge.

I froze, caught off guard by my kid logic. Tammy worked with Mom, so it felt safe. The moment passed with a laugh, but it hinted at something brewing—new connections weaving into our life, stirring both hope and uncertainty after so many transitions.

That evening, Tammy and Richard filled our apartment with warmth. The clatter of plates and bursts of laughter bounced off the walls as we dug into Mom's spaghetti. Tammy, her blonde hair catching the light, leaned over to me with a grin, whispering, "Your mom's perfect for my dad. I just know it." Her certainty sparked a flicker of hope in me, a quiet thrill at the thought of our families tangling together like vines.

After that night, Richard didn't waste time. He asked Mom out again and again, each date lighting her up like a lantern. One Saturday, he even roped me in, inviting us to Six Flags. I can still feel the rush of the roller coasters and hear Mom's squeals mixing with Richard's goofy cheers as we looped through the air. At home, their joy spilled over. Richard would strum his guitar, and Mom's voice wove through the chords. Their laughter seeped through the thin walls. I'd press my ear to the plaster, smiling at how alive she sounded.

Six months flew by, and one evening, under the glow of our porch light, Richard asked my mom to marry him. Mom's "Yes!" echoed in my chest, a wild mix of excitement and relief washing over me. After years of just the two of us, our growing family was taking shape.

I couldn't wait to call Richard my stepdad. His easy grin and big heart made loving him effortless, and Tammy as a stepsister felt like a bonus prize. (Someone to swap secrets with!) But not every piece fit smoothly. Mark and I stumbled through the coming shift that would be their marriage, our bike-riding camaraderie fraying at the edges. He'd grown quiet, his usual chatter replaced by a distant stare, and I'd snap at him over nothing, frustration bubbling up without warning. The looming merge of our families wasn't the seamless joy I'd pictured. It was messy, jagged, and confusing.

But Mom and I had clawed our way through so much—the kidnapping, living in fear, starting over—and I'd prayed for a dad who wouldn't break me again. God answered with Richard, a man who overflowed with love and light. Discipline wasn't his game;

he'd rather belt out a tune or crack a joke until we were all doubled over, tears streaming from laughter instead of pain. And here's the wild part—I'd known him first. I'd been slumped on his couch with Mark, munching popcorn weeks before he ever met my mom. God had woven him into my life like a quiet gift, letting me trust him as a friend before he became family. That twist still makes me smile. How many kids get to pick their stepdad before their mom does?

Before my mom and Richard got married, our lives took a surreal turn…NBC was crafting a movie about my kidnapping.

One of the men who'd helped rescue me had sold the story, and now they wanted Mom's voice to shape it. I'd sprawl across her bed, the comforter bunching under me, as we pored over the script. She'd scribble out inaccuracies with a frown, and I'd read "Lauren's" lines in a dramatic whisper. She chuckled at my attempts to sound tough. We'd collapse into giggles, the absurdity of a movie about *us* sinking in. So many kids vanish across borders, stolen by a parent, but few ever come home. That script held my pain, my survival, and I couldn't believe it was real.

In January 1993, when I was thirteen years old, *Desperate Rescue: The Cathy Mahone Story* aired on NBC, featuring Mariel Hemingway playing Mom's part. That Monday night felt like a spotlight on our scars. The film got most of it right—the fear, the chase—but it skipped the divine thread that held us together. No scenes showed Mom fasting for three days, her voice raw from prayer, or the men racing through Jordan's dusty streets as she begged God for my safety. It didn't capture the miracle of passports and visas aligning to slip us into Israel. Watching it, I felt the pang of my father's betrayal laid bare, but the healing grace that followed remained unseen.

Life shifted fast after that. NBC whisked us to LA for interviews and promos, a whirlwind adventure for my mom and I to enjoy. A sleek limo came to our DeSoto apartment to pick us up. Its leather seats were cool against my legs. It was the first time I'd ever ridden in one. I pressed my nose to the tinted window, grinning as we rolled to the airport. Another limo waited in LA, sleek and surreal. Uncle Dan greeted us at a glitzy hotel with a bear hug.

Before launching its fall lineup, NBC held a major press event—one central location where commercials were filmed, interviews conducted, and buzz built around both new series and returning favorites. It was a whirlwind of energy and celebrities. On day one, we explored Universal Studios.

But the next day was the real event. Our interviews for the made-for-TV movie collided with the network's media frenzy. Conference rooms and hallways buzzed with stars from *Saved by the Bell*, *Blossom*, and *Days of Our Lives*. I was overwhelmed, caught in the chaos of fame and flashing lights.

Then I saw him—Mario Lopez, A.C. Slater in the flesh, walking confidently past us. I froze. My Uncle Dan, unfazed, flagged him down for a photo. My heart pounded as I stood next to him, my hands trembling while I tried to smile. I couldn't believe I was standing beside a real TV star.

Mariel Hemingway swept in too, her presence warm and real as she shook Mom's hand. "Cathy, I'm so sorry." She laughed, cutting herself off mid-sentence. "I gave you a thick country accent. I just assumed!"

Mom's laugh rang out, pure and bright, and Mariel's eyes softened. "Your strength blows me away," she said. "I'm honored to play you."

That moment stitched a thread of pride through my hurt. My mom, a woman who'd fought for me, had been seen by someone who mattered. The interviews rolled on, and small rooms with lone reporters gave way to a grand ballroom for Mom and Mariel. Chairs scraped, cameras hummed, and questions flew until the chandelier above swayed, crystals clinking.

It was an earthquake rippling through, subtle but sharp.

Everyone froze, staring up, except my mom, who was oblivious. "What's going on?"

I stifled a laugh.

We flew home, the glitter of LA fading into memory, and soon after, Mom and Richard said, "I do." That wedding marked a pivot away from the shadow of my father's wounds and toward something new. We moved into Richard's apartment; boxes piled up like promises of a fresh start. At first, it was a thrill. New walls, new rhythms.

Tammy bunked with us for a stretch, and sharing a room with her felt like hitting the jackpot. Suddenly, I had a big sister, ten years older, all sparkle and sass. We'd stretch across our shared room, and she'd tease me about my messy hair as we swapped stories under the glow of a thrift-store lamp. She was her dad's mirror—joy spilling out, laughter lighting every corner. I secretly loved when she'd "break up" with her boyfriend; she'd sweep me off to Six Flags. Roller coasters rattled my bones, then we'd cap it with Braum's banana splits. Cold, creamy bliss dripped down our chins as we giggled. Those days softened the ache of my father's absence, filling gaps I'd carried too long.

But beneath the sweetness, change stirred unease. The movie had peeled back my wounds. My dad's betrayal and the years lost made it hard for me to trust again. Richard's love was a balm, steady where my father's had faltered, but blending our lives wasn't all laughter. It was a dance of healing and hoping, each step testing my heart's scars against a future I wanted to believe in.

The shift hit me hard. For years, it had been just Mom and me. Two against the world, a tight knot no one could unravel. Now,

Richard's presence tugged at that thread, asking me to share her and let him in. The word "Dad" loomed like a storm cloud, heavy with the weight of my biological father's wounds: betrayal, abandonment, a childhood stolen. I couldn't say it to Richard, not yet. He never pushed, never even hinted at wanting it. His quiet patience gave me room to wrestle with it, to sift through the pain on my own terms. "Dad" meant hurt, but Richard was warmth, laughter, a steady hand. But those old scars held me back, whispering that love from a father could break me again.

That first year of their marriage buzzed with newness, a whirlwind of change I couldn't quite catch up to. It was a taste of the family I'd craved, but it didn't last. Blending our family was like stitching a quilt from torn scraps, beautiful in theory but tough in practice.

Only later did I piece together why it was hard for Mark and I. His world had just cracked open. His parents' divorce still raw, the sting of seeing his dad only on weekends cut deeper than I'd guessed. Tammy had stumbled on the truth. Their mom's affair had shattered their home, but Mark, at age eleven, couldn't grasp the why behind it all. Now, his dad was marrying my mom, moving in with us, and Mark's weekends weren't even his anymore.

I had my own wounds too, from years of hiding, and losing my dad to Jordan's chaos. Together, we were like two bruised kids bumping into each other in the dark, neither of us sure how to heal or connect. Our fights weren't just kid squabbles; they were echoes of bigger hurts we couldn't name.

And months after their marriage, Tammy got her own place, and soon after, Mom landed a job managing a new apartment complex. We packed up again, this time to a sprawling two-story setup. Two units had been fused into one, with walls knocked down to create a maze of space. Mom's office doubled as our home, and I got my own front door, a tiny kitchen, and even a bathroom to myself.

At thirteen, it felt like a dream to have my own slice of freedom, a key jangling in my pocket like a badge of independence. But the thrill faded fast, replaced by a hollow ache. Alone in that cavernous space, the silence pressed in, amplifying the loneliness I'd buried. We'd traded closeness for square footage, and I missed the nights I'd crawl into Mom's bed, spilling every thought that crossed my mind. And now she was a newlywed, focused on Richard, and I was adrift, caught between the family I'd gained and the one I'd lost.

School didn't help. I started eighth grade at a new place, the fifth school in five years. It was near Mom's job, and a campus with no safety net for my dyslexia and dyscalculia. Every day, I'd slip out of class, shoulders hunched, to walk a few blocks down the road to Masters Academy, a school for kids like me, either struggling with books or behavior. The shame burned hot as I left my peers behind, their whispers trailing me out the door. I'd slump in my seat at Masters, the chalkboard a blur of numbers I couldn't tame, feeling like an outsider twice over.

Sports might've bridged the gap, but constant moves had robbed me of a shot at teams or tryouts. Friends came easier, but middle school was a beast. For the first time, I didn't fit. One girl, though, got it. Her dad had left wounds, too, and we clung to that shared hurt, navigating the halls like two lost souls in a storm.

Richard, though, was a gift, no question. No kid could dream up a better stepdad. He'd belt out tunes on his guitar, eyes crinkling with joy, more eager to make us laugh than lay down rules. But his light couldn't fully pierce my dark. Sharing Mom with him felt like losing her, a space once mine now split in two. They'd disappear into their newlywed bubble, giggles echoing from their room, and I'd retreat to mine, the vastness of our new home swallowing me whole. At thirteen, it was my lowest point: new school, old shame, and a heart still bleeding from my father's cuts. God had answered my prayers with Richard, yet the bitterness lingered—a stubborn root I didn't even know was there—choking out forgiveness I wasn't ready to give.

In that quiet, I'd trace the scars my biological dad left. What was he doing now? Anger flared, then sadness would sink in. Why couldn't I know him? Why did his choices shred my normal? If God was good, why had He let this happen? I'd prayed for a dad, and Richard was here, steady and kind, but the hole gaped wider. I'd imagine calling my father, my pulse racing at the thought of his voice, awkward, distant, like those rare phone calls we'd fumbled through.

Mom urged me to reach out, tears in her eyes as she said, "I don't want you to regret not knowing him for yourself." But fear locked me in place, the hurt too raw, the love I still craved from him a wound I couldn't face.

Romans 8:26–28 became my lifeline in that haze: "The Spirit helps us in our weakness… intercedes for us… And we know that in all things, God works for the good of those who love Him." (Romans 8:26–28 NIV) Richard's love was healing, but it stirred the mud of my past, dragging old pain to the surface. I didn't confront it; I hardened around it, building walls instead of bridges. Alone in my half-apartment, I'd sit with those questions, the weight of my father's absence pressing down, searching for an escape from a life that felt pieced together and fragile.

When I built up the courage to call my dad, it was always the same, a stiff ritual.

"How are you? How's school? I miss you," he'd say, his voice crackling through the line. He'd call me "baby" and tack on an "I love you," but the words landed like stones, awkward and hollow. How could he love me when he didn't even know me? How could I be his "baby" when we were strangers bound by a frayed thread?

What I craved wasn't platitudes; I wanted him to say, "Lauren, I'm so sorry I hurt you. I'm sorry I tore you from your mom and broke your world." I ached for magic words to erase the pain, anger, and void he'd left, but they never came. Looking back, I see I was chasing a fix he couldn't give. Only God could mend that shattered piece of me.

That ache festered, and I started to unravel. At thirteen, I'd slip out my window into the night, the cool air biting my skin as I ran with kids who didn't ask questions. We'd dodge streetlights, flirting with trouble. Petty stuff, but enough to feel alive.

Mom was lost in her newlywed glow with Richard, while I drowned in a silent storm. She saw me fraying, with my sullen stares and sharp edges; she knew I was hunting for answers she couldn't provide.

I had so many unanswered questions for my father. Did he know there was a movie about what he'd done—our story played out on screens for strangers to watch? Did he know the press had hounded us? That I'd been forced to change my last name, to live quietly and carefully, hidden because of the choices he made?

His letters kept coming anyway—pleading, apologetic, relentless. They piled up at my grandmother's house like ghosts of a life I'd lost, each one reopening wounds I wasn't sure had ever closed. He wanted to see me. He wanted a chance to explain.

Eventually, my mom told me the decision was mine, if I felt ready. A face-to-face meeting might stitch something back together—or at least calm the noise in my heart. I didn't know which I needed more.

My father was no longer overseas. He had returned to the United States quietly, re-entering a life he had once torn apart. When he first came back to Texas, he was arrested and spent a brief period in jail before posting bail. From there, he was placed on probation, restrictions that would remain in effect until I turned eighteen. My mother was alerted as soon as he re-entered the country. She knew he was back, knew where he was living, and knew he had rebuilt a life with his wife and children in Vermont.

His return revived fears we had worked so hard to quiet, but it also stirred something more complicated inside me. As painful as it was, I wanted to see my father again. I wanted to understand who he was and why he had taken me—what had lived inside him that led to those choices. I also longed to see my stepmother and siblings. They were innocent in all of it, yet I had lost them as family when I lost my father. His return reopened wounds, but it also reopened questions I had never stopped asking, and a hope—fragile and uncertain—that answers might finally be within reach.

The plan was cloaked in caution. He still thought we lived in Florida, where he mailed his letters, a shield Mom held onto tightly. She concocted a story. We'd be "visiting friends" in Dallas, where his brother lived, and could meet at the Galleria Mall. She swapped our Texas plates for old Florida ones, her hands steady but her eyes darting, and booked us a hotel to dodge any trail back home.

As the day crept closer, my gut churned with a wild mix of fear and anxiety gnawing at me, curiosity burning brighter, desire overpowering it all. I *wanted* to see him, to claw back what he'd stolen, to know the man behind the voice. My siblings would be there, too, a fragile lifeline easing my dread. Six years had passed since Jordan, six years since he'd ripped me from Mom, and now, at age thirteen, I stood on the edge of facing him again.

The buildup was electric. We pulled into the mall's sprawling lot, the glass towers glinting under a Texas sun, and my pulse hammered like a drumroll. Mom squeezed my hand as we stepped inside, into the bustle of shoppers. "Lauren, we can leave anytime," she said. "You don't have to do this."

But I did. I had to.

Richard flanked us, his easy grin a buoy in the tension, promising safety with every quip. My breath hitched as we neared Bennigan's, the restaurant's green sign looming. Would he look the same? Would he see me—really see me?

Then, there he was. He emerged from the crowd, his smile wide and unguarded, arms open as if time hadn't fractured us. He hugged me, kissed my forehead, spoke to me in his thick, foreign accent, a stranger's voice in a father's body. Tears broke free, hot and messy, as fear crashed into excitement.

He acted like Jordan was a blip, like six years hadn't stretched between us, but for me, it was a chasm. That hug felt wrong—stiff, unfamiliar—yet he *was* my dad, not some ghost. My siblings rushed in, their faces bright, and talking to them flowed easy, a balm against the awkwardness.

Richard cracked jokes, Mom hovered like a hawk. Dinner blurred by, and when he asked if we could meet again the next day, I nodded, exhausted but tethered to the fragile hope of knowing my dad and siblings again. He suggested a park, handing my mom the location before we parted ways that night.

The next morning, a strange mix of emotions settled over me—anxiety, curiosity, and emotional exhaustion all tangled together. Part of me was afraid to see him again, afraid of the memories it might stir. But another part of me still longed for something normal, something that felt like a family.

So the next day, Mom, Richard, and I drove to the park he had chosen. I tried to steady my breathing as we pulled into the parking lot, bracing myself for another quiet meeting with my dad and siblings.

But the scene waiting for us was nothing like what I expected.

We arrived expecting swings and picnics, but Dad had brought an entourage of relatives I didn't know, women in flowing Jordanian dresses, voices weaving between Arabic and English. They swarmed me with kindness, hands brushing my hair.

I froze, overwhelmed. Then a loudspeaker pierced the air from a mosque nearby, calling to prayer. My chest seized, memories of Jordan flooding back—dust, fear, isolation.

Mom saw my panic, grabbed my hand, and yanked me to the car. "Lauren, I'm so sorry," she gasped, wrapping me tight. "I didn't know he'd bring all to a park near a mosque."

Dad stood clueless as she snapped at him. The mosque, the crowd—it was too much, a cruel echo of the past I couldn't outrun.

Back at the hotel, I broke. "Why that park?" I sobbed. "A mosque in Dallas? I felt like I was back there!" I'd wanted to see my dad and my siblings, not plunge into old nightmares. The fear of him taking me again, the dread of losing Mom, the loneliness of Jordan all roared back, raw and unrelenting.

He begged for one more day, but Mom shut it down. Two days had gutted me; I couldn't take more. That night, curled against her, with my emotions all over the place. I'd chased his apology, a fix, but it wouldn't come. Psalm 147:3, NIV whispered through my haze. "He heals the brokenhearted and binds up their wounds." (Psalm 147:3 NIV) I clung to it. God was peeling back my layers, slow and steady, but I had to let Him in to face the anger and forgive what Dad couldn't mend.

Some women in the Bible had scars that mirrored mine. Take Leah in Genesis 29. Laban, her father, tricked Jacob into marrying her instead of her radiant sister, Rachel. Laban cloaked her in deception, thrusting her into a loveless union, her worth trampled. She lived overshadowed, yearning for Jacob's heart. Her father's rejection was a wound that festered. Yet she praised God through it, and He blessed her. She became the mother of Levi, whose genealogical line led to Jesus. Reading this story as an adult hit me hard. Hurt by a father, healed by faith. My wounds ran just as deep, but like Leah, I had to fix my eyes on Jesus, spill my pain, and let forgiveness bloom slow and messy, but real.

CHAPTER SIXTEEN

THE HOUSE THAT BUILT ME

Hurt can feel like a shadow you can't outrun, a quiet weight that dims even the brightest days, especially when left by a father's hand. But God doesn't leave us there, trapped in that ache. He sends a village of friends, mentors, and unexpected kin to lift us when we're sinking, to uncover the pain we've buried so we can breathe free again. If we stay stuck, clutching our wounds like a shield, healing slips through our fingers.

That box—the one I mentioned at the beginning of this story—sat quietly through the years, tucked away but never forgotten. Inside were the pieces my mother had carefully gathered: her journals, cassette tapes, newspaper clippings, magazine articles, even the movie made about our rescue. She kept it all, not to trap us in the past, but to safeguard the truth until the right time. We both knew what it held—answers, context, and memories sharp enough to cut—but neither of us was ready to lift the lid. Preservation, I would learn, doesn't soften pain. Even sealed away, the wounds my father created seeped into our lives, surfacing in unanswered questions, heavy silences, and moments when the past pressed against the present. The box waited—not as a threat, but as a quiet reminder that healing would eventually require courage, not just survival.

After my mom and I moved to Florida, our contact with the Lamberts became limited to occasional phone calls. They were no longer part of our daily lives, and I deeply felt the absence of their steady presence. By the time we eventually moved back to the Dallas area, Rick and Bev had relocated to Lindale—about a two-hour drive away. The distance made visits rare, and in the four to five years since my rescue, we'd only seen each other a handful of times. During that stretch of time, I began to spiral. I was angry at God, aching with the absence of my biological father, and consumed by a loneliness that settled into my bones. My mom and Richard were immersed in building their new life together while I quietly unraveled. I started sneaking out, craving acceptance in the fleeting glances of a neighbor boy. He was two years older, and the attention he gave me felt like something I needed to earn—so I followed him into risky corners, streetlamp shadows, and late-night dares.

It had been one or two years since we'd last seen the Lamberts in person. I was able to spend a little time with Miranda, Luke, Rick, and Bev during Mom and Richard's wedding, but that day was a blur. Between the ceremony, the reception, and a house full of guests, there was barely a moment to connect. The excitement of the wedding—and my parents' focus on merging two households into one—meant there wasn't much space for quiet conversations or heartfelt check-ins. When Rick and Bev came to visit us in DeSoto later that year, their presence stirred something in me. Bev's sharp eyes noticed what others hadn't—the slump in my shoulders, the forced tone in my voice. She knew. Something was wrong. We swapped small talk over glasses of iced tea, the clink of ice covering my discomfort, until I quietly slipped out and left them to catch up with Mom and Richard.

Alone in the living room, Bev asked my mom, "What's going on with Lauren? She's either sad or in trouble, but something's not right." No sugarcoating, just truth, which was Rick and Bev's way.

I imagine it unfolded like this: "Cathy, you've got to get her out of here, or you'll lose her. She's on a dark path, and it's time for a big move." They weren't wrong. My hidden hurt, fury at my dad, and longing for a family I'd lost was spilling out, poisoning me. Friendship, though, was about to pull me back.

Lindale, Texas, waited two hours east, a sleepy dot on the map with a Brookshire Brother's grocery store, a Kid Jones gas station, and a Dairy Queen where locals lingered over soft serve. Rick and Bev had landed there in the early '90s, financial strain nudging them closer to family. They'd found an old farmhouse, its sagging porch and peeling paint a fixer-upper's dream.

The Lambert farmhouse in Lindale, Texas—the house that helped rebuild my life.

The house was small and run-down, the kind of place most people would pass by without a second glance. It needed more than a little love—it needed *vision.* With the owner's nod, they traded sweat for lower rent. Rick sanded the worn floors until they glowed, and Bev scrubbed years of neglect out of every corner. The place had its quirks—a clawfoot tub, creaky stairs that moaned with every step—but set foot in its kitchen, and you were wrapped in love like a well-worn quilt. They couldn't have known then how that tired old house would become the inspiration for Miranda's song, "The House That Built Me"—a haven for countless souls, mine included.

The move was happening, though I didn't feel it yet. That day in DeSoto, Bev's words lit a fuse. Mom listened, her brow furrowing as Rick nodded, their voices low but firm. I was teetering into rebellion, and they saw what I couldn't—staying stuck meant losing more than I'd already lost. Lindale wasn't just a change of address; it was a reset, a chance to unearth the pain I'd buried under anger and bad choices. The Lamberts' farmhouse loomed ahead, not fancy but a place where healing could begin. And yes, that blonde-haired girl flitting through its halls was Miranda, my lifelong friend, my little sister, long before she'd sing about that house and bring Grammys home. When I hear her voice belting "The House That Built Me" now, tears fall with my memories of friendship, of being seen, of a village that refused to let my hurt define me.

I was about to turn fifteen when Bev and Rick threw me a lifeline. "Come stay with us in Lindale."

Mom nodded, her eyes soft with trust, and I packed a duffel, oblivious to the bigger plan brewing in Bev's heart.

That summer stirred with life. I spent mornings making breakfast with the Lamberts in their kitchen and afternoons chasing Miranda and Luke through sun-dappled fields, their shrieks echoing off the trees. We spent evenings at Prairie Creek Church with Pastor John Offutt, where worship music sunk into my bones. Every night, I'd collapse into bed with dirt under my nails, buzzing from kid sports and family chaos.

Their farmhouse pulsed love in every creak of the floorboards, and hard work wove itself into the rhythm of each daily chore.

We'd gather at dusk around a scratched oak table, plates piled high, swapping stories of our day. I missed Mom and Richard, but the Lamberts' orbit felt like home—a taste of family I'd been missing without knowing it.

As summer faded, I returned to DeSoto with sun on my skin but a storm beneath it. My time with the Lamberts had been filled with warmth, laughter, and the steadiness I craved—but part of me still longed for the city, for the familiar pulse of home. I was torn between two worlds, caught in a quiet ache I couldn't name. But the Lamberts saw through the smile I wore. They didn't let go. Their love turned persistent, their concern steady and strong. They pressed my mom and Richard with a gentle urgency: "Move to Lindale. It's what she needs."

Rick dangled a gem—twenty-five acres teeming with oaks whispering promise, for sale at a great price, less than five miles from their place. Confronting someone about their kid is a tightrope, and swallowing that truth is harder still. But Mom saw it. I'd come back from the Lamberts' brighter, lighter, only to sink again into that familiar gloom of anger at my dad's ghost, loneliness gnawing me hollow. One weekend, we piled into the car, and drove with tires pulling toward Lindale to see Rick's find.

I wasn't ready for more upheaval. That summer had been fun with Miranda's giggles and Luke's tag-along grin, but now, change loomed like a thunderhead. Bev pulled me aside during a visit, her gaze piercing the walls I'd built. "Lauren, talk to me," she urged.

I bristled, arms crossed, clinging to my dark corner. My father wounds festered hurt I couldn't voice and shame I wouldn't share. Hiding felt safe, but it's a flimsy shield; the pain always seeps through.

We pulled into the Lamberts' driveway, the tires crunching over gravel, dust rising like a veil between where I'd been and where I was going. As the house came into view—small, worn, and full of character—my chest tightened with a storm of emotions. I loved them deeply. Rick and Bev, Miranda and Luke—they were my family, the kind that wrapped you in warmth just by being near. But there was also an ache of everything I couldn't make sense of. Too much had shifted—inside me and around me—and I didn't know how to carry it.

But as soon as the door opened, the weight lifted just a little. Rick's tangy barbecue sauce filled the air, sweet and smoky and familiar. Bev was in the kitchen, chopping vegetables with her usual rhythm, and Rick stirred the pot like it was sacred work. Miranda and Luke came running out with wide smiles, the dogs tumbling behind them in a blur of paws and laughter. Their home was humble, but it breathed life and love in every corner.

Miranda and Luke tugged me outside the moment we arrived. Chickens scattered around our feet as we gathered warm eggs into a basket, laughing as rabbits darted just out of reach. We bounced on the trampoline beneath a wide Texas sky, our shrieks echoing across the yard—until the familiar call for dinner pulled us back inside.

Around the table, the smell of smoked ribs and grilled chicken filling the room, Mom dropped a bomb: "We're thinking about looking at land nearby." My fork paused mid-air. My stomach flipped. I knew they had talked about this, but I wasn't sure that it would really happen. Before I could ask questions, Rick chimed in, his eyes lighting up as he described the plot just five miles from their place—twenty-five acres of thick, tree-covered property.

After dinner, we climbed into the car and rumbled down a back road, dust swirling in our wake. Rick wanted us to see the land from the back side, where its beauty wasn't hidden behind trees. As we turned a bend, the view opened wide—a hill crowned with tall oaks, a red barn glowing in the distance like something out of a postcard. It was quiet. Serene. Almost magical. But still, something in me pulled back. As breathtaking as it was, I wasn't ready to move again.

Anger flared as we toured it. "Why are we moving *again*? I'm a city girl. Dallas lights, not country dirt. I don't ride horses, I don't care for rodeos, and I don't want this!" It wasn't about urban versus rural; it was my heart, brittle and shadowed. The devil wanted me stuck there in the city, festering, but God saw more.

Bev pulled my mom aside and said it as plain as possible: "Don't let a fifteen-year-old's emotions make this decision." My parents listened. They bought the land, uprooted everything. Richard started sketching blueprints like a man on a mission, and we got to work. Chainsaws roared as my mom and Richard cut through trees and thorn-covered brush, some of it two or three inches thick. I pulled the tangled mess into piles, arms scratched, sweat dripping. I couldn't see their sacrifice—only my own. I was leaving behind everything familiar, still wrestling with pain I didn't know how to name. But the Lamberts' steady presence made the change feel a little less like a loss. And they also softened the blow. That first year, while the house was being built, my mom and Richard let me live with Rick and Bev so I could start school on time. It was a decision wrapped in love, even if I couldn't see it then.

I dragged my feet, but love won out. Living with Miranda and Luke was a salve. Miranda and I shared a room and whispered secrets under quilts in the dark.

I had no say. I didn't have much say in the decision. Bev and Mom were both iron-willed women—protective, determined, and convinced they knew what was best for their kids. In many ways, they were right. They had carried the weight of the rescue, the danger, the fear of losing me—but this time, losing me emotionally, not physically. If they believed Lindale would give us safety and a fresh start, then the plan was already set in motion.

But inside me, another move felt like one more earthquake. I was tired of starting over—new schools, new houses, new people asking questions I didn't know how to answer.

Weekends, Mom and Richard drove in from Dallas, trading city desks for hammers and brush fires. Once, Mom's blaze nearly torched the hill. Flames licked high until the neighbor farmer doused it, his laugh cutting through the panic.

Building that house was grit and grace. They carved a half-mile road from the highway to the top. Their hours on I-20 were a testament to their dedication to finishing the task. I couldn't yet grasp why. I was still too mad to see it and too hurt to care, but the Lamberts' table changed that.

Night after night, we'd circle their oak slab with plates clinking. We divvied up the jobs—me setting forks, Luke fetching garden carrots, Miranda scrubbing pots. Laughter spilled over mashed potatoes, stories stitching us tight. It was family, raw and real, and it smoothed my rough edges. My walls built from father wounds, from years of loss, softened a little each meal. God was doing that new thing, "…streams in my wasteland," (Isaiah 43:19 NIV) shifting my direction through love I couldn't dodge. I'd fought the move, but here, amid the clatter, my heart thawed.

Once I was actually living with the Lamberts and not just visiting for the summer, Bev decided it was time to get me plugged into the youth group. Faith wasn't just something the Lamberts talked about; it was woven into their everyday lives. Their home was filled with prayer, worship music, and open Bibles, and they lived what they believed. Prairie Creek was their church home, and each of them served with purpose. Rick played guitar on the worship team every Sunday morning. Miranda sang on stage beside him during the main service, her voice rising with confidence. Bev poured herself into the youth ministry, showing up every Sunday and Wednesday night with snacks in hand and a heart wide open. It wasn't long before I was swept into their rhythm, stepping into a community that felt both unfamiliar and strangely like home.

During the summer, I tagged along to one or two youth group events—just enough to get a glimpse of what was coming. But when fall rolled around, things picked up quickly. Weekly meetings kicked off in full swing, gearing up for the school year. And Bev? She already had a plan (because of course she did). She knew every kid in that youth group by name, and before I even walked through the door, she'd been telling them about me.

That first Wednesday night, she walked me straight into the church building with the confidence of someone on a mission. She didn't hesitate; she just marched right up to Julie and Bekah, two girls she knew would be safe and kind. They greeted me with warm smiles, the kind that melted away the fear of being the new girl. In a small town like Lindale, a new face was big news, and Bev had made sure mine was met with open arms.

Bev's introduction was intentional, pairing me with the kind of friends who could help lift me up instead of pull me further down. That night, as worship music filled the room and hands lifted in surrender, something shifted. I felt God starting to mend what had been broken, touching the places my father's absence had left aching. And with the Lamberts by my side, I was beginning to believe healing was possible.

By now, I was no stranger to starting over. I'd bounced between states, homes, and schools more times than I could count. Each move meant a new cafeteria, a new set of rules, a new crowd I didn't belong to. And here I was again—another first day, another school, another version of me trying to fit in.

This time felt a little different, though. The youth group at church had given me a few familiar faces in the hallway, and that softened the blow. But the anger and frustration I carried hadn't disappeared—they'd just burrowed deeper, buried beneath my fresh start.

School was a blur, a maze of lockers and laughter that I couldn't yet join. I drifted through the days, keeping my head down, until Bev—always with a plan—began bringing us to the Friday night football games.

I didn't expect much. But under the glow of the stadium lights, something cracked open. The field was lit like a stage, and the whole town poured in to watch. The roar of the crowd, the rhythm of the drums, the electricity in the air—it was intoxicating. Students crowded the bleachers, huddled in groups, laughing, shouting, belonging. And for the first time in a long time, I felt a pull—not just to the moment, but to the possibility of fitting in.

In this tiny town, church and school wove together seamlessly. Kids I prayed with on Sunday sat beside me in class on Monday. Soon, I was nudging Bev. "Can I go to youth group Sunday night? Wednesday too?" My defenses had softened, and light seeped into the cracks. God wrestled with me, but this time, I wasn't alone. Friends encircled me, their prayers a steady rhythm. I'd never seen so many kids love Jesus and each other with such unguarded joy.

Three months later, Lindale felt less like a sentence and more like a gift. Friendships took root, what once were only names became faces, and faces became family. Coach Phillips, my health teacher and the athletic trainer, spotted my dream of physical therapy and tossed me a chance. "Want to be a student trainer?"

I said yes, trailing him onto the field, the grass still damp with morning dew. That fall, I stepped into the role of student trainer for the football team, learning how to tape ankles, ice down bruises, and keep my cool when players dropped to the ground in pain. I was there at games and practices, lugging coolers, refilling water bottles, wrapping wrists, and offering encouragement.

After classes, I headed straight to the field for practice, and every Friday night, I stood on the sidelines under the lights, adrenaline and the smell of Gatorade in the air. I traveled with the team to away games, part of a small crew that kept the athletes going. I darted between huddles, weaving past cleats and helmets, handing out water and checking on injuries. Their grunts, laughter, and shouted plays became a strange sort of music to me—one that reminded me I belonged, even if just at the edge of it all.

Then came the shock.

They voted me Football Sweetheart for homecoming.

Me—the girl who'd sulked her way into town, whose parents were still nailing boards into our half-built house. In mere weeks, these peers had claimed me, their votes whispering, "You belong." God was weaving a tapestry of provision. New opportunities, new bonds, and blessings stacking up like firewood for winter.

Homecoming night approached, and I needed an escort for the halftime walk across the field. For anyone who's lost a father young, the fear of an empty arm at life's big moments cuts deep. This was one of those moments. Richard, my stepdad of three years, was a rock, but Rick had held me since my first breath. Amid that turmoil, God's hand became clear. He provided Rick Lambert, a steady light and the closest thing I'd ever had to a father.

Rick loved me like I was his own, a gift I'll forever cherish. His kids, Miranda and Luke, shared him without hesitation, and I clung to that grace. Father's Day, however, often reopened wounds of loss and betrayal, my father's actions having stolen my childhood and flipped my world upside down. Yet every year, I picked out a card for Rick. Because of him, I wasn't left out. With his broad shoulders and big heart, Rick loved fiercely, stern when he needed to protect, tender when it counted most.

Rick wasn't just a father figure; he was a teacher too. A former police officer and private investigator, he carried a quiet authority, especially around guns. One crisp afternoon when I was sixteen years old, he took Mom and me to the range, the air sharp with gunpowder. He knelt beside me, his calloused hands guiding mine as he explained safety. His voice was calm until I spun around, gun in hand, oblivious to the danger.

"Never point a gun at anything you don't intend to shoot!" he barked, his tone slicing through the haze. My heart froze, tears pricking my eyes, certain I'd ruined everything.

But then he softened, his hand on my shoulder. "Lauren, I'm not mad. I just want you safe." That moment clicked. Rick's love held firm, even when I stumbled. Unlike my father, he wouldn't hurt me.

God sees our fractures and meets us there, I've learned. He sent Rick, someone who'd known me from the beginning, to mend what was broken like a true father. I'll never forget the day my husband and I met Rick and Bev at the Pink Pistol, Miranda's store in Lindale, our hearts full of excitement as we slid an ultrasound photo across the table. "We're pregnant."

Their faces lit up. Rick grinned wide, Bev's eyes glistened, and my chest swelled. This was the family I'd craved, especially in milestone moments like that.

When I asked Rick to walk with me at homecoming, Richard's grace shone bright as he stepped aside without hesitation. That night, under the glare of lights and the crowd's roar, it hit me:

"Football Sweetheart" wasn't just a title. It was proof God was fighting for me, pulling me into safety, love, and healing. He placed Rick in my path as a father figure, easing that old ache with every step we took across the field.

Rick Lambert walking me onto the field at Homecoming—showing up for a moment my biological father never could.

Pain had burrowed deep in me, a tangle of thorns I didn't know how to uproot. God, though, was patient, peeling back layers I'd locked away. I'd prayed into silence, feeling unheard, but He'd been listening all along. My friends Amy, Julie, Erica, Leslie, John, Tom, Daniel, Johnathan, and Kenny glowed with families I envied—parents still married, homes surrounded with stability.

Julie's world especially stung; she was blonde and radiant. She got to be the cheerleader I'd always wanted to be, and her dad attended every game. Her house seemed to be full of love with her mom teaching, a sister giggling, and grandparents dropping by. I loved them, but jealousy gnawed at me. Why couldn't I have that?

Healing began with honesty—a jagged, trembling thing, especially among peers. Church offered Life Groups, Sunday night gatherings in cozy living rooms, Bibles splayed open on coffee tables. It's one thing to sit in a pew, another to bare your soul in a circle of trust.

One night, under the soft glow of a single lamp, I let the anger, hurt, and my childhood's ragged edges spill out. My voice cracked as I spoke of the kidnapping, the endless days in Jordan, the father wounds that still ached beneath my ribs. I confessed the longing I'd carried for years: that my biological dad would say the magic words, offer an apology to mend it all. Tears blurred my vision as I admitted how Julie's seemingly perfect family pierced me with envy, a reminder of what I'd lost. But as my friends leaned in, their hands warm on my shoulders, a truth settled in. Healing wouldn't come from my earthly father. It would come through my heavenly Father and through this circle He'd placed around me.

Those friends, through their hugs, their quiet listening, and their gentle accountability, showed me His love in ways I could feel. They were a phone call away when I stumbled, a steady reminder that I wasn't alone in my chaos. Their lives weren't picture-perfect either, a revelation that softened my shame. Bev's prayers wove us tighter. Her gentle questions drew out our hidden struggles—hurt, disappointment, rage—one raw confession at a time. I learned that healing begins when you allow yourself to be vulnerable, to share your pain with others who care. That's where I found freedom.

Back then, we didn't have social media's endless scroll to fuel our comparisons, but the lie that everyone else's life shines brighter has echoed since the Garden of Eden. I'd believed that once, measuring my brokenness against the polished surface of my friends' lives. But in that room, as our Life Group shared their own scars from fractured homes, silent fears, and faith stretched thin, the light broke through. No family is flawless, no heart unscathed. The enemy thrives in the shadows of those lies, but when we gather in prayer, the truth burns bright. That season didn't erase my past, but it taught me this: Freedom isn't found in hiding our pain; it's found in sharing it. In those messy, honest spaces, God does His deepest work.

Forgiveness came slow, a gradual process filled with setbacks and small victories. My friends wept with me as I wrestled to forgive my dad. Not because he asked me to, but because I needed release. It wasn't a single moment of absolution, but a series of choices to let go of the anger that had weighed me down. God showed me I could forgive without excusing, without forgetting. It took years, with stumbles aplenty, but when it settled, I felt lighter. My dad's name no longer choked me; phone calls carried less venom and the Jordan box was more approachable. God was walking me through it, and I had my friends praying for me when my own words ran dry.

As I stood in the doorway of the Lamberts' house, my temporary sanctuary, I took one last look at the room that had been my refuge. The Lamberts had given me more than just a place to stay; they had given me a sense of belonging, a family when I needed it most. But now, it was time to move on. Just a few miles down the road, our new house awaited, a symbol of permanence in a life that had been defined by constant change, from apartments to my grandmother's home, always moving, always adapting.

This was different. This was the first real house I could call my own, built with love by my mom and stepdad. As we drove the short distance, I felt a swirl of emotions: gratitude for the stability I'd found with the Lamberts, excitement for this fresh start, and a hint of nervousness about what lay ahead. The house was a beautiful two-story with a wide front porch; it had large windows that welcomed the sunlight and a backyard brimming with possibility. It was a place where I wouldn't have to pack up and leave, where I could finally hang pictures on the walls and know they'd stay. This home would carry me through the rest of high school, into college, and through the challenging moments of reconnecting with my biological father. More than just a structure, it was a foundation—a place where I could plant my feet and grow.

Lindale, the speck on the map I'd once cursed, became my haven, its quiet streets framing my best years. The devil fights to keep you from Jesus, but God's pull prevails. I'm grateful for my parents' sacrifice, for the Lamberts' open door, and for Bev's steady hand guiding our group through high school. True healing isn't tidy or swift, but it's born in community, forged in prayer, and sealed by a God who never lets go.

Yet, as I settled into our new home, a symbol of stability and growth, I couldn't help but think about my father. I had recently found out he would be returning to Dallas to help his brother open a Middle Eastern bakery. This proximity would give me the chance to reconnect with him. Could I face him again, now at the age of seventeen, and find the healing I so desperately sought? The thought both excited and terrified me, but I knew that this was the next step in my journey. What would it feel like to stand before him, to confront the past and perhaps build something new? Could I open myself up to the hurt again, or would it break me once more? With faith and family holding me firm, I unpacked my life in our new beautiful home, poised for what lay ahead.

CHAPTER SEVENTEEN

FINDING MY VOICE

"*A father to the fatherless, a defender of widows, is God in his holy dwelling."* (Psalm 68:5 NIV)

I sat cross-legged on my four-poster bed, the carved wooden posts rising like silent sentinels around me. Sunlight poured through the huge window of my beautiful bedroom, casting warm golden patches across the soft quilt that cradled me. Beyond the glass, the rolling hills of Lindale stretched out in quiet splendor, a soothing contrast to the storm brewing inside me. This room was my sanctuary where I could escape the world's noise and wrestle with the ache that never quite left my chest. That ache had a name: Ali. He was a man I yearned to know, despite the deep wounds he'd carved into my life. What lay ahead were steps toward knowing my father, meetings that would force me to untangle the mess of my father wounds.

A father's love shapes something deep in a child. When it is missing or broken, the wound doesn't stay neatly contained; it settles into the hidden places of the heart. My father's absence and the pain he caused left scars I couldn't ignore. If I didn't let Jesus walk me through that hurt, those wounds would fester, shaping me in ways I didn't want.

And still, despite everything, part of me reached for him. I wanted to hear his voice and have the kind of honest, easy conversation daughters often take for granted. I wanted him to know the person I had become. God stirred courage in me to try, and my mom, knowing how much I carried, supported that fragile hope.

In 1998, my father lived in a different state with my stepmother and their five children, very far from me. We'd kept in touch through letters and phone calls, but each exchange felt like navigating a minefield. I longed to know him, to connect with my siblings, yet the conversations were stilted and strange. He spoke to me as if we shared a history, but to me, he was a stranger wearing the title of "dad." I'd sit in my room, the phone heavy in my hand, working up the nerve to dial his number. The ringing would echo in my ears, and when he answered, my heart pounded so fiercely I could hear it thumping against my ribs. "Hello," I'd manage, my voice small.

"My baby Lauren, I love you," he'd say, his words warm but jarring. The room seemed to close in around me. Why was he calling me his baby? How could I respond to his professed love? My tongue felt tied, caught between not wanting to hurt him and not knowing if I could say those words back. They stuck in my throat, heavy with years of pain.

Two desires warred within me. Part of me longed for a relationship with my father—to understand the man behind the voice and reconnect with the siblings I barely knew. But another part of me wanted to close the door completely, afraid that opening it again would only expose old wounds. Every phone call left me emotionally drained, stirring memories of betrayal and loss I had tried to bury.

Then everything changed. With my dad now in Dallas helping at the bakery, just a two-hour drive from Lindale, the distance that once separated us shrank. Texas and Vermont no longer stood as a wall between us. He called often, his voice crackling through the line, asking to visit me. My stomach twisted at the thought. Having him in my home felt too intimate, too raw. I wasn't ready to let him into my safe space, to share the life I'd built without him. But I couldn't deny the pull to know him. And knowing him meant facing him and stepping into the fear I'd carried for so long.

I turned to my mom, spilling my tangled thoughts across the kitchen table. She'd seen me wrestle with this for years, watched me cry and question and heal in pieces. I told her I needed to know who my father was, but she searched my eyes, making sure I was ready to face him again. The last time I'd seen him, years before, the encounter had left me shaken, tears streaming down my face, even as it stitched a small part of me back together. We talked it through, her voice steady and kind, until she and my stepdad agreed to drive me to the bakery. "I'll support you," she said, her hand resting on mine. "I know you need this, even if it's hard." She'd take me to uncle's bakery—the same uncle who'd appeared on our doorstep weeks after we fled Jordan—triggering a memory of when she'd pointed a gun at him and demanded answers. That same man now ran the bakery, and my mom was willing to walk through its doors with me. I watched her that day, her smile soft as she stepped past her own fears, giving me room to face mine.

The day arrived, and I stood in my room, hands trembling as I pulled on my shoes. Sunlight still danced through the window, but my mind churned with excitement and dread. In a few hours, I'd climb into the car with Mom and my stepdad for the two-hour drive from Lindale to Dallas. I was about to meet my Uncle Amir for the first time since my kidnapping, his bakery a bridge to my father. And there, I'd reunite with Dad, a man I barely knew yet couldn't escape. Questions swirled like a storm in my head. What would he look like now? I had not seen him since that meeting in the mall when I was twelve years old. Would he recognize me at the age of seventeen? Could I find something real beneath the awkwardness? My heart raced as I grabbed my bag, the hills outside my window fading into the background. The drive stretched ahead, a ribbon of asphalt carrying me toward answers I wasn't sure I was ready to hear.

As I pushed open the door to the bakery, warm air rushed toward me carrying the scent of fresh pita bread, za'atar, and mint. The smell stopped me in my tracks. For a moment, I wasn't in Dallas anymore—I was back in the markets of Jordan, surrounded by sounds and memories I had tried for years to forget.

My stomach churned with a rising tide of fear as I stepped inside. The sound of Arabic conversations swirling around me like a haunting melody. Men and women in traditional clothing moved gracefully through the space, their vibrant patterns a stark reminder of a past I wasn't ready to face. Then, through the haze of my racing thoughts, my dad emerged from the kitchen, his chef's apron dusted with flour, a wide, genuine smile lighting up his face. His joy at seeing me softened the edges of my anxiety, and as he ushered us in with an offer of steaming tea and warm pita, he proudly gave us a tour of his bakery, a small haven he'd built with his hands.

My uncle appeared briefly to greet us, but the awkwardness between us was palpable; he quickly excused himself, retreating to the safety of his work.

We settled at a small wooden table, the hum of Arabic news playing on a television in the background, its cadence blending with the clatter of baking trays and the chatter of customers. It was surreal sitting in a Dallas bakery while feeling as though I'd been whisked back to Jordan, surrounded by the same sounds, smells, and the familiar sight of my dad across from me.

"So," he said, gesturing around us, "what do you think of the bakery?"

"The bread smells good," I replied, surprising myself. "Just like over there."

He nodded, a small smile crossing his face. "Bread is bread," he said. "It follows you."

I asked about my siblings—*his* children—because that was easier than asking about him or offering pieces of myself. "How are the kids?" I asked. "How is Nora, my stepmother?"

"They're good," he said quickly, relief flickering across his face. "They're growing fast. They ask about you."

I nodded, unsure what to do with that. My mom stayed close, her chair angled toward me, her presence a quiet anchor. I wasn't ready for her to step away, not with every sound and scent threatening to pull me apart.

We avoided heavier truths, circling safe topics—the bakery, the children, the weather—until the visit drew to a close. It wasn't reconciliation or resolution, just a brief reintroduction to a relationship I'd spent years surviving rather than understanding.

Sitting across from him, I felt the tension I had carried for years. Part of me longed to know my father, while another part guarded the wounds he had left behind. The words of Romans 12:21 (NIV) echoed quietly in my mind: *"Do not be overcome by evil, but overcome evil with good."* I didn't know what reconciliation would look like, but I knew I didn't want bitterness to define my life.

In the weeks following our bakery visit, my dad's calls became more frequent, each one laced with a quiet hope to visit my home. At first, I hesitated, but as I prayed and reflected, a sense of readiness began to grow within me, bolstered by countless conversations with my mom and stepdad. We spent evenings huddled around the kitchen table, weighing the decision. Finally, we agreed to invite him over, and I spent the days leading up to his arrival in a whirlwind of preparation. I cleaned the house meticulously, as if tidying every corner could somehow order the chaos of my emotions. Yet, as the doorbell rang and I opened the door to see my dad standing there, a flood of anxious thoughts surged back. This time, though, the fear of him taking me was gone. I was older now, no longer the vulnerable child he once knew, but the tangle of emotions remained: a deep pull to know my biological father, yet a longing to close this painful chapter for good.

We gathered in the living room, an unlikely group: me, my mom, my stepdad, and my biological dad, all sharing the same space. I never imagined this moment would be possible, yet here I was, sitting face to face with the man whose absence had shaped so much of my life. We moved to the dinner table, keeping the conversation light as we savored the meal my mom had lovingly prepared. I couldn't help but marvel at her grace; not only had she welcomed my dad into our home, but she had also cooked for him, a quiet testament to God's love and forgiveness. Her actions spoke louder than words, teaching me how to extend the same grace I felt called to offer. I noticed it, even if my dad didn't.

Sitting across from him, I couldn't ignore our striking similarities—the same olive complexion, the same thick dark hair. It felt surreal sharing a room with the man who was both a stranger and a part of me. Fear, curiosity, and unresolved hurt tangled inside me as I wondered what life might have been like if he had never taken me all those years ago.

My dad leaned back in his chair and began talking about his children and my stepmother, subjects that felt safe because they let me learn about the family I'd been separated from without exposing too much of myself.

"Your brother just started school," he said, a note of pride in his voice. "He's always asking questions. Curious like you were."

I nodded, holding onto every detail. "Does he like sports?" I asked.

"He tries everything," my dad replied. "And your sister—she's the quiet one. Always watching."

I pictured them as he spoke, wondering if they knew the real reason I'd been missing from their lives. Did they think I'd chosen absence? That I simply didn't care? I wanted to ask if he'd ever told them the truth—what he'd done, what he'd taken—but the words stayed lodged in my throat. He didn't offer them either.

"So," he said after a pause, "how's school going for you?"

"It's good," I answered quickly. "Busy." *Safe.*

As he talked, a bitterness surfaced beneath my calm. I had always imagined growing up surrounded by siblings, a full family table, shared memories. Instead, I sat across from the man who had stolen that from me—the reason I didn't know my brothers and sisters, the reason my stepmother was a stranger, the reason I felt like an outsider to my own blood. I pushed the thoughts down and steered us back to lighter ground—classes, my parents, even the weather.

We talked a little longer before he stood to leave. When the door closed behind him, I stayed still, letting out a breath I hadn't realized I'd been holding. It wasn't healing or forgiveness—just a small, cautious step toward understanding who my father was now, while the deeper questions waited quietly for a braver day.

Later that evening, I found myself grappling with the weight of the day. I sank into my couch. Seeing my dad had stirred up a complex mix of feelings: the ache of old wounds, the flicker of hope for something new, and the lingering fear of being hurt again. I replayed our conversation, each word and gesture heavy with meaning. The hurt of my past clashed with the possibility of healing, leaving me both exhausted and restless. While processing the day,

I asked for the strength to forgive and the wisdom to navigate this uncertain path. Though the visit had been a step forward, it also reminded me how much of the journey still lay ahead, a journey I knew I couldn't walk alone.

Facing my fears had stirred up the hurt I'd carried for years, but it also planted a seed of hope in my heart. After returning home, my dad reached out to my mom with a new request: He wanted me to visit his family in Vermont to meet all my siblings and spend time with my stepmother. The idea filled me with a mix of excitement and trepidation, but I felt emotionally stronger, ready to take this next step. My siblings, after all, were innocent in the heartache my father had caused, and I longed to build a connection with them. After heartfelt discussions with my mom, I told her I was ready, my voice steady with resolve. I wanted this chance to know my other family.

I flew alone, my stomach twisted into a tight knot as the plane touched down. Thoughts of meeting my siblings—and seeing my stepmother again—raced through my mind as I walked through the airport toward baggage claim.

When I reached baggage claim, I spotted my dad right away. He stood stiffly beside my oldest sister and brother. My sister's warm smile and my brother's shy wave loosened something in my chest as they hurried over to grab my bags.

But the relief didn't last long. As soon as we stepped outside to the curb, my dad froze. The car was gone. His frustration erupted instantly—sharp, rapid Arabic spilling from his mouth as he turned on my siblings. His voice echoed with irritation, drawing glances from passing travelers. Then he looked at me, jaw clenched, and said the car had been towed.

We trudged across the lot to the tow office, where a gruff man sat behind thick glass and demanded two hundred dollars to release the car. My dad didn't have the money. I did—thanks to the emergency cash my mom had quietly tucked into my bag. My siblings shifted uncomfortably, their faces burning with embarrassment, while my own nerves—already stretched thin—felt ready to snap.

I kept asking my dad if I could use the payphone to call my mom, my voice shaking more each time. When I finally reached her, calling collect, I could hear the concern rush into her voice as I explained what had happened.

"Mom, I'm okay," I said quickly, "but Dad's car was towed from the airport. Can I use my money to get it back?"

"Yes, of course, Lauren," she said gently. "And I can be on a plane tomorrow if you need me."

Her calm steadied me. I told her I was okay—even as my hands trembled—determined to push forward, to prove I could handle this, and to believe that somehow, everything would be fine.

The drive to my dad's house in Vermont was quiet in all the wrong ways. He stared straight ahead, hands tight on the steering wheel, the tension in his jaw saying more than his silence ever could.

"So…what's Texas like?" my brother asked from the backseat, his voice hopeful, almost cheerful.

"It's hot," I said with a small smile. "Really hot."

My sister leaned forward between the seats. "What do you study?"

"Athletic training," I answered. "I'm in school for it."

"That sounds cool," she said quickly, eager to keep the conversation going. "Do you like it?"

"I do," I said, grateful for the questions and for the way they pulled me out of my own thoughts and gave us something normal to hold onto. My dad said little, his anger simmering beneath the surface, while my siblings filled the car with kindness—asking about school, my friends, the things I liked to do back home.

By the time we pulled into the driveway of their modest house, exhaustion had settled over all of us. The front door opened before we could knock. My stepmother stood there, her face lighting up as she wrapped me in a hug that felt unexpectedly like home.

"You must be tired," she said softly. Then she turned sharply toward my dad, her words spilling out in Arabic, her tone firm and unyielding. He said nothing, just lowered his eyes. She sighed and faced me again. "I'm so sorry," she said gently. "Your mom called me. She told me everything."

Hearing that brought a rush of gratitude I wasn't prepared for. In that moment, standing in the doorway, I realized I was held—protected—by two women who wanted the same thing for me, even across distance, language, and everything my father had broken.

That week became a precious gift, a chance to connect with my siblings in ways I'd only dreamed of. I spent one-on-one time with each of them, learning their quirks and sharing stories of my own. My oldest sister and I bonded over late-night talks in her room, giggling over shared tastes in music, while my younger brother talked to me about sports and friends, his eyes bright with pride. My stepmother spoiled me with affection, taking me and my oldest sister to the mall, where she bought us matching outfits, Clinique makeup, and piles of clothes that made me feel seen and cherished. Spending time with my siblings and stepmother felt effortless, a natural rhythm of laughter and connection, but my interactions with my dad remained strained. He often spoke to me in Arabic, growing frustrated when I couldn't respond in the language I'd long forgotten. He'd call me his baby and tell me he loved me, his voice thick with emotion, but I couldn't bring myself to say those words back. Our past was still a silent barrier between us I wasn't ready to cross.

When I returned to Texas the following week, I was emotionally drained but deeply grateful for the trip. The time with my siblings and stepmother had been a balm to my heart, filling a void I'd carried for years. I wanted to know them, and I wanted them to know me—to understand that my absence from their lives had never been my choice. As I unpacked my suitcase, pulling out the clothes my stepmother had bought me, I felt a quiet joy at the memories we'd created. My dad called occasionally after the trip, but his calls were less frequent, and I welcomed the space. I needed a break to process everything, to focus on school and church, and to let the whirlwind of emotions settle. The trip had been a bridge to my other family, a step toward healing, but I knew the journey with my dad would take more time.

It was the start of my junior year at Lindale High School, a whirlwind of activity that kept me on my toes. Between classes, church activities, time with friends, and traveling with the football team as the student trainer, I barely had a moment to breathe. That fall, my dad returned to Dallas to help at the bakery again, and his calls became more frequent. At first, he asked if we could meet, but soon he was requesting another visit to my home. By then, October had arrived, and Halloween was just a week away. For most, it was a time of costumes and candy, but for my mom and me, Halloween carried a heavy weight, marking the anniversary of my kidnapping—a day that always dredged up painful memories—so we had stopped celebrating years ago. When my dad asked to visit, I told him I was too busy with school, hoping he'd understand the unspoken reason behind my refusal. I couldn't bring myself to tell him the truth, assuming he'd remember the significance of the date.

That Friday, the weekend of Halloween, I was at home with my parents, trying to find some calm amidst the emotional storm the season always brought. A sudden knock at the door jolted me from my thoughts, and when I opened it, I saw my dad standing there, his unexpected presence sending a wave of fear crashing over me. I froze, my heart pounding, before retreating to my parents' bedroom in a panic. "Mom, he's here," I whispered, my voice trembling.

"Who's here, Lauren?" she asked, her brow furrowing with concern.

"It's him; it's Ali. He's at the door. I told him not to come, but he's here." I slipped into their bathroom, my mom following close behind as tears welled up in my eyes.

She knelt in front of me, her gaze steady and full of love, and said, "Lauren, I've watched you cry and struggle for so many years. This is your chance to let it all out. Let him see your tears, let him see your anger, get mad at him." Her words struck a chord deep within me, and I nodded, wiping my eyes.

"You're right," I said, feeling a flicker of resolve. As my mom stayed in her bedroom to pray, I took a deep breath, walked back to the door, and let my dad in.

He greeted me with a bright smile, oblivious to the storm inside me, and said, "I wanted to surprise you."

Keeping my voice steady, I replied, "We need to talk. Let's sit in the living room."

That day remains etched in my memory, a turning point where God filled me with an unshakable peace as I walked toward the living room, guiding the words I needed to say. For the first time, I wasn't afraid to be honest, no longer the people-pleaser trying to keep the peace. I was ready to confront my dad with the truth.

Sitting across from him, I looked into his eyes and asked, "Do you know why I didn't want you to visit today?" He stared at me, confusion clouding his face. "Do you not remember that Halloween is the anniversary of when you kidnapped me?"

His response was a quiet shock. "No, Lauren. I had no idea."

My voice rose with a mix of disbelief and pain. "How could you not know? How could you not remember? Every Halloween since you took me, I've remembered. The memories come flooding back, and I refuse to go out on this day. You took me from my mom, from my home, from everything I ever knew, and you changed my life forever. I changed my last name and lived in hiding because of you. After all of that, my mom still invited you into our home, and then you show up today, uninvited, showing no respect for her or for me. Since you're here anyway, you need to see my tears, my anger, and all the hurt you've caused."

He sat there, stunned, and all he could muster was, "I'm sorry. I didn't know."

But I wasn't done. God gave me the strength to push forward, to ask the hard questions without crumbling. "Dad," I said, the word feeling foreign on my tongue after so many years of absence, "do my siblings know why I'm not part of their lives? Have you ever told them what you did?"

He shook his head. "No, but Lauren, they know you love them. They understand."

My heart sank. "So they have no idea? They just think I chose not to be part of their lives? They don't know you kidnapped me? Do they even know about the movie, the magazine articles, the talk shows? Have *you* seen the movie? Because I have a copy, Dad. They need to know what you did."

My mom had been right. I needed to say those words, to release what I'd carried for so long and to let my dad see the depth of my pain. That conversation didn't change him; he offered no real answers, no profound apologies that could undo the past. But it set me free.

Speaking my truth didn't change my father, and it didn't erase the past. But it changed something in me. For the first time, the anger and questions I had carried for years were no longer trapped inside. I walked away realizing that true healing wouldn't come from my father—it would come from God, who had been with me through every step of the journey.

After our emotional confrontation, my dad seemed to grasp the depth of my hurt, and his phone calls became less frequent as he returned to Vermont. During the next year, my senior year, I nurtured my connection with my oldest sister and stepmother, who reached out often with warmth and care. When they expressed their desire to attend my high school graduation, I felt a mix of nerves and excitement but agreed they could come. The entire family made the long drive, and my dad even invited relatives from the Dallas area to join us. At that time, most of Lindale knew my story, a tale of kidnapping and reconciliation that had spread through our small town over the years. On the day of my graduation, as I walked into the ceremony, I had a feeling everyone in the arena would know exactly who my family was, their presence a visible testament to the journey we'd all been on.

The graduation took place at Tyler Junior College and was held in the basketball arena, a spacious venue buzzing with anticipation. Rows of chairs for my senior class were arranged on the polished hardwood court, facing a stage adorned with the school's colors, while additional seating lined the sides and stretched up to the second floor. As I took my seat among my classmates, I glanced up to the second-floor balcony and saw my dad and his family standing together, a striking sight that drew whispers from those around me. My dad, aunts, and uncle were dressed in traditional Jordanian clothing, a bold contrast to the sea of caps and gowns below. There was no mistaking them; they were undeniably my family, and yes, that man at the center, beaming with pride, was my biological father.

After the ceremony, my mom invited everyone—my dad, his family, all of us—back to our home. She cooked a full, homemade meal to celebrate my graduation, moving quietly around the kitchen with practiced ease. At the time, I didn't recognize what she was doing. I was too young, too overwhelmed by the moment and the history sitting at the table. But years later, when people ask me how I forgave my dad, my mind goes back to that afternoon. I see my mother standing at the stove, cooking for the man who kidnapped me, the man whose choices had cost her everything—financially, emotionally, physically. She never gave a speech about forgiveness. She lived it. Long before I understood grace, my mother showed me what it looked like in action.

Reflecting on that unforgettable graduation day, I realized God had been leading me on a profound journey to reconnect with my father, a path marked by difficulty but also by divine purpose. He understood my deep desire to live without regrets, gently teaching me to trust Him through every uncertain step and surrounding me with people whose encouragement and wisdom arrived at just the right moments. Their presence reminded me I was never alone in this healing process. Yet, even as I stood at this milestone, my story was far from complete. Not all journeys end as we imagine, and God had more in store for me, more lessons to unfold.

CHAPTER EIGHTEEN

REDEEMED

As I left the familiar embrace of Lindale behind and stepped into the uncharted territory of college life at UT Arlington, I felt a thrilling sense of freedom, ready to spread my wings and discover who I truly was. The world seemed wide open, brimming with possibilities, from chasing my dream of becoming a physical therapist to navigating the vibrant chaos of campus life, complete with late-night study sessions, sports team travels, and the electric buzz of college parties. Yet, beneath the excitement, a quiet drift began to take hold, pulling me away from the faith that had once been my anchor, leaving me to wonder how I'd find my way back. Little did I know, God was weaving a story of redemption through the people and challenges that lay ahead and continuing to heal those father wounds I still had buried deep inside.

Throughout high school, my learning disabilities had forced me to work harder than most, a challenge that often left me feeling like I was running uphill while others sprinted ahead. My high school counselor, skeptical of my dreams, urged me to choose a less competitive path, warning that physical therapy school would be out of reach with my grades. But Coach Phillips, the head athletic trainer at Lindale High, saw my potential and helped me apply to the athletic training program at Tyler Junior College. To my delight, I was not only accepted but also awarded a scholarship, followed by another from the Texas Rehabilitation Commission in recognition of my learning challenges.

After a year and a half at TJC, where I thrived as a student athletic trainer, I transferred to UT Arlington with yet another scholarship, continuing my work with the university's sports teams. My heart was set on becoming a physical therapist. Despite my passion, my college counselor echoed the same doubts as before, cautioning that my test scores made physical therapy school an impossible dream. Yet, I pushed forward, completing my undergraduate degree in just three and a half years. Through every obstacle, I felt God's hand at work, revealing a plan and purpose for my life that transcended test scores. He had gifted me with talents and determination, and my mom, my unwavering cheerleader, never stopped reminding me that I could achieve anything I set my mind to.

College life at UT Arlington brought a whirlwind of new experiences. Away from the grounding presence of my church and life group, I found myself going out more often, drinking, and slowly losing who I was—the person I'd fought so hard to find.

At one of those college parties, surrounded with track athletes, I met Abby, a high jumper whose smile and spirit mirrored my own. We both felt out of place amidst the thumping music and crowded apartment, so we stepped outside to catch our breath, settling on the cool concrete steps of the building. As we talked under the starry Texas sky, we discovered a shared sense of longing, both of us Christians who felt adrift in the college scene, wrestling with guilt over the parties we attended. I shared about my complicated history with my dad, and Abby shared her own struggles with her father, forging an instant bond between us.

While I was at UT Arlington, my dad reached out again. It had been about two years since I had seen him at my high school graduation. He had returned to Dallas to help my uncle at the bakery.

His request to visit stirred a familiar unease, and I knew I couldn't face him alone. I turned to Abby, my trusted friend, who agreed to join me for lunch at a restaurant near the bakery.

Sitting across from my dad, with Abby by my side for support, I tried to keep the conversation light, but the awkwardness between us was palpable.

He spoke to me as if no time had been lost, filling the space with easy questions and familiar tones that didn't match my memories. "So what are you studying now?" he asked, leaning forward like this was a continuation of a life we'd shared. I answered carefully, telling him about working toward my BS in athletic training, my words measured and polite, my body still despite the nerves humming underneath.

Abby, sensing the heaviness settling in, smiled and stepped in. "She keeps half the athletic department running," she said with a grin. "If someone's hurt, she's the one we all look for." Then she nodded toward herself. "I'm the high jumper—so I owe her my legs."

The tension eased just enough for laughter to slip in. My dad chuckled, nodding like this was knowledge he was entitled to, and I smiled back, learning in real time how to balance courtesy, curiosity, and fear—all at once.

I asked him about my stepmother and the kids—questions that came easier than asking about him or offering anything about myself. Talking about the children felt like neutral ground. In truth, it was a form of self-protection. I wasn't ready to hand him pieces of my life he hadn't earned. How much could I really trust him after everything he had taken from me? Keeping the focus on them allowed me to stay present without surrendering too much, a quiet boundary I held onto as tightly as I could.

But as always, my father wanted more than I could give him. He wanted a deep connection with me without accepting what he did was wrong. It felt like he wanted to sweep everything under a rug and not take any responsibility for all the chaos, hurt, and trauma he caused. My desire to have him back in my life kept me trying over and over again, and after every meeting I felt empty and drained.

After a few more visits, each one as challenging as the last, I realized I wasn't ready to have him in my life. The emotional weight was too heavy, the wounds too fresh. I chose to step back, maintaining contact with a few of my siblings and my stepmom, whose warmth I cherished, but letting my dad go for the time being. In that decision, I felt a quiet assurance that it was okay to set boundaries, to prioritize my own healing, and to trust that He would guide me through this journey in His perfect timing.

During my senior year of college, I poured my energy into securing a spot in physical therapy school. Countless hours were spent boosting my grades and preparing for the GRE, a grueling process that tested my determination. I applied to two programs, and to my astonishment, both welcomed me with open arms. School counselors had warned me, predicting I'd fall short, but their doubts had only fueled my resolve. Through relentless effort, tutoring sessions, late-night study marathons, and heartfelt prayers, an incredible opportunity emerged.

Ultimately, I chose UT Health Science Center in San Antonio, Texas, a decision that felt divinely guided. Months later, my stepdad's job relocated him to the same city. This alignment reassured me I was on the right path. That summer, before my first year of physical therapy school began, my parents moved from Lindale to San Antonio, and I settled back into their home, living with them until my final year.

Around the time I graduated from UT Arlington, my relationship with my biological father faded entirely. His calls ceased, and I was too consumed with school to notice the growing distance. But life has a way of filling the gaps. During my second semester of physical therapy school, a classmate named Paige introduced me to Brett Burns, the man who would become my husband. We clicked instantly, tying the knot just six months before I graduated.

On my wedding day, my stepdad, Richard, walked me down the aisle—a moment that swelled my heart with gratitude and left no room for regrets. Richard was a remarkable man who loved me unconditionally, as if I were his own. Growing up, I'd often wondered who would take on that role when my big day arrived, a question every little girl ponders as she dreams of her wedding. When the moment came, I knew without a doubt it would be him, and I felt immense pride in his presence.

My stepdad Richard walking me down the aisle on my wedding day.

When I became a wife, a quiet conviction stirred. I needed to reconnect with a church, to realign my life. But the transition wasn't easy. I'd left behind the cozy, small-town churches of my past for the sprawling expanse of a big city. Stepping into those massive sanctuaries left me overwhelmed, a stranger in a sea of faces. Discouraged, I abandoned the search almost as quickly as it began.

A turning point came when my oldest child, Cooper, was about a year old. Paige noticed my longing to get back into church. She was on the same quest herself. One day, she called with an invitation that sparked hope. "Lauren, there's a Mentoring Moms group at Oak Hills Church in San Antonio. Want to come?" Her voice carried the encouragement of possibility, and I jumped at the chance.

"Yes!" I blurted, barely letting her finish.

Then she hesitated. "But it's on your birthday. Are you sure?" Paige, with her knack for remembering everyone's special days (she still texts me birthday reminders for friends), wanted to be certain. I laughed. "Absolutely! This feels right. It's where I need to be."

Together, Paige and I stepped into the conference room at Oak Hills, greeted by a scene that felt like a gift. Tables adorned with elegant decorations lined the space, and a spread of food beckoned from the side. We scanned the room. Most seats were taken, but we spotted one table with space—Megan's. We settled in, unaware that this moment would mark the beginning of a decade-long bond. That night was Megan's first-time volunteering as a mentor for Mentoring Moms, a detail we'd learn later. The evening unfolded with a speaker's message, followed by Megan introducing herself. She led us in a Q&A and closed with a prayer, her kindness radiating through every word. Paige and I exchanged glances as we left, a shared certainty settling in.

Megan was the mentor we'd been craving, someone to guide us and lift us up in prayer. From then on, we met monthly, gradually bonding with the women at our table, savoring meals we didn't have to cook or clean up, a small but cherished reprieve.

Three months later, life delivered a devastating blow when I suffered a miscarriage. The pain sliced through me, leaving me isolated in a sea of grief. I turned to Paige, who encouraged me to share my burden with our Mentoring Moms group. Five days later, we sat together at a table surrounded by women we were still getting to know. After the speaker concluded her message, our group gathered around Megan's table, and she invited prayer requests.

As I began to speak, tears streamed down my face, my voice quaking under the weight of loss. Though I barely knew these women, their eyes shimmered with empathy as I poured out my heart. One by one, they encircled me, offering warm hugs and sharing their own tales of sorrow. I realized I wasn't alone; others had walked this painful path too. They prayed over me, their words a soothing balm, their presence a vital lifeline.

Just as He had in my previous life group, God met me there, stitching together bonds from the threads of strangers' shared grief. That evening ignited a connection that has endured. Ten years later, we still meet every Thursday night under Megan Green's unwavering leadership, lifting up prayers for each other's children, some now in college, once little ones we supported through their elementary years. What started as a hesitant leap of faith on my birthday has grown into a bedrock of love, healing, and community.

The following year, Brett and I welcomed our second son, Caleb. Then, on December 23, 2018, tragedy struck again with the sudden passing of my stepfather, Richard. His death left a lingering ache in my heart. My dear friend Abby once told me I'd had to mourn the loss of a father twice, and she was right. I'd grieved the end of my relationship with my biological father, Ali, and now I mourned Richard, the man who raised me. Through it all, God walked beside me, guiding me through the healing process and giving me the strength to confront my biological father and offer him forgiveness aloud.

A month after Richard's passing, I stopped by my mom's house to pick up the kids. She greeted me with startling news. "Your dad called today," she said casually.

Confusion jolted me. "My dad? You mean Ali?" I still grappled with the reality that Richard, the only father I'd truly known, was gone.

She nodded. "Yes, Ali. He tracked down my number. He asked how you're doing and if he could talk to you. I told him I'd pass along his number, and you could decide."

Stunned, I took the slip of paper and slipped it into my pocket. My mentor, Megan, had always encouraged me to pray before acting or speaking, a piece of wisdom that became my anchor.

For weeks, I carried that number, praying each time Ali crossed my mind: *God, give me direction. What do I do with this? Guide me; keep me steady.* Then, one day, a quiet certainty settled: *Now is the time, Lauren. Call him.* Why now, so soon after losing Richard, I wondered. Alone in my car—my refuge from two energetic boys—I held the number, whispered a prayer, and dialed. It had been twelve years since I'd last spoken to Ali, my senior year at UT Arlington now a distant memory.

His voice, rich with an Arabic accent, answered, and my heart raced. "Hi, Ali. It's me, Lauren." I couldn't bring myself to call him Dad; that title belonged to someone else.

"Lauren! Hi, baby! It's so good to hear your voice. Oh, how I've missed you. How are you? I love you," he said, his excitement tumbling out.

I paused, collecting my thoughts. "I'm good. Mom told me you called, and I just wanted you to know I'm okay."

"I'm getting older, and I've thought of you often over the years. You're my oldest child, and I've always loved you. I want to know you and your family. I'd love to meet your husband and children."

I took a deep breath before responding. "I forgive you. I believe in Jesus, and because of that, I forgave you long ago. I'm not angry anymore."

His reply came softly, laced with regret. "Thank you, Lauren. I'm sorry I hurt you. So many years have passed without speaking. I'd love to meet your husband and children, if that's possible. I'll always be your dad."

My heart steadied as I spoke. "I've forgiven you, Ali, but I don't want a relationship. I've built a good life, a great job, an amazing family. Richard was the father who raised me. He was there when I graduated physical therapy school, he walked me down the aisle, and he held my boys when they were born. He passed away recently, but he loved me like his own, and he was a good father."

A brief silence settled between us—heavy, but not hostile. We said goodbye gently, a chapter closing not with bitterness but with grace and clarity.

In that pivotal conversation, I shared Jesus with my father once more, fully aware that his salvation was never mine to carry.

For years, I'd lifted my biological father up in prayer, trusting that my role was to intercede while God handled the rest. But I'd learned a profound truth: God sees everything. He sees the wounds we carry, the desires of our hearts, and every step we take through life's trials. When we place our trust in Him, He moves in His perfect timing, weaving redemption in ways we can't always predict.

My story isn't finished, and neither is Ali's. Perhaps one day he'll surrender his life to Jesus, a possibility that flickers with hope in my mind. But I've released that outcome to God, knowing it's His work, not mine, to complete.

In May 2023, a spark ignited the desire to write this book and share my story. Fear gripped me at first. I had no idea where to begin, but I turned to prayer, seeking His guidance to light the way. In April 2024, I launched the *Redeemed* podcast, armed with nothing but a laptop and a microphone, recording from the floor of my closet. Now, as I write this in January 2026, it's been almost two years and ninety episodes, with the journey still unfolding. That simple act of obedience set off a chain of divine connections I never could have foreseen. Through the podcast, God reintroduced me to the very men and woman who had risked everything to rescue me from Jordan in 1987. Two months after the launch, I found myself interviewing each member of that courageous team, their voices breathing life into memories I'd held for decades.

Then, in September 2024, a remarkable chapter unfolded. My mom, Rick, Bev, and I traveled to North Carolina for the first-ever Desperate Rescue Reunion. There, I reunited with JD Roberts and his wife Linda, Dave Chatellier, and Don and Judy Finney. For two days, we gathered around a table, enjoying Beverly Lambert's home cooking. We savored her famous meatloaf recipe (in Miranda's cookbook), while they recounted my rescue mission. I sat in awe, hanging on every word as they relived each detail, each moment etched in their minds.

The timing proved even more sacred than I could have imagined. Just six months after our reunion, JD Roberts passed into heaven to be with Jesus. I'll forever cherish God's perfect orchestration, which allowed me not only to see JD one last time but also to capture his voice and wisdom on my podcast for generations to hear. Those recordings, those moments, and those artifacts are treasures of a story still being written—one of redemption, reconnection, and unshakable faith.

Reunited with the men who risked everything to help bring me home. Their courage changed the course of my life.

If you carry the sting of a father's wounds, I feel the weight of your pain, shame, trauma, and heartache, and I am truly sorry for all you've endured. But hear this: That trauma does not have to define you. My deepest prayer is that, through my story and the *Redeemed* podcast, you'll catch a glimpse of the heavenly Father's relentless love—a love that pursues you, longing to heal your deepest hurts and mend the broken places. I'm no different from you, no more special or deserving. I simply said "yes" to Jesus and took a trembling step of faith. Yet, that step wasn't taken alone. It was God who surrounded me with a community: my mom, the Lamberts, my Prairie Creek life group, Megan Green, and faithful friends who held me steady, pointing me back to Jesus when I faltered. They fueled my faith, and now I want to offer that same lifeline to you.

I urge you to pray, to listen for God's whisper, and to step boldly out of your comfort zone when He calls, even when that means forgiving the one who wounded you most. There is a profound freedom in forgiveness, a release from the chains of bitterness that keep you tethered to that hurting place. You don't have to stay stuck any longer. The power of prayer can anchor you, the strength of community can lift you, and the act of forgiveness can set you free. My journey is proof that God is still writing stories of redemption, and yours is no exception. Say yes, lean into the people He provides, and trust that He's chasing after you with a love that never lets go. Your healing, your hope, your future—it's all waiting on the other side of that step.

ACKNOWLEDGMENTS

This book exists because of the courage, faith, and generosity of many people who stood with me through some of the most difficult and redemptive chapters of my life.

First and always, thank you to my mother. You not only fought to bring me home, but you taught me how to forgive when anger felt justified and how to trust God when fear felt overwhelming. Your faith shaped my healing, your strength anchored my hope, and your love showed me that forgiveness is not weakness, but freedom. This story is as much yours as it is mine.

I am deeply grateful to the men and women who played a role in the rescue and in bringing me safely home. Dave Chatellier, JD Roberts (in loving memory), Don Feeney, Judy Feeney, Jim Hatfield, and Al Zapanta—your courage, integrity, and perseverance changed the course of my life. I will forever carry gratitude for the risks you took and the lives you impacted through your service.

I want to especially honor the memory of JD Roberts. Your life mattered, your work mattered, and your role in this story will never be forgotten. Thank you for standing for truth and helping bring light where darkness once lived.

Rick and Beverly Lambert, thank you for being a refuge for both my mother and me when we returned home. Your support during those fragile early years meant more than you may ever know. Thank you for opening your home, your hearts, and your lives to me during my high school years, and for walking alongside us with love, steadiness, and faith when everything felt uncertain.

To my family and friends who have prayed, encouraged, and stood by me through seasons of healing and reflection—thank you. Your presence carried me through moments when words were not enough.

I am deeply grateful to my agent, Kristen Terrette of Martin Literary Management, for believing in this story and stewarding it with care, wisdom, and integrity. Thank you for championing this book and helping guide it into the right hands.

To my editor, Debra Englander, and the entire publishing team, thank you for treating this story with sensitivity, respect, and excellence. Your commitment to honoring both truth and healing has been a gift.

To the pastors, mentors, counselors, and faith-filled friends who pointed me back to hope when fear tried to define my future—thank you for reminding me who God is and who I am in Him.

Above all, thank you to God—the One who rescues, restores, and redeems. When fear once ruled my life, You became my protector. When brokenness felt final, You proved redemption was still possible. This book is a testimony of Your faithfulness.

And to the reader—if you have ever felt unprotected, forgotten, or afraid, I pray you find in these pages a reminder that healing is possible, hope is real, and redemption is never out of reach.